Beyond Violence

Figure 1. Outline map of Northern Ireland: Main cities,
           towns, and villages

Beyond Violence

Conflict resolution process in Northern Ireland

MARI FITZDUFF

United Nations
University Press

TOKYO · NEW YORK · PARIS

international conflict research

INCORE

United Nations University Press
The United Nations University, 53-70, Jingumae 5-chome, Shibuya-ku, Tokyo, 150-8925, Japan
Tel: +81-3-3499-2811   Fax: +81-3-3406-7345
E-mail: sales@hq.unu.edu (general enquiries): press@hq.unu.edu
http://www.unu.edu

United Nations University Office in North America
2 United Nations Plaza, Room DC2-2062, New York, NY 10017, USA
Tel: +1-212-963-6387   Fax: +1-212-371-9454
E-mail: unuona@ony.unu.edu

United Nations University Press is the publishing division of the United Nations University.

Cover design by Joyce C. Weston

Printed in the United States of America

UNUP-1078
ISBN 92-808-1078-2

Library of Congress Cataloging-in-Publication Data

Fitzduff, Mari.
Beyond violence : conflict resolution process in Northern Ireland / Mari Fitzduff.
    p.   cm.
Includes bibliographical references and index.
ISBN 92-808-1078-2
1. Conflict management—Northern Ireland. 2. Violence—Northern Ireland. 3. Social conflict–Northern Ireland. I. Title.
HN398.N6 F58 2002
303.6'9'09416—dc21   2002009065

CONTENTS

LIST OF FIGURES

LIST OF ABBREVIATIONS

ACT	All Children Together
ANC	African National Council
BBC	British Broadcasting Corporation
CAJ	Commission on the Administration of Justice
CCRU	Central Community Relations Unit
CIRAC	Centre for Independent Research and Analysis of Crime
CLMC	Combined Loyalist Military Command
CRC	Community Relations Council
CRTLC	Conflict Resolution Training Learning Consortium
CTG	Cultural Traditions Group
DCAL	Department for Culture Arts and Leisure
DPPB	District Policing Partnership Board
DUP	Democratic Unionist Party
ECONI	Evangelical Conference on Northern Ireland
EDI	Equity, Diversity, and Interdependence
EMU	Education for Mutual Understanding
ETA	Euskadi 'ta Askatasuna
FAIT	Families Against Intimidation and Terror
FEA	Fair Employment Agency
FEC	Fair Employment Commission
IFA	Irish Football Association
INCORE	Initiative on Conflict Resolution and Ethnicity
IPCC	Independent Police Complaints Commission
IRA	Irish Republican Army
LVF	Loyalist Volunteer Force
NGO	Non Governmental Organization
NICEA	Northern Ireland Council for the Curriculum, Examinations and Assessment
NIWC	Northern Ireland Women's Coalition
NORAID	Northern Aid Committee
PAF	Protestant Action Force
PAFT	Policy Appraisal and Fair Treatment
PSNI	Police Service Northern Ireland
PEG	Political Education Group

PRG	Peace and Reconciliation Group
PUP	Progressive Unionist Party
RISCT	Research Institute for the Study of Conflict and Terrorism
RUC	Royal Ulster Constabulary
SAS	Special Air Service
SDLP	Social Democratic and Labour Party
TSN	Targeting Social Need
UDA	Ulster Defence Association
UDP	Ulster Democratic Party
UDR	Ulster Defence Regiment
UFF	Ulster Freedom Fighters
UUP	Ulster Unionist Party
UVF	Ulster Volunteer Force
WAVE	Widows and Widowers Against Violence
WEA	Workers Education Association
YMCA	Young Men's Christian Association

PREFACE

The beginning of the end?

The Shankill Road, a staunchly Protestant area of Belfast, is a busy place on a Saturday afternoon as families go about their weekend shopping, stopping to chat with their relatives and friends. 23 October 1993 was a bright autumn day and the street was packed with people enjoying the unexpected sunshine. When the bomb exploded in the local fish shop, ten people were killed in the blast, including two children and the bomber himself, who turned out to be a member of a Republican paramilitary group.[1]

The following day I made my way to the scene of the murders, to leave a wreath of sympathy. There was just a pile of rubble left to indicate where the fish shop had been. In front of it, a mound of flowers and letters for the families and friends of the dead had begun to grow. Many of the messages of sympathy to the Protestants of the Shankill Road were from Catholics angry at the murders that had been committed in their name.[2] Some of these messages from Catholics told of sons in jail, of relatives murdered by Republican or Loyalist[3] paramilitaries, and all spoke of their desire for peace.

A week later, in Greysteele, a quiet village in the northwestern part of Northern Ireland, the paramilitaries struck again. This time it was Loyalists who attacked what they thought was a Catholic bar, opening fire indiscriminately and killing seven people. And once again the bereaved, this time mostly Catholics, were not left to mourn by themselves. Their local Protestant neighbours came to join in their wakes and their funerals, and even chided their politicians for not joining with them in such collective grieving. These responses were a welcome change from the days and years when such violent acts would almost inevitably have resulted in a desire for some communal, and aggressive, reprisal against the other community.

In the months that followed, the killing continued. It was mostly individual and sporadic, but included another pub attack by Loyalists in which six Catholics were killed while watching a World Cup football match. Although the murders continued, the signs of hopes began to multiply. More and more, the communities crossed their sectarian barriers to mourn with one another. Protestant shipyard workers called a strike when a Catholic colleague was killed. Catholics cradled a dying British soldier after the Irish Republican Army (IRA) shot him. Protestant and Catholic community workers walked their streets together, openly professing their solidarity. Clerics (at last) began to cross the sectarian divide, to grieve at each other's funerals.

By the summer of 1994, the search for peace had become relentless. The preceding months had been ones of feverish mediation and negotiation between governments, politicians, and paramilitaries. And at last, on 31 August, came the announcement: "... the leadership of the IRA have decided that as of midnight August 31, there will be a complete cessation of military operations."

Six weeks later the Combined Loyalist Military Command (CMLC), representing all the main Loyalist paramilitaries, followed suit by announcing their own ceasefire, on the condition that there was no return to violence by the IRA. They apologized to all those who had been innocent victims of their violence, and asked that all in Northern Ireland should: "firmly resolve to respect our differing views of freedom, culture and aspiration and never again permit our political circumstances to degenerate into bloody warfare."[4]

These announcements from the IRA and the CLMC, the main paramilitary protagonists in a war in Northern Ireland that has lasted over 30 years and cost over 3,600 lives, marked a new and hopeful dawn in the often bloody history of the island of Ireland. This emphasis by both organizations on wanting to move into the democratic process marked the beginning of a new stage of the peace process in Northern Ireland.

In the years that followed, the ceasefires were not easy, with occasional breakdowns, with continuing wrangling between the political parties about how and when to organize all-party talks, and frequent confrontations about the decommissioning of paramilitary arms. Despite such difficulties, the politicians did eventually deliver an Agreement on Good Friday[5] 1998 – the Belfast Agreement – which was to lead to a power-sharing government between most of the political parties in Northern Ireland, as well as guarantees on issues of equality and cultural diversity for all communities. By 2001, notwithstanding the various wrangles on policing and decommissioning that were to follow the Agreement, all the major political parties had together agreed on a programme for government for Northern Ireland on issues such as education, health, and economic development that would be of joint benefit to all of their constituents.

From violence to politics

Conflicts that are of the length and depth of Northern Ireland do not end, but they can and do change. What eventually brought the people of Northern Ireland to the point where their politicians eventually agreed to move from the use of violence into the use of politics to manage their differences, and to agree to share political power to accommodate each other's right to cultural and political diversity? The creation of the road that has made such progress possible and enabled the signing of the Belfast Agreement has been the result of the development of many conflict resolution initiatives in the fields of equality, diversity, and security work, as well as political and community dialogue, which are outlined in this book. The unfortunate length of the conflict (30 years) has provided the region with the time to develop a variety of systematic ways to constructively address many of the causes and manifestations of the conflict. Such activities not only contributed substantially to the development of the peace infrastructure that has made progress possible, but also helped to develop many frameworks, both conceptual and structural, that should continue to positively inform progress beyond violence and into increasing political cooperation.

This book is written in the hope that it will be of some relevance and assistance to others who are struggling to manage and resolve ethnic, religious, political, or cultural conflicts in their own areas.

Over the years of the conflict in Northern Ireland people have learnt a great deal that was valuable from the efforts of many people involved in conflict areas elsewhere, but often, acquiring the practical information that was needed about such programmes, was surprisingly difficult. While acknowledging that there are substantial differences in each conflict, the hope of this book is that the information it contains about the conflict resolution programmes that have been developed in Northern Ireland will make acquiring such information a little easier for others for whom time is often at a premium, and need is ever urgent.

My own part in the work began in 1983 when, angry and weary with the conflict that had constrained and darkened most of the life of my family, I decided to enter the fray of peace-building in Northern Ireland. The journey involved me in many explorations into the rapidly developing world of conflict resolution. Finding that little indigenous training for such resolution was available, I set up a conflict resolution training project for Northern Ireland, with a particular emphasis on local issues and needs.[6] Through the universities, I also set up the first courses in Northern Ireland on understanding and dealing with conflict, particularly for policy makers, and practitioners in the statutory and voluntary sectors. In 1985, I jointly undertook an analysis (see Frazer and Fitzduff, 1986) for an advisory body to the government (Standing Advisory Commission on Human Rights) on the adequacies or otherwise of existing strategies for resolving the conflict and in particular of existing community relations work.[7] The review found such work to be inadequate, unstrategic, and poorly funded, incurring as it did less than 1 per cent of the security budget.

Spurred by the report, in 1988 the government set up a central unit, the Central Community Relations Unit (CCRU) at the heart of government to oversee the development of the work of conflict resolution, and in 1990 the unit set up the Community Relations Council (CRC), an independent agency dedicated to improving relationships between the communities and fostering conflict resolution in Northern Ireland. The council was given a remit to undertake development work with agencies and groups of people interested in promoting good relations between the communities and constructively addressing the causes and resolution of the conflict, and to assist with funding such work. Its remit also included the provision of advice to government on issues that affected the community divide such as planning, economic and community development, and education. As first director of the CRC, from 1990 to 1997, I have been privileged to be part of some of the many developments outlined in this book, and a close observer of the others.

A complex endeavour

Perhaps the first, indeed the most obvious lesson we have learnt through the years, as our conflict successfully defied any simple solutions, is that resolving a conflict, particularly one that is generally defined as intractable, is a complex and interlocking process. In many ways the task is like working on a jigsaw, where the successful putting together of just a few pieces may well leave the picture as a whole still in fracture, and uncertain. We have learnt that it is impossible to separate the violence from an apparent lack of political creativity. We know that political discussions have often failed because of the lack of trust between the politicians. We know that people often resent their politicians' apparent inability to deliver on agreement, but we also now understand that the politicians often feel they cannot move beyond their communities' perceptions and fears. We know that addressing structural inequities is an essential part of conflict resolution but also that many of these can only be redressed if there is adequate economic development.

Only by acknowledging and dealing with the various strands of such complexities have we been able to achieve a significant movement towards unravelling the various gridlocks that have so constrained our progress. It is interesting to see that this necessity, for a much more comprehensive approach to conflict resolution development, has gradually become recognized as an increasingly important factor in conflict resolution (see Lessons Learned, 2000).

We have found the practice of developing "pieces of peace" (Rothman, 1992) to be a useful one, offering as it does both a manageable way of addressing localized and institutional conflicts and a means of gaining experience and confidence for groups moving on to address the more macro questions of political peacemaking. Such a concept provides a very useful approach for groups and institutions, often daunted and discouraged by their sense of the overwhelming need to end all violence as quickly as possible. Many of these pieces of peace, slowly and surely developed over the years, provide the main substance of this book, which outlines the main approaches that have been devised to address the substantial issues of the conflict.

These approaches include programmes designed to address equity issues (Chapter 2); work within and between groups and communities at all levels to increase understanding and cooperation (Chapter 3); work undertaken with children and youth to address their particular needs in a divided society (Chapter 4); cultural work that can address the necessities and problems of cultural diversity (Chapter 5); work that is required by security forces to ensure the containment of violence (Chapter 6), the problems of communities addressing paramilitarism (Chapter 7); and work designed to facilitate political discussion and mediation (Chapter 8).

The book also contains a chapter (Chapter 1) on the history and of the main dimensions of the conflict, which will be particularly useful for those unfamiliar with the parameters of the situation. There is a chapter on the training or preparation work that has been designed to increase people's capacity to work in the area of conflict resolution (Chapter 9). Chapter 10 looks at how successful these programmes have been, and finally there is a chapter outlining some of the lessons learned about the work (Chapter 11). Inevitably, because of the limitations of a single book, it will be impossible to do justice to the work that has been undertaken in Northern Ireland under the above headings, and this will be frustrating for some readers. For those who are particularly interested in work on improving community relations, I recommend the website of the CRC at http://www.community-relations.org.uk/. For those who wish for more information on most of the other initiatives, I recommend that they contact the CAIN website http://cain.ulst.ac.uk/, which site also includes a very extensive bibliography on Northern Ireland.

A global need

There has rarely been a time when the need for positive and effective programmes to deal with conflict has been more necessary. The last decade of the millennium saw over 100 conflicts, most of which were intrastate conflicts, and their number looks set to continue.[8] Many of these conflicts, which are the substance of my current work as Director of INCORE[9] echo the kinds of issues with which we have been struggling in Northern Ireland. These include dealing with cries for self-determination, leveraged by armed struggle; containing destructive urges towards ethnic cleansing in either subtle or manifest forms; addressing state tendencies to fuel conflict through excluding some communities from power and respect; and the urgent need to find creatively agreed constitutional and political frameworks through which to address these conflicts. Such issues have been the gist of our conflict resolving work for many years.

Even the great historian of warfare John Keegan has come to the conclusion that positive conflict resolution work is the only hope for the future of our world (Keegan, 1993). Let us hope that such a conclusion will, with increasing energy, be supported and resourced by all our institutional and individual power makers and power brokers throughout the world and that the complex and challenging work of the construction of peace will be increasingly endorsed for the crucial and indispensable work that we in Northern Ireland know it to be.

1

A divided island

Plantations and division

Civil violence broke out in Northern Ireland in 1969, and has continued to the present, although it has very significantly diminished since the ceasefires of 1994. This episode of violence was a continuation of a context of conflict that had begun in the twelfth century, with the colonization of Ireland by the neighbouring island of Britain. As part of that colonization, millions of acres of land were given to English soldiers who had served in wars against Ireland. Over the years, many of these "settlers" eventually integrated into the local communities throughout the eastern and southern parts of the island. However, the northern part of the island remained mostly Irish.

In 1609, the British government decided to attempt a more comprehensive plan of colonization, particularly in the northern parts. They invited settlers, mainly from Scotland, to take up offers of land in the northern part of the island.[10] These settlers, who came throughout the 17th and 18th centuries, did not, in general, integrate with the indigenous Irish. In part, this was a deliberate strategy on the part of the British to secure the segregation of the natives from the settlers, and initially the settlers were not even permitted to employ the indigenous Irish on their lands and in their houses. However, another major reason was that following the recent Reformation, the settlers practised a different version of Christianity, i.e. Protestantism, while the Irish whose land they colonized were mainly Roman Catholics[11] who still adhered to Rome for their religious leadership. Many of the settlers also had close industrial ties with Britain, which they maintained, as they set about developing a very successful industrial base in the north of the island.

Inevitably, the native Irish harboured great resentment towards the settlers, and in turn, the settlers felt continually under threat from the Irish. In land settlement terms, the colonization of Ulster was particularly successful, e.g. in 1703, 14 per cent of the land of the island was owned by Irish, whereas in Ulster, only 5 per cent of the land remained in indigenous ownership (Darby, 1997: 20). By 1921, only 10 per cent of population of the southern part of the island was Protestant, while the corresponding figure for the northern part of the island was 70 per cent.

Throughout the centuries since colonization began, there had been frequent attempts (many violent) by the Irish people to achieve independence from Britain. Although these were successfully resisted, the pressure on the British government to grant some form of limited independence to the island continued to increase, and in 1920 Britain agreed to this. Northern Protestants, however, feared such independence because they were afraid that their faith would suffer in a mainly Catholic Ireland, where they believed their religious freedom would be restricted. They also feared the poorer economic state of the rest of the island, compared to their own relatively prosperous and more industrialized region.

The Protestants (usually referred to as "Unionists" because of their desire to retain union with Britain) threatened to use force if they were coerced into a united Ireland and began to mobilize private armies against such an eventuality. In an effort at compromise, the then Prime Minister of Britain, Lloyd George, insisted that the island be divided into two sections, the northeastern six counties, and the rest of the island, each with its own parliament. Irish Catholic leaders were divided over this suggestion, but the offer was eventually accepted, under significant pressure, by those leaders who were sent to conduct treaty negotiations with the British in London, and who were anxious to avoid a return to what was becoming an increasingly bloody conflict in Ireland. The suggestion of a division of the island was also accepted by the Unionists, although reluctantly, as their first wish was for the whole of the island to remain within the United Kingdom of Britain and Ireland.

The decision to partition the island led to bitter and violent civil conflict between the Irish who accepted partition and those who rejected it. Eventually, in 1923, those who accepted partition achieved a victory, and the Irish Free State was formally created. In 1938 it adopted the status of a republic, under the official name of Eire, although it is known internationally as the Republic of Ireland.

Green and Orange states[12]

The establishment of the two separate entities of the Republic of Ireland and Northern Ireland ensured the development of two sectarian states north and south of the border that divided them. The majority of the 4 million citizens of the Republic are Catholics, a fact that has been consistently reflected in the ethos and laws of the state since independence. Contraception only became legally available in the 1980s and many chemists still refuse to sell it. Divorce only became available in 1995 and abortion is still illegal. The Angelus, a Catholic call to prayer, is still broadcast twice a day on the national broadcasting station. The 10 per cent of Protestants who found themselves living within the borders of the Republic at the time of partition have now dwindled to 4 per cent.[13]

At the time of partition in 1921 Northern Ireland had a population of about 1.5 million people, a million of whom were Protestant and mostly Unionist.[14] Most of the Catholics in the region were angry to find themselves living within the new state because they feared discrimination against them. Their fears proved well founded. When Protestants took power in Northern Ireland they established what was essentially a Protestant state, which effectively discriminated against Catholics in housing, jobs, and political representation. Although there are still Unionists who deny that there was any significant discrimination against Catholics during the time that the

Unionist Party held power in Northern Ireland from 1921 to 1971, the existence of such discrimination, which provided the main focus for the civil rights campaigns of the late 1960s has been well documented (Cameron Report, 1969; Rose, 1971).

For many Unionists, discrimination was valid because of their fear that Catholics were not loyal to the state, and that the very existence of Northern Ireland was threatened by what they saw as a subversive minority. This fear would appear to have been very prevalent, as exemplified by the following statement made in 1948 by the Unionist member of Parliament for Enniskillen in County Fermanagh, speaking at the annual Unionist Party conference:

> The Nationalist majority in the county ... stands at 3,684. We must ultimately reduce and liquidate that majority. This county ... is a Unionist county. The atmosphere is Unionist. The boards and properties are nearly all controlled by Unionists. But this is still a millstone around our necks ... I would ask the meeting to take whatever steps, however drastic, to wipe out this Nationalist majority.[15]

Peoples apart

The existence of such sectarian hostility was an inevitable product of a system of plantation that was designed to ensure the continued separation of settlers and natives in order to maintain orderly governance by the British. Unlike the earlier plantations, where gradual integration between natives and settlers on the island became the norm, the later influxes led only to an extremely divided society, which has maintained most of its divisions to this day. Such divisions have successfully combined to create what Levine and Campbell (1972) have termed a "pyramid-segmentary" structure – where segregation became the norm and in which different categories of a social, political, cultural, and theological nature rarely cut across one another.

Nowhere is this segregation more evident than in living territories (Murtagh, 1999). In rural areas many of the smaller villages are completely "owned" by one tradition or the other; ownership is easily recognized from the flag flying on lamp posts and houses, from murals and graffiti painted on the walls, from kerbstones painted in the different national colours and through the presence of churches and Orange and Hibernian Halls.[16] The organizations that flourish in these areas are generally segregated: farmers belong to different farmers' unions, the Women's Institute (a rural women's organization) is mainly Protestant, and in rural areas in particular much of the social life of both communities is based around the separate churches.

City lives are often no less separated. The many leisure centres are usually associated with a particular tradition, in some cases because they do not open on a Sunday (a Protestant tradition) or because of the name of a centre, or the symbols or flags displayed therein. Border areas within the cities are usually well defined by flags and graffiti, and painted kerbstones. In addition, there are 19 sectarian borders or "interfaces" in Belfast city where high so-called peace walls have had to be built between neighbouring streets, to divide the communities from each other because of persistent rioting or murders.

The education system is almost totally segregated (Gallagher, 1998). The state schools, in theory open to all denominations and religions, are rarely attended by Catholics, who make up fewer than 5 per cent of their pupils, and their attendance at such schools is frowned upon by the Catholic church. Whilst integrated schools have begun to flourish in the last decade (see Chapter 4) they as yet only cater for about 5 per cent of the school-going population. Youth clubs are also usually separate, and organizations such as the Scouts and Girl Guides have different groups for Catholic and Protestant youth.

Sports in Northern Ireland also generally reflect the denominational split. Catholics generally play Gaelic football, camogie, and hurling, games indigenous to Ireland. Protestants generally play rugby, hockey, and cricket at school, games more usually associated with Britain. While both communities play soccer/football, support for teams is mainly given on a denominational basis, and the game has on occasion given rise to violent expressions of sectarianism by both players and spectators alike. Even where communities enjoy the same sport, for example, boxing, bowls, or athletics, these tend to be organized around churches or youth clubs that are mostly denominational and thus prevent mixing.

Cultural celebrations, and especially those marches and festivities that celebrate particular victories or commemorate losses for either community are often divisive and sometimes violent occasions. Activities such as music and dancing are usually related to particular identities, for example Irish, or Scottish/British. The use of the Irish language has often been a particularly divisive issue between the communities.

Even work does not usually provide an opportunity for mixing, as most work situations (with the exception of the public sector) are segregated and this is particularly true of small businesses, which make up the bulk of the businesses in Northern Ireland.

There are of course some exceptions to such separation. The centres of some towns, and particularly Belfast, provide some degree of capacity for mixing between the communities, in their various pubs, theatres, restaurants, and shopping areas, and these have increased since the ceasefires of 1994. There is also a substantial number of mixed marriages; estimates for which usually suggest about 10 per cent of all marriages are "mixed", i.e. between Catholics and Protestants, and they now appear to be a growing phenomenon. However, as residential territories are generally segregated, participants in such marriages are often subjected to intimidation.

This overall situation means that it is quite possible for a substantial number of people, particularly those within working-class urban areas or in rural areas, to study, live, work, and socialize almost completely, for most of their lives, within their own community, and not develop close or sustained relationships with someone from another community. Even where such contact does happen, which is more commonly among the middle classes who have greater access to shared work and leisure facilities, such contact is usually notable for its often polite, but calculated, avoidance of any acknowledgement or discussion of differences, in the belief that such discussion is bound to be contentious. In the words of Seamus Heaney, the Nobel prize-winning local poet, the key concept for most such conversations remains, "Whatever you say, say nothing."

Police hegemony

Within this divided context, the police have usually been seen as not only consolidating the divisions, but as largely representing and supporting the Unionist, Protestant, hegemony. In 1922 a new police force for the state was established, the Royal Ulster Constabulary (RUC), and it was recommended that one third of its recruits should be drawn from the Catholic population. In the event, political pressures and threats, both from Unionists and from Catholics themselves who were suspicious and rejecting of the new state, ensured that the quota of Catholics was never filled. By the late 1920s only 17 per cent of the force were Catholics (Farrell, 1983), by 1969 the proportion of Catholics in the police force had dropped to just over 10 per cent, and by 2000 the figure was 7 per cent. The innate suspicion of the power systems of the Northern Ireland state shared by most Catholics inevitably led them to remain suspicious of what they saw as the biased power of the police. This was inevitably to compound the problem when the conflict erupted in the late sixties.

Civil conflict 1969

Given such patterns of separation and a police force seen as largely biased, it was not surprising that the civil rights marches against Catholic discrimination in 1968 (peaceful in the first instance) were met with suspicion and fear by the Protestant Unionists. Ever conscious of their status as a minority group within the island of Ireland and their long-felt fear of subversion by Catholics wanting to force them into a united Ireland, the Unionists reacted with anger, and in some cases with violence, to Catholic demands for equality. When it became obvious that those Unionists who were in power were not willing (or felt themselves unable) to address quickly enough the demands for civil rights that were being made, the campaign gradually developed on the part of some people into a violent campaign which was based on the belief that equality was impossible within the existing state structures, and that the only solution was a united Ireland.

Revival of the paramilitaries

The major supporters for the use of violence were the Irish Republican Army (IRA), who were the descendants of the most forceful military group that had fought for independence in 1921. They were a very small group in 1969, but as the conflict began to descend into sectarian violence, some Catholics, fearful for their safety in the riots that followed the civil rights marches, began to ask the IRA for protection. By early 1970 IRA members were confronting British troops who had arrived on the island to assist with riot control. During the following months the violence of the IRA grew into extensive bombing campaigns directed against civilian, public utility, and military targets. Recruitment to the group was helped by security mismanagement, which was manifested in such activities as internment (imprisonment) without trial in 1971, which was only directed against Catholics, despite evidence of Protestant violence. In 1972, the killing of 13 unarmed men during a civil rights demonstration by Catholics in Derry/Londonderry significantly increased community tension.[17]

The Loyalist paramilitaries, called "Loyalists" because of their profession of loyalty to the Queen who is monarch of Britain, also began to re-emerge in the sixties. The Ulster Volunteer Force (UVF) saw themselves as the descendants of the militia who emerged in response to the threat of a united Ireland in the earlier part of the century. They were worried by the civil rights reforms suggested by the Prime Minister of Northern Ireland, Terence O'Neill, and they saw such reforms as threatening the existing Protestant supremacy in Northern Ireland. Recruitment to the ranks of the Loyalist paramilitaries was substantially increased when violence erupted on to the streets in 1969. In almost all the working-class areas of Belfast the men, both Catholic and Protestant, formed themselves into vigilante groups in order to protect their streets; many of these vigilantes subsequently joined the paramilitary groupings. Among the Loyalists, these groups were mainly the UVF and the Ulster Defence Association (UDA).

The number of active paramilitaries who were Republican was estimated in 1991 to be about 200–300 (RISCT, 1991) although obviously many more supporters assisted the military campaign by providing safe houses, hiding weapons, and providing finance. The number of active Loyalists was estimated in 1992 to be around 150–200 (RISCT, 1992), although they too had active and passive support from many more people in their communities. Despite their small numbers the paramilitaries have carried out most of the horrific bombings, shootings, kidnappings, racketeering and intimidation that have characterized the last 25 years of the conflict in Northern Ireland, and have been responsible for approximately 90 per cent of the deaths in Northern Ireland.

The politicians

One of the main difficulties in bringing paramilitary violence to an end has been the almost total failure of the communities' elected representatives to concur upon possibilities for a political agreement, either within the region, or within the island. The objectives of the politicians do not differ significantly from the objectives of many of the paramilitaries, and during the conflict, the constitutional political parties frequently accused each other of colluding secretly with the different paramilitaries.

Almost all Catholics want a united Ireland, and throughout the conflict the main democratic proponent of the desire for this political option is the Social Democratic and Labour Party (SDLP) which usually polls about 20 per cent of the vote. Sinn Fein, which is seen as the political wing of the IRA, usually polls between 10 and 16 per cent of the electoral vote in Northern Ireland, and about 2 per cent in the Republic of Ireland.

Almost all Protestants still wish to retain the constitutional link with Britain. There are two main Unionist political parties, the Ulster Unionist Party (UUP) and the Democratic Unionist Party (DUP), which between them poll just over half of the total vote. The Alliance party is generally seen as a more moderate political party, containing members from both Protestant and Catholic communities. It has variously polled between 6 and 10 per cent of the vote.[18]

During the late 1990s several small political parties emerged which were to add some new political voices to the development of political agreement in 1998. The first of these was the Progressive Unionist Party (PUP) and the Ulster Democratic Party (UDP). Both of these parties recruited heavily from ex-Loyalist paramilitaries and they brought an additional perspective to Unionist politics, which in many cases was to prove constructive. Another new party, which emerged in the late 1990s, was the Northern Ireland Women's Coalition (NIWC). This is a cross-class, cross-community women's group, which was borne out of women's local community social action. They were committed to gaining a consensus among all parties to a just and equitable political agreement to the conflict in Northern Ireland. Both the PUP and the NIWC have gained sufficient electoral support to have two seats each in the new political assembly established in 1999.

In general, the main rift that has divided most political parties, as well as the main focus for the paramilitary campaigns, is the question that pertained in 1921 – whether or not Ireland should be a country politically united under the governance of Dublin, or whether Northern Ireland should remain under the sovereignty of Britain.

Given the history of the divisions on the island, it is not surprising that reaching an agreement on how to share it should be so difficult. Although a reluctant agreement to divide the island was reached through partition in 1921, the agreement in fact satisfied no one. And following the 1921 agreement, little was done by the parties in the North or the South to ensure the necessary contact and reconciliation work that might have diminished old suspicions and angers in the two parts of the island. Even more disastrously, little work on agreed systems of government, justice, and resource sharing was attempted between the two communities in the north.

When civil rights demands for Catholics came to the fore in 1969, the existing government, a Unionist monolith, proved itself unable to cope, and the British government was forced to introduce direct rule from London in 1972. The British government suspended the Protestant-dominated government and set up a coordinating Northern Ireland Office to take control of Northern Ireland from London. A Secretary of State implemented this direct control and four ministers were appointed by the British government in London – a situation that prevailed from 1974 until 1999. It is probable that the lack of local influence by politicians has enabled many politically sensitive reforms addressing issues of equality and diversity (see Chapters 2, 3, 4, 5, and 6) to be successfully implemented in Northern Ireland. Enlightened legislators, civil servants, and members of civic society, sometimes working in conjunction with various British ministers, undertook most of the reforms and activities outlined in this book.

Since 1972, there were many attempts by the British government – and since 1995 by the British and Irish governments – to persuade the representative political parties to come to some agreement about how to share power in Northern Ireland (see Chapter 8). The closest the British government came to achieving such an agreement was in 1974, when the constitutional parties (that is, those parties who are committed to using only the democratic process, and not violence) agreed to a form of power sharing in government. This initiative survived for only five months before it was destroyed by the Loyalist paramilitaries who brought the region to a standstill by strike actions and road blockages.

The British-Irish dimension

In the mid-eighties, the British government, with great reluctance, and only because of the continuing violence, turned its attention towards external initiatives that were beyond what they had hitherto perceived as the intrastate nature of the problem. In 1985 the British and Irish governments signed the Anglo-Irish Agreement. This was an international agreement lodged with the United Nations which formally recognized that any change in the status in Northern Ireland could only come about with the consent of the majority of people in Northern Ireland. It also, for the first time, acknowledged that the Irish Republic had a legitimate interest in Northern Ireland, by establishing an intergovernmental conference where both governments could discuss matters of policy affecting Northern Ireland. Although the Republic of Ireland was to be involved only in an advisory capacity and had no executive or veto powers, the policy areas for discussion were substantial, including political, legal, and security matters, and cross-border cooperation. The Irish government was also explicitly entitled under the agreement to comment on justice and equality bodies operating in Northern Ireland, as well as on those bodies involved in security matters. The Agreement also committed both governments to promote an agreed, devolved government that would secure widespread acceptance between both communities.

The Agreement was widely backed in Britain, and in the Republic of Ireland. It was rejected by the Unionists, who saw it as diluting the union with Britain, and by Sinn Fein, who saw it as confirming partition. Despite the widespread opposition of Unionists to the Agreement, it has proved to be an extremely important key to the development of an eventual political solution, as it considerably increased the capacity of both governments to address the conflict as a joint problem.

By the mid-eighties, following the Agreement, it became obvious to many people within Sinn Fein that a continuing military campaign by the IRA would not necessarily achieve a British withdrawal from Northern Ireland. It was also obvious to the British army that, although it could contain the conflict, it could not, given the existing community support, defeat the IRA through military means. Sinn Fein therefore began to explore the option of creating a much more widely based Nationalist political front in order to progress towards their aim of a united Ireland. They had also begun to change the nature of their political demands, softening the requirement for a stated time frame for a British withdrawal, recognizing the need for Unionists to consent to a united Ireland, and asking the British government to be persuaders to that consent.

After another round of failed political talks in 1992, from which Sinn Fein were excluded because of their support for violence, John Hume, the leader of the SDLP, and Gerry Adams, the leader of Sinn Fein, started to dialogue in 1993 to see if they could achieve a breakthrough in the stalemate which saw violence continue and no political solution in sight. These discussions continued for most of 1993, and eventually a series of principles was agreed upon which they hoped would make it possible for the IRA to end the violence with some sense of honour.

Towards the end of 1993, it was also revealed that the British government, through intermediaries, had been having secret talks with Sinn Fein/IRA, directed at ending the violence. These talks had focused on how such an ending could be achieved, and how Sinn Fein could be included in talks once they had eschewed violence.

Ceasefires – 1994

In 1993 both Irish and British governments agreed to the Downing Street Declaration in the hope that such a declaration would provide a sufficient excuse for the IRA to end its campaign. In it, the governments agreed that a decision on the future of the Union was to be ratified by referenda both north and south of the border, thus allowing for the "self-determination of the people of the island of Ireland" which Sinn Fein had said was necessary if the violence of the IRA was to cease. Although the Downing Street Declaration was declared by Sinn Fein to be insufficient to satisfy its political aspirations, on 1 September 1994, the IRA began a complete halt to its military operations in order to try to achieve their aspirations through the political process. Six weeks later the Loyalist paramilitaries also called a ceasefire, and asked to be included in the coming political negotiations.

In February 1995, the British and Irish governments produced another document – The Framework Document – that outlined the British government's perspective on a possible framework for internal government in Northern Ireland, and their joint thinking on a political agreement between the two governments and cooperation on an island-wide basis. However, the issue of decommissioning began to significantly threaten the process. In March 1995, the British government made paramilitary decommissioning a requirement for entry into political talks. The IRA felt it was sufficient that they had called a ceasefire, and that this should suffice for entry into the talks. In an attempt to resolve the issue, an International Body on Decommissioning was set up, chaired by US senator George Mitchell, and it reported in January 1996, advocating a set of six principles that should underline the process of political dialogue.[19] In response to these principles, the IRA called an end to their ceasefire in February 1996, accusing the British government of wasting the opportunity for peace. The IRA exploded a huge bomb in London's Canary Wharf, which was a commercial flagship project at the heart of the redevelopment of the London docklands, effectively bringing an end to their ceasefire. The Loyalists maintained their ceasefires.

Belfast Agreement 1998

In May 1997, a new Labour government, led by Tony Blair, won a massive parliamentary majority, which gave the new British government more room to manoeuvre on the peace process. It quickly set about drawing Sinn Fein back into dialogue. The British government gave commitments to Sinn Fein on policing reform, employment equality, action to address contentious parading[20] by Protestant Orangemen through Catholic areas and the transfer of Republican prisoners from jails in England to jails in the Republic of Ireland. Crucially, Labour announced that decommissioning was secondary to actually getting people into talks and the demand for decommissioning prior to entry into the talks was dropped. The IRA declared another ceasefire in July 1997.

For the first time ever, talks which included all the parties to the conflict, that is the two governments, all the major political parties, and parties representing the main paramilitary organisations, began in September 1997. The talks were chaired by US Senator George Mitchell and despite many difficult days, including periods when both Sinn Fein and the UDP were expelled from the talks for limited periods because of continuing violence by the parties with which they were associated, the talks continued. In April 1998, after 48 hours of intensive non-stop negotiations, all parties (except the DUP) finally accepted the Belfast Agreement.[21]

In the Agreement, the parties accepted that the constitutional future of Northern Ireland was to be decided by the people of Northern Ireland. The citizens of Northern Ireland would have the right to an identity that was British, or Irish, or both, including holding passports associated with such identities, and the Irish State would drop its territorial claim to Northern Ireland.

In addition, there would be a power-sharing assembly within which the parties would allocate chairs and vice chairs on an agreed basis, and a cross-community consensus would be necessary for agreement on issues of major relevance to both communities. A North-South ministerial body would be set up to deal with issues of common concern, and a British-Irish Council would also be established, which would draw members from the newly evolved Welsh and Scottish Assemblies, as well as members from the Northern Ireland Assembly, and members of the British and Irish governments.

A number of other issues were also addressed in the agreement, e.g. the setting up of an Equality Commission and a Human Rights Commission, the development of social, economic, and cultural inclusion policies, the need to recognize the needs of victims, the acceleration of paramilitary prisoner releases, the normalization of security arrangements as the threat of violence diminished and the setting up of independent commissions for the criminal justice system, and for policing.

It was also agreed that the Agreement would need the ratification of the majority of people on the island of Ireland, both North and South. A copy of the Good Friday Agreement was sent to every household and the Agreement was put to a referendum. Despite the reluctance of many Unionists who saw the Agreement as a sell-out to terrorism, and the reluctance of some Republicans, who saw it as a sell-out on their goals of a united Ireland, the Agreement was passed with a Yes vote by over 71 per cent of the people of Northern Ireland, and 94 per cent in the Republic of Ireland.

Post-Agreement tensions

Following the Agreement, Northern Ireland had a long and difficult summer. There were significant tensions between what came to be known as the 'Yes' camp (those in favour of the Agreement) and the 'No' camp (those against the Agreement). In August 1998, a bomb exploded in the market town of Omagh, in County Tyrone, which killed 29 people, both Protestant and Catholic. The bomb was the work of the RIRA, a disaffected Republican group. The shock of the attack was such that it had a sobering affect on the political leaders, and in September 1998, David Trimble, the leader of the UUP and now First Minister designate in the new Assembly, met Gerry Adams, the leader of Sinn Fein for their first ever face-to-face meeting. Gradually, the various aspects of the Agreement began to be implemented.

The main sticking point continued to be decommissioning, and in the face of the refusal of Sinn Fein/IRA to accept any definite date for it to start, the UUP abstained from the establishment of the power-sharing executive in July 1999. There was much frustration, with all parties accusing each other of intransigence. The political parties and the governments again asked Senator George Mitchell to conduct a review of the decommissioning process in September 1999. This review reported in November 1999, and in December

1999, the IRA confirmed that it would appoint a representative to the Independent Commission on Decommissioning. This representative was appointed, and the power-sharing executive set up simultaneously on 2 December 1999 with its full quota of 10 Ministers, four of whom were from the UU, four from the SDLP, two from the DUP, and two from Sinn Fein. A UU (Unionist) First Minister was appointed, and an SDLP (Nationalist) Deputy First Minister.

By 2001, in spite of almost two years of devolved government, it was obvious that many sectarian tensions remained at community level, and they continued to be played out through continuing sporadic violence on the streets. Decommissioning continued to be a significant source of tension, and although the IRA eventually agreed to start some actual decommissioning in October 2001, achieving a conclusion to the process of decommissioning by both Republicans and Loyalists is likely to prove contentious for some years yet. Although many issues of policing reform had been agreed by 2001, e.g. the SDLP had, for the first time in history, joined the policing board, and Catholics had begun to join the new police service in significant numbers, there is still not total agreement on some issues of police reform. And public parades are likely to remain contentious for some years to come. However, the Agreement does appear to provide many of the necessary processes through which to resolve a lot of the remaining difficulties. In particular the power sharing and consensus mechanisms enshrined in the process have been designed to ensure that the politicians engage in a continuing balancing process on issues of community need. By 2001, the main parties, including those who have developed from violence into politics, had invested a significant amount of energy into developing a programme for government for Northern Ireland, and this augers well for the continuation of the political process.

Although it is quite possible that at some stage the remaining differences may temporarily disrupt the continuation of power sharing between the parties, which would mean a resumption of informal shared authority over Northern Ireland by the British and Irish governments, the bones of any final agreement are unlikely to be different from those of the Belfast Agreement.

The cost of the conflict

More than 3,700 people have died in the conflict since the civil rights movement in 1969 (about 2.5 per cent of the population) and over 30,000 have been injured.[22] Almost 60 per cent of the killings have been carried out by Republican paramilitaries, and almost 30 per cent by Loyalists. Just over 10 per cent of the killings that have occurred were carried out by the security forces, many in contentious circumstances (Fay et al., 1997). Most of the killings happened in particularly difficult urban areas where there were substantial inter-faces between the communities. Within a one-square-mile area of north Belfast, for example, there have been over 600 murders during the period of the troubles. The numbers of people killed in the con-flict reached a maximum of 467 per year in the mid-seventies, but fell to approximately 80 people per year in the period 1984–93. In addition to those killed in Northern Ireland 200 people have been killed in the Republic of Ireland, in Great Britain[23] and Europe, as a direct result of the conflict. No one has ever been held to account for most of the murders and over three quarters of Republican murders, and over half of Loyalist murderers go unsolved. There is also sig-nificant disquiet by many over the fact that very few in the security forces, who were responsible for approximately 10 per cent of the killings, have ever served sentences for such killings. The legacy of the conflict in grief, anger, and hate within and between the com-munities remains substantial. Continuing to maintain a stable po-litical agreement in the light of this legacy, as well as the need to address the remaining issues that still separate people in Northern Ireland, is likely to need significant commitment at both the politi-cal and the community level for many years to come.

2

Equity work

Patterns of inequality

In 1968, a young, single, Protestant woman called Miss Emily Beattie was allocated a public council house in the County Tyrone village of Caledon. She was the secretary to a Unionist parliamentary candidate, and could by no means have qualified as a priority candidate for such housing, given the number of Catholics, many with children, who were waiting on the housing list. This incident exemplified the kind of injustice that was angering an increasingly middle-class Catholic population, many of whom had benefited from the provision of free education through the 1947 Act, and were now much less likely to acquiesce in the face of perceived discrimination than had been the case in the past. The protest meetings that followed gradually snowballed into violence between those calling for more civil rights for Catholics[24] and between Protestants, and police, who saw such protests as disloyalty to the state.

Such feelings about discrimination were not new − since the inception of the state in 1921, many Catholics believed that there had been systematic discrimination against them. Their perceptions were confirmed by the findings of the first official inquiry by the British government into such matters, which was undertaken when the troubles erupted in 1969 (Cameron Report, 1969). In its reporting on the civil disturbances of 1968 and 1969, the Cameron Commission concluded that a sense of injustice had been a major contributory factor in engendering the violence.

The existence of discrimination, which provided the main focus for the civil right campaigns of the late 1960s, has been well documented (Rose, 1971). When Protestants took power in Northern Ireland they established what was essentially a Protestant state, which effectively discriminated against Catholics in housing, jobs, and political representation. Membership of the Orange Order, a wholly Protestant society, was often essential for progress in politics and business. One of the main grievances was the "gerrymandering" (or rigging) of voting boundaries to discriminate against Catholics, and the existence of a weighted voting system which favoured Protestants. The most striking example of gerrymandering was in the city of Derry/Londonderry.[25] The city had a large majority of Catholics but the voting wards were designed so that the city council would always contain a substantial majority of Unionist councillors, despite the minority numerical status of Unionists. The practice of allocating multiple votes to the owners of large businesses also favoured the weighting of the Protestant vote.

Such arrangements ensured that Unionists dominated most local councils, and that employment and housing allocation patterns were consequently biased. For example, in 1969 in the local Dungannon district, not one of the council's administrative, clerical, and technical employees was a Catholic, even though Catholics constituted about half the district's population (Cameron Report, 1969). In 1959, 94 per cent of the 740 most senior civil servants were Protestant (Barritt and Carter, 1962). Catholics were also in the main excluded from other major areas of employment in the private sector and in state subsidized industries such as shipbuilding, as these were also Protestant-owned or controlled.

When the latest phase of violence began in Northern Ireland, it therefore erupted largely around issues of inequality. The British government declared in August 1969 that "every citizen of Northern Ireland is entitled to the same equality of treatment and freedom from discrimination as obtains in the rest of the United Kingdom" (Bardon, 1992: 672). Following this statement, a series of legislative reforms to address existing inequalities was introduced, first by the Northern Ireland parliament, and, after it had been dissolved in

1972, by the Westminster parliament. In 1973 the British government established the Standing Advisory Commission on Human Rights to monitor the effectiveness of laws against discrimination. In addition, responsibility for contentious areas of work was taken from the local district councils and centralized.

Reform

Housing reform

Control of all public housing allocation was transferred to a regional authority, the Northern Ireland Housing Executive. This body began its work in early 1971, and faced immense problems from its beginnings. It faced not only discriminatory patterns in housing, but also the results of decades of neglect which had resulted in a badly rundown housing stock – it was estimated that about 20 per cent of the existing houses were unfit to live in. The Housing Executive succeeded in having housing prioritized. Their work has been so successful that by 1992 surveys showed that, in great contrast to the grievances of 1969, Catholics and Protestants alike were equally satisfied with both the allocation and the services of the Housing Executive.[26]

The upgrading, and the fairer allocation of housing provision, may also have had an additional positive consequence. Because paramilitary strongholds tended to exist in the more rundown and ghettoized enclaves it has been suggested that the effective efforts of the Housing Executive may have contributed substantially to the significant fall in levels of violence in the region in the 1980s when compared with the high levels prevailing in the 1970s (Bardon, 1992: 793).

Voting reform

The British government, following its intervention in 1969, quickly introduced voting reforms. House ownership was no longer a prerequisite for voting rights, and the multiple votes given to business owners were abolished. Local council boundaries were redrawn more accurately to represent the reality of citizen distribution, and a proportional representation system of voting was introduced which increased Nationalist chances of gaining some power where their numbers were substantial enough, and increased the number of councils under Nationalist control. Apart from some minor disputes that still erupt when such boundaries are reviewed in response to changing populations, and continuing suspicions of impersonation in elections (called the "vote early-vote often system"), the processes of democracy have ceased in the main to be a source of contention between the communities.

Employment reform

The Cameron Report and other reports confirmed such major disparities in employment levels. In 1971 it was estimated that 17.3 per cent of Catholic males were unemployed, compared to 6.6 per cent Protestant males (Gallagher, 1991). Addressing such an imbalance was to prove to be an extremely difficult task, particularly in the area of male long-term unemployment, and given the relevance of unemployment issues in support for violence. A number of studies that have considered the characteristics of those who supported Sinn Fein (the political wing of the IRA) have showed that such support is at its maximum among young male unemployed Catholics with lower levels of occupational skills. The New Lodge district of north Belfast has almost 56 per cent male unemployment, is completely Catholic, and has a high support for Sinn Fein. A similar picture may be seen in Catholic west Belfast, in the Bogside in Derry/ Londonderry city, and in Crossmaglen in south Armagh. Other studies show that cities and towns with large Catholic ghettos and with high unemployment rates have the highest levels of violence (Poole, 1990).

The link between unemployment and violence is also noticeable on the Protestant side. The Shankill and Crumlin Road areas of west and north Belfast are the highest areas of both Protestant unemployment and Loyalist paramilitarism. Studies in Derry/Londonderry city also show a similar connection between unemployment and Loyalist paramilitarism on the Waterside, a traditionally Protestant part of the city.

At the outbreak of violence in 1969, the Parliamentary Commission Act (NI) established the office of the Northern Ireland Commissioner for Administration. The office had powers to investigate complaints of misadministration by government departments, including discrimination on grounds of religious or political belief. In 1972 a commission was established to promote fairness in staff recruitment in the local councils, which had been noted for their discriminatory nature, and the government established a working party to look at employment practices in the private sector. In 1973 the Northern Ireland Constitution Act provided for a legislative assembly for Northern Ireland and made void any legislation by that body which discriminated on the ground of religious or political belief. The Act also established the Standing Advisory Commission on Human Rights.

In 1976 the Fair Employment Act was passed, making discrimination in employment on religious or political grounds unlawful and a Fair Employment Agency (FEA) was established to receive complaints of discrimination in employment and to investigate further the extent to which there was inequality. Employers were encouraged voluntarily to promote principles of equality and to sign a declaration to that effect. In 1982 the government announced that tenders for government contracts would not normally be accepted by firms unless they held an equal opportunities employer certificate issued under the Fair Employment Act.

From the mid-eighties, however, the 1976 Act came under increasing pressure for reform, as government statistics continued to indicate that despite the Act, the unemployment gap between Protestants and Catholics in Northern Ireland was not declining. In an attempt to accelerate the process, a new Act was therefore introduced in 1989 under which the Fair Employment Commission (FEC) replaced the FEA. The FEC was given extra resources and powers by the government in pursuit of its task. These included a new body to handle cases of alleged discrimination, and the requirement that all employers with 25 or more employees had to register with the FEC and had to monitor the religious composition of their workforces. In addition, indirect discrimination was made illegal, such as the use of a criterion for recruitment or promotion that could indirectly indiscriminate against a member of one community in favour of another, when the criterion was not job-related. In addition, the guidelines issued with the Act described legal affirmative action policies that employers could implement in their attempts to lessen the existing imbalances within their workforces.

By the early nineties, however, after two decades of government attempts to address equity issues in Northern Ireland, the indicators showed that the Catholic community remained seriously disadvantaged. This was particularly true in the case of long-term unemployment, where Catholic men were still twice as likely to be unemployed as their Protestant counterparts. Existing legislation and monitoring measures had only marginally alleviated that figure, from 2.5 times higher in 1971 to 2.2 times higher in 1993. In addition, 45 of the top 50 unemployment black spots areas in Northern Ireland were almost exclusively Catholic.[27]

Research into the reasons for the continuing disparity was also showing that although direct discrimination against Catholics was still playing a part in maintaining discrimination, the steps needed to redress the situation were now seen to be far more complex than merely introducing monitoring and legislative procedures.

The fact that Catholics rarely sought employment in security and security-related services was a problem; the evidence showed that if they were equally employed in these sectors the differential would be significantly decreased (Boyle and Hadden, 1994). The continuing recession, which was afflicting all European countries, meant that employment creation and job turnover were extremely low, which reduced the chances for Catholic entry into many industries. In addition, differentials in education were identified as a significant factor in limiting employment equity.

Education reform

Throughout the history of Northern Ireland, children from Protestant schools generally had higher qualifications than pupils from Catholic schools. In part this was due to the fact that there were fewer places available in Catholic grammar (academic upper-stream) schools than in Protestant grammar schools and figures also showed considerable disparity in nursery school provision, with three times more places available in Protestant areas than Catholic areas.[28] Catholic opportunities for employment also appeared to be limited by the fact that a lesser emphasis had traditionally been given to the teaching of science and technology in Catholic schools, and more time was given to the teaching of the arts, and particularly religion. Such practices limited the range of occupations available to Catholics upon leaving school.

Reforms aimed at changing funding arrangements for the maintained (mainly Catholic) sector were introduced in 1992. A formula was agreed for funding which took account of social deprivation, provided 100 per cent capital funding for maintained schools, which had previously only received 85 per cent of such funding, provided extra resources for the building of more grammar school places for Catholic children, and provided for a review of the necessity to address nursery school provision, and a review of the curriculum to ensure that both Catholic and Protestant schools offered a broad and balanced curriculum. Through the latter it was hoped to redress the deficiencies of Catholic schools in the provision of more science and technology education and thus increase the ability of Catholics to find employment in those sectors where they have traditionally been underrepresented.

Targeting social need

In 1990 the British government decided that the existing legislative measures to address inequity were not still not enough to reduce existing differentials, particularly that of unemployment. Catholics within the overall system of employment were doing better in recruitment terms and in some cases, particularly in government agencies (employing 40 per cent of the workforce in Northern Ireland) Catholics were achieving entry and promotional prospects at a disproportionately higher rate than Protestants. Overall, however, Catholic unemployment figures remained depressingly high.

In addition, the 1990 census identified some continuing discrepancies between the communities that were in need of attention. While direct discrimination in housing allocation was no longer a problem, there still remained a significant difference in patterns of tenure and in overcrowding. Health indicators also showed differentials, with disability at all age levels being significantly higher among Catholics.[29]

Faced with a major challenge of the continuance of marginalized ghetto areas (mainly Catholic, but also some Protestant areas) and the obvious link between such areas and the use of paramilitary violence, the government decided that a major initiative was needed to address such alienation. Thus, in the early 1990s, it set up a new initiative, called Targeting Social Need (TSN), under the auspices of the Central Community Relations Unit (CCRU). The objective of this programme was to tackle areas of social and economic differences by targeting government policies and programmes more sharply in those areas or sections of the community suffering the highest levels of disadvantage and deprivation.

Under this initiative, all government departments were in the first place required to analyse and monitor the impact on the community of their policies and actions and any differentials in such impact between the two sections of the community. Where a differential was found to exist, scope for remedial action was to be considered. In addition, a variety of new schemes were implemented, and existing schemes were augmented to ensure that they made a more effective contribution to the mitigation of disadvantage. These initiatives included work designed specifically to address disadvantage in Belfast such as the Making Belfast Work scheme (with funding of approximately $25 million per year) that was designed to assist community participation and development, including economic development, in the most deprived areas of Belfast.

Extra attention was also given under the TSN programme to providing further opportunities for training, to increasing development work for indigenous industry creation, particularly in the most marginalized areas, and to ensuring that individual job creation agencies further biased their work towards those areas that were most seriously disadvantaged.

Action for Community Employment, a scheme primarily aimed at the long-term unemployed, was given substantially more resources, as long-term unemployment is proportionately higher among Catholics. More money was made available for housing renovations and for community development, which the government agreed was often the first step necessary for communities to develop in confidence and expertise to a level enabling them to begin to address the hard necessities of economic and job development. In addition, five areas of particular rural disadvantage, all of which were Catholic areas, were also chosen for extra funding and development.

Policy and fair treatment

As well as the above initiatives, designed to address issues of inequality by addressing the wider context and not just the legislative need, the government in 1994 introduced a new initiative called Policy Appraisal and Fair Treatment (PAFT) also under the auspices of the CCRU.

The object of this initiative was to ensure that, in practice, issues of equality and equity conditioned policy making and action in all spheres and at all levels of government activity, whether in regulatory and administrative functions or through the delivery of services to the public. The guidance given through the initiative was designed to ensure that considerations of equality, equity, and non-discrimination (not just in relation to religious/political affiliation, but also in relation to other areas of inequality such as gender, race, disability, marital status, sexual affiliation) were built in from the outset to the preparation of policy proposals, including legislation and strategic plans for the implementation of policy and the delivery of services. These guidelines applied to all Northern Ireland government departments and all government agencies.

Belfast Agreement

Following the Belfast Agreement, many of the responsibilities for equality are now the responsibility of the Equality Commission which was set up in October 1999, taking over the responsibilities of the FEC (religion), the Equal Opportunities Commission (gender), the Commission for Racial Equality for Northern Ireland, and the Northern Ireland Disability Council. The new Equality Commission is also responsible for relevant matters in the extension of the Fair Employment and Treatment (NI) Order 1998 which covers equality issues in the provision of goods, facilities, and services and the management and disposal of premises.

Equality schemes and impact assessments (as advocated in section 75 of the Belfast Agreement) have now become the prime requirements of a multifaceted approach to equality, including elements of the first Programme for Government produced by the new Assembly of politicians. There is also now an Equality Unit within the Office of the First Minister and Deputy First Minister, which is deemed to be the driving force on issues of equality, including TSN, and promoting social inclusion.

Conclusion

Many of the initiatives designed to introduce more social equity into the structures and systems of Northern Ireland have had some considerable success. Complaints are no longer heard about rigged voting, unfair housing allocations, or unequal educational funding. Although Catholics are still disproportionately represented among the long-term unemployed, twice as many Catholics are now employed at senior management level than were employed 10 years ago. Although they are still less represented in the very senior positions in both the civil service and the private sector, after the exclusion of security-related occupations (where employment was rarely sought by Catholics) the representation of Catholics in the public sector had reached the overall representative rate for Catholics in the economically active population (Equality Commission, 1999).

The range of initiatives undertaken since 1970 have begun to bear significant fruit, and have substantially changed the capacity of Northern Ireland society to provide for equal opportunities for its citizens, both Catholic and Protestant alike. They also provide for a background of equity in employment, education, health, housing, and social services, as well as representation on all public sector boards, and this is likely to prevent the re-emergence of nationalist violence in the future. The delegation of responsibility for equality matters to the Office of the First and Deputy First Minister, which lies at the heart of the new power-sharing assembly ensures that equality issues will remain at the core of the work of the government in the future, and will ensure that such issues will not have the capacity to destabilize a society that has been so convulsed by issues of equality in its history.

3

Community dialogue and cooperation

A divided society

Within a particular one square mile area of north Belfast there have been over 600 murders during the period of the troubles. Only a few yards, or a street corner, or the colours on the kerbstones will differentiate between the territory of the "Taigs" (slang word for Catholic) or the "Prods" (Protestants). Increasingly over the past few years their separation has been assisted by the erection of massive "peace" walls designed to offer some element of security to both beleaguered communities. When people do by chance meet as they go about their business, most of their meetings are limited by an instinctual treating of the other as different – one of "them." It has been established that by the age of eight, many children have learnt to tell the difference between a Catholic and a Protestant, through having learnt the subtle combination of accent, name, and background clues that ensures such "telling."

Such almost immediate differentiation means that even where meetings do occur, they are circumscribed by a caution that will usually prevent any open and honest dialogue, particularly about issues that are pertinent to the conflict. Indeed such caution is often justified, and those facilitating contact between the communities have learnt to respect the need for caution, particularly in an area such as north Belfast, where murderers and their families often live in close proximity to the families of their victims. It is not unknown for dialogue groups to discover that they contain the relatives of both victims and perpetrators amongst their members. Such meetings exemplify the strange conjunction in Northern Ireland whereby people often live near to each other, and can learn enough about each other's movements to ensure murder, but their relative physical closeness rarely produces positive relationships that can ensure both honesty and respect, and develop the necessary trust that needs to underpin any political agreement.

This chapter addresses the ways in which people involved in conflict resolution work tried, and are still trying, in increasingly strategic ways, to find ways to develop such positive relationships in Northern Ireland, and programmes to sustain such relationships. In Northern Ireland such work was usually called "community relations work" although at various times other terms have been fashionable, e.g. anti-sectarian work, interdependence work, coexistence work, or peace-building work.

Contact necessities

Faced with such a divided society, and an ongoing, violent conflict, two main approaches to the divisions are possible. The first is to ignore these divisions, both communal and personal, and hope that when a political solution is eventually agreed upon this will in itself be sufficient to ease and develop the bonds between communities. With a political solution achieved, and violence diminished, communities can then settle themselves, perhaps into benign apartheid, where communities continue to live, work, learn, and play separately, but are at least agreed about existing constitutional arrangements, and violence has ceased. If such agreement is effective enough, and fears about domination or coercion are addressed, then they may begin slowly to cooperate across the communal divide as needs and functions arise.

The second approach is to believe that while such physical and mental separation exists between communities, fears and misunderstanding about each other's ultimate intentions will continue, and will thus make the achievement of any agreed political solutions between the communities even more difficult, and more difficult to sustain. The latter belief is what has informed most of the community relations work in Northern Ireland.

Achieving quality contact

The assumption that increased contact between communities will improve relationships has been a substantial belief that has informed the programmes of most of the peace groups that have grown up over the decades of the conflict. A study undertaken in 1985 (Frazer and Fitzduff, 1986) showed that there were approximately 47 "peace" groups in existence. Some of these, such as Corrymeela, an inter-church group, had been established in the mid-sixties, but many others had arisen in response to the ongoing conflict. One of the most notable of these was the Peace People, established in 1976 in response to an aborted IRA operation which had caused the deaths of three children. The majority of these peace groups relied on the assumed effectiveness of contact in changing attitudes and behaviour.

However, the presumption that increased contact will necessarily improve relationships has been questioned over the past few years (Hewstone and Browne, 1986; Cairns, 1994; Ryan, 1995: 129–52). It is now accepted that to be of significant use, such contact has to be of a qualitative nature, which means that where possible contact should be undertaken in a context where group identity, and not just individual identity is acknowledged, where differences are articulated rather than avoided, and where superordinate goals (usually social needs goals in the first instance) are agreed for co-operative work by groups. It is also important that such contact is developed within a context that builds up structures for the continuance and sustainability of the contact.

In addition such work should ideally cater for the fact that attitudinal and behavioural change factors will vary according to individual learning and personality needs, for example, how much they need to 'belong' to groups, and whether they are primarily motivated by rational, or by emotional needs (Fitzduff, 1989b). There is a requirement, therefore, to provide a variety of possible change factors for use in programme development.

In resourcing such work, many groups have found it useful to phase in the work gradually. In the first instance, some groups such as the Women's Information Group, set up in the early nineties by a group of women concerned with common social problems in their Belfast communities, concentrated on less contentious issues around which to meet each other – for example crèche provision, women's education, unemployment needs. Later, some within the group felt both confident enough, and trusting of each other, to begin to address contentious issues of policing and paramilitarism within their communities. This gradually phased development was characteristic of many groups, such as community development groups who mainly concentrated on developing their own segregated communities, but developed the confidence and courage to reach out to the other community on common social problems, and subsequently to address specific issues of cultural and political tension (O'Halloran and McIntyre, 1999; Jarman and O'Halloran, 2000).

Single-identity work

Such work also showed the importance of the need for, and the legitimacy of, *single-identity* work. Single-identity work is work within groups that are either Unionist/Protestant or Nationalist/Catholic and is aimed at increasing the confidence of a group in terms of its identity and capacity. Without such pre-contact work, it was discovered that contact itself can be burdened with so much defensiveness that it can be hostile and counterproductive. Such single-identity work also often succeeded in developing the necessary leaders who could reach out beyond their ghettoized identities to connect with the other side. This work was recognized to be so important that it eventually received significant funding, provided such programmes were seen eventually to lead to cross-community dialogue (Hughes and Donnelly, 1998).

Cross-community work

By the year 2001, there were over 130 organizations that facilitated opportunities to enable people to meet across the community and institutional divide, and to address questions of differences, including issues of politics, policing, equality, and identity. In such workshops can be found local politicians, trade union officials, prisoners, prison officers, community, church and youth leaders, police and soldiers, former paramilitaries, teachers, and others. To detail here all of the work in the many areas where such work has developed over the past few years would be impossible,[30] but several case studies have been selected to exemplify the range of work undertaken.

The Interface Project

The Interface Project was an integrated community development/ community relations project that was developed along the 19 interface areas of Belfast, where violence has been at its highest. Through this project, following two years of single-identity work, which addressed issues of common social problems, local skilled mediators eventually succeeded in bringing together community development groups to look at ways in which they could together address the need to break down the emotional and physical walls that separated them. This project, and others along the interface, which were eventually to include many ex-prisoners as they returned to their communities, was to provide a fertile space for dialogue between paramilitaries and communities in the years preceding the Agreement (O'Halloran and McIntyre, 1999).

The Peace and Reconciliation Group

The Peace and Reconciliation Group (PRG), based in Derry/ Londonderry, was set up in the eighties to deal with the hostile relationships existing in the city, and in its early days it dealt particularly with the problems of rumours and counter rumours that contributed significantly to the spiral of violence. By using the services of contacts within each community (often ex-prisoners) it maintained a watchful eye on escalating stories of possible attack and counter-attack, and often prevented these from stimulating full-scale violence within the city by clarification of such rumours. Subsequently, the group has been significantly involved in working on developing training for community sensitivity with the police and army, whose actions in trying to maintain law and order were often counterproductive, particularly within Nationalist areas where they were usually treated with distrust, but also in some Loyalist areas. The group also spent much of its time facilitating contact between those who were most violently involved with each other, and on facilitating dialogue between the communities, especially at times of particular tension, such as parading times and breakdown of cease-fires.

Counteract

Counteract, which began in the early nineties, was a group which functioned under the auspices of the trade unions, and whose task was to end sectarianism in the workplace. At the beginning of the troubles in 1969, workplaces were not only mostly divided, but where there were some workplaces with both Protestant and Catholic workers, such workers as were in the minority often suffered from harassment, and in some cases, murder. At particular times of the year, and especially on those days and during those events commemorating historical gains or losses for each community, tensions would be extremely high. Counteract began a series of programmes with both employers and workers, aimed at eliminating such hostility: workplace awareness programmes, anti-sectarian programmes, and, eventually sectarian harassment officers who were responsible for ensuring the end of such harassment. They have now succeeded in almost ending the sectarian tension that used to make life so miserable, and often dangerous, for many workers from both communities.

North Belfast Community Development Centre

North Belfast has suffered more from political and sectarian violence than any other area of Northern Ireland. It is a region criss-crossed by Catholic and Protestant areas, with a high rate of murder between the communities. Communal riots are a particular feature of the area, and particularly during the summer, when the "marching" season is at its highest. Since the mid-nineties, the North Belfast Community Development Centre has concentrated on cross-community dialogue between community leaders from different traditions, to enlist their help where possible in limiting such violence. A particular feature of such work has been the use of mobile phone networks, where leaders are issued with mobile phones to keep them in touch even when it is difficult to go into each other's areas. These are particularly useful to alert each other of trouble brewing on each side, and in developing integrated strategies to avoid the worst of such confrontations. Such programmes have notably limited the communal violence that was such a significant Saturday night feature of the area, particularly in the summer (Jarman and O'Halloran).

Mediation Network

In the late 1980s, a small group of people, including the author, got together to promote the work of mediation in Northern Ireland. Although such work had begun to develop several decades previously in the US it was only represented in Northern Ireland in areas such as trade union and marital/family mediation, and not at all in the political sphere. Aware that Kraybill and Buzzard (1982) and others from the US had been using such techniques to apparent good effect in ethno-political conflict, the group set up a new organization dedicated to extending the use of mediation to the political and neighbourhood spheres. Such work was not without significant challenges – including threats to many indigenous mediators from both sides of the paramilitary divide – but the pool of mediators available to undertake politically and culturally contentious mediation gradually increased. The group set up the Mediation Network in 1991 and the usage of mediators gradually became more common. Within a decade, they were being used by governments and by public bodies and others as an increasingly useful tool for dialogue in politically contentious situations.

Churches

Church membership and attendance in Ireland, both in the Republic of Ireland and in Northern Ireland, are amongst the highest in Western Europe, and the churches are very important centres of social and leisure activity, particularly in rural areas where church attendance numbers are at their highest. For much of the conflict, however, with a few honourable exceptions, such as the Quakers and some individuals from other churches, churches have either denied that addressing the conflict was their business, or have given a religious endorsement to political and cultural allegiances.

It has therefore been very difficult for the churches to put much emphasis on cross-community and reconciliation work. And in many cases churches, and their congregations, have deliberately blocked such work. In the mid-eighties, it was still possible for a Presbyterian clergyman to be forced out of office by his congregation because he crossed the road one Christmas Eve to shake hands with the local Catholic priest, in a very minor gesture of reconciliation. A decade later, he was still receiving threatening letters about his action. And when the first integrated schools were set up, the Catholic Church refused to set up religious support for Catholic children attending such schools.

Some of this has begun to change. Since 1990, there has been a large increase in the number of church-based organizations concentrating on community relations. The Evangelical Conference on Northern Ireland (ECONI), an evangelically based organization, undertakes substantial internal work with its congregations aimed at increasing tolerance, and was one of the first Protestant organizations to involve Sinn Fein publicly in dialogue. All the main churches were involved in setting up Youthlink, an organization whose purpose is to foster youth work across the community divide. The Young Men's Christian Association (YMCA) began to develop programmes dealing with identity and sectarianism, and set up projects to foster community relations. During the mid-nineties, the role of a few clergymen, both Protestant and Catholic, was crucial in developing dialogue between Sinn Fein and the Dublin government, and in helping the Sinn Fein leadership to understand Unionist thinking.

Some of the local churches have begun to play an increasingly important part in facilitating tolerance through activities such as shared social action, shared Bible study groups, interdenominational worship, joint services and demonstrations following murders, participation in cross-community justice groups, setting up interdenominational clergy groups and inviting clergy of other denominations to preach in their churches. Training for student and incumbent clergy to prepare them to deal with such issues and in developing community relations, is now being undertaken by all the major churches under the auspices of a variety of church-based reconciliation groups such as Corrymeela, a reconciliation group set up in the sixties to foster dialogue between the churches. However, research shows that there is still a very long way to go in ensuring a positive role for the churches in helping to ameliorate sectarian divisions in Northern Ireland.

Mainstreaming community relations work

In a society that is divided along religious, cultural, or political lines, it is important that work that increases interaction and dialogue, and that develops focused options for cross-communal cooperation, is incorporated as much as possible into every aspect of society. In Northern Ireland, it was felt by those interested in community relations work that such divisions are so detrimental to the development of trust that every opportunity possible should be taken to incorporate and integrate such work into as many institutions as possible.

District councils

In ensuring such integration, district councils were the first institutions to be formally targeted. Northern Ireland has 26 local councils, which have, with varying degrees of resources and responsibility, been charged at differing times with local decision making about planning, community services, housing provision, and rate setting. Almost without exception such councils have exemplified the hostility that has pervaded much of Northern Ireland's public life. They were significantly responsible, in many cases, for the kind of discriminatory behaviour that led directly to the civil rights movement in 1969. Their abuse of power was so obvious that in 1969 they were stripped of many of their existing powers in housing, social services, health care, and education services, and responsibility for such work was put into the hands of more central agencies. The councils' functions were then limited to burying the dead, garbage collection, and the administration of the community and leisure centres. This limit in their powers did not, however, decrease the acrimony with which many of them continued to conduct their business. Council chambers in many cases continued to be marred by party wrangling, walkouts, physical intimidation, and discrimination. Although a few positive signs emerged in the seventies about possible cooperation in Derry City Council, and in Dungannon where some Nationalists and Unionists began a tentative "responsibility-sharing" regime, the picture in relation to the councils, and in particular their capacity to help to improve community cooperation, was bleak.

Despite the inauspicious signs, a decision was made in 1989 by the Central Community Relations Unit (CCRU) to try to involve the councils in an initiative designed to improve community relations in their areas; it was a brave decision, given their history. Councils were invited to draw up their own plans to develop cross-community programmes in their area, and to look at possibilities for promoting greater mutual understanding and respect for different cultural traditions. Government funding was offered for these programmes, and for one or two staff persons for each council to develop them. The grant aiding was conditional on councils agreeing on the programmes on a cross-community basis.

All district councils are now involved in the programmes, although it took four years to persuade all of them of the merits of the work, and to encourage them to cooperate on an agreed agenda for it. Much of their work has developed substantially since the initial beginnings, helped by an extensive evaluation, which looked at the kinds of activities that differing councils were undertaking, and the kinds of effect these programmes were having on community relations in their respective areas (Knox and Hughes, 1994).

The evaluation discovered that high-profile events such as large community festivals, inter-schools sports projects, cross-community dances etc. which were aimed at attracting large audiences and increasing general consciousness rather than in-depth discussions, were least effective in changing attitudes or behaviour. On the other hand, community, economic, and social development work, undertaken on a cross-community basis, which provided opportunities for communities to become involved with one another on a sustained basis and which were aimed at increasingly tangible cooperation over a sustained period, were probably the most effective in achieving attitudinal and behavioural change on the part of the participants.

Cultural traditions projects, which addressed the need for communities to begin to see their cultural differences as a possible source of richness, and not as a threat to each other, were also seen as useful. Those most frequently developed were cross-community music and drama festivals, cultural "fairs," and study series addressing historical and cultural issues. Also useful were focused community relations work projects, which specifically focused on the need for in-depth and often difficult discussions to happen between communities so as to establish the cultural and theological differences between them. These workshops often took place over a few days, were sometimes residential and were sometimes structured as a problem-solving workshop.

The evaluations showed that such programmes showed positive gains, even in the early years of their development. All council chief executives interviewed in the evaluations agreed that the attitude of councillors towards community relations had changed significantly since the introduction of the programmes and that much of their initial hostility and anxiety about the work had disappeared. Perhaps even more significantly, in areas where such projects had been in place for two years, as opposed to those only starting, random population surveys showed that people within those areas had seen what they believed to be an improvement in community relations. Subsequently, the Partnership Boards, set up in 1996 to distribute part of the $500 million funding from the European Community, which was given to consolidate peace in the post ceasefire situation, have had active participation from the district councils, who now work alongside businesses, trade unions and the community and voluntary sector in developing and delivering programmes to consolidate the peace.

Sporting progress

The idea of addressing divisions through sport is a very ancient ideal, best exemplified by the idea of the Olympic games. In Northern Ireland, however, research has shown that sport is more frequently used to reinforce divisions than to unite communities (Sugden and Harvie, 1995). This issue is now being significantly addressed, and sporting activities are being used with increasing frequency to provide opportunities for increased cultural understanding and cross-community cooperation.

By the late eighties, television and radio began to increase their coverage of games traditionally played by the Catholic community, which had been consistently under-represented in the media. This both balanced a previous discrimination and permitted many more Protestants to enjoy such games, even if only at a safe distance on the television. Many local newspapers, which in Northern Ireland are mostly representative of one or other community, began to increase their coverage of the sporting events of the other community, possibly as much to increase their sales, as to promote community relations!

Substantial work began in 1991 between the Sports Council and the CRC to develop programmes that would help to break down the existing divisions in sport and assist its capacity to improve, rather than maintain, divisions. In 1995, the Sports Council appointed a full-time community relations officer to ensure that such a community relations need would inform, where possible, the further development of sport. Work has been undertaken with and by the various agencies responsible for sport. One example is the Irish Football Association (IFA), responsible for the promotion of soccer. While soccer is one of the few games played by both communities, many teams were single identity and games between teams of different identities frequently led to displays of sectarianism and violence, particularly by club members and spectators. Such games often necessitated a large police presence. Such trouble was common not only in Northern Ireland, but also in neighbouring Scotland, which also had some teams that were seen as being either Catholic (e.g. Celtic) or Protestant (Rangers). Northern Ireland supporters, who travelled frequently to these games, often created violent trouble both on and off the Scottish pitches.

However, many of these teams are now making substantial efforts to field a mixed team of players, and are using various methods to limit the use of the matches as opportunities for contention. Such work is gradually proving successful in limiting the sectarian hostilities that have traditionally attended football both in Northern Ireland and in neighbouring Scotland.

Sporting skills are now increasingly being taught on a cross-community basis; rugby and Gaelic core skills, for example, are now taught together where possible. Some schools are now providing sports from both traditions as part of their curriculum, particularly in integrated schools. Taster courses in each sport are now more frequently provided across the community, for example, the Irish Rugby Football Union is now targeting more participation by Catholics in the game by means of Saturday morning sessions with children in Catholic areas. Other new and creative ways are being found by some associations to promote contact and respect between differing sporting traditions; several have set up experimental "mixed rules" games where the participants play games that are a mixture of their traditional games, for example hockey and hurling. Efforts are also being made to introduce more "neutral" games such as basketball, which are free of historical connotations and which are gaining in popularity.

Institutional anti-sectarian work

During the nineties, all organizations, including government departments, public bodies, educational institutions, community, voluntary, and social bodies were encouraged to undertake anti-sectarian activities (Logue, 1993) to help them become more inclusive. Such work included ensuring a community balance in their employees, and auditing their customer ratios to ensure that they serve all communities where possible. Many now routinely undertake anti-sectarian work to address negative attitudes and behaviour within an organization and train their staff to increase their ability and confidence to work in and with any community. Where necessary, they undertake anti-intimidation work with trade union officials, management, and staff to prevent and deal with intimidation and to encourage an ethos within their organization to ensure that it respects the cultures of all communities. Increasingly many groups such as government training agencies, schools, and community organizations are encouraged to provide opportunities for their members to meet on an on-going cooperative basis and to train their staff to develop and encourage such contact and prioritize such work as part of their programme development.

Such work is not easy, involving as it does people in management who are often themselves fearful of contact, but substantial strides have been taken in developing work in many areas including businesses (CRC, 1997), social services (Barry and Higgins, 1999), and service delivery (Dunn and Morgan, 1999). This approach has been further assisted by the statutory requirement placed upon most major institutions in 2000, following the Belfast Agreement, not just to address issues of equality, but also issues of "good community relations." This requirement has significantly increased the necessity for organizations to develop their expertise in this area, and many are drawing substantially upon the previous learning of other institutions in the field who have already voluntarily begun to develop such work (Fay et al., 1997).

Venues and transport

One of the main problems facing any group that wishes to facilitate contact in Northern Ireland is that the venues available for such meetings are extremely limited. Apart from some city or town-centre hotels, few venues are seen as "neutral" by both communities. In order to address this problem, grants were made available, mainly from European Community funds, for community groups, district councils, and others to build new venues which could be used with feelings of safety by both communities. Training was also provided for management committees to develop these venues to ensure that, for example, the committees are mixed, and the use of symbols in venues is carefully considered in order not to exclude any one community. Agreements were made, where such centres are to be used for traditional sports and pastimes, that these should take place in a balanced fashion so as to ensure that the buildings continue to represent the interests of all communities. All groups receiving public monies now routinely carry out such work.

In addition to the building of new venues, considerable efforts are now being made to ensure that existing single-identity buildings review their use by only one community, and take steps to diminish the difficulty people from the other community have in using them. Community groups and church groups are encouraged to invite and "host" groups from differing areas to spend some time in what were deemed to be alien premises, and work is also undertaken with groups to encourage them to venture into other areas. Community groups are encouraged to alternate their meetings from one venue to another to provide balance, and to give the participants a chance to gradually become more comfortable in each other's premises. Analysis has been made of possibilities for increasing the use of premises such as libraries and integrated schools, so as to ensure that people who wish to organize integrated events are more creative in their use of existing facilities.

Such work, begun in a consistent way since 1990, has proved to be very successful and the number of "neutral" venues that can be used by cross-community groups has increased considerably. Perhaps of even greater interest for long-term relationships is that work encouraging the integrated use of existing premises, "owned" by one or other community is also proving to be successful. Increasingly such premises as Orange halls, and churches, are becoming more useful as places for integrated meetings, as fear and suspicion diminish through experience of such use.

In some cases the lack of available transport to facilitate contact has also proved a problem. Traditional public transport patterns have grown up to take account of differing divisions. Belfast (where almost 50 per cent of the people of Northern Ireland live and work) is an example of the problem: the existing patterns of transport are radial, reflecting the segregated nature of the city. Thus in order to undertake a cross-community visit to an adjoining area, a journey into the centre of town and out again is often required (CRC, 1992). Initial work addressing the problem has concentrated on the use of buses or minibuses to enable movements of groups from one area to another, and grant-aiding was made available for such needs. More concerted efforts, with more permanent possibilities are now being organized to ensure that problems of segregated transport disappear (Smyth, 2000). All transport companies (which are mostly public) are now being encouraged to address existing transport patterns to ensure that cross-community contact can happen on a more extensive basis and what are now being developed are more circular patterns that can increase contact capacity throughout the city in a way that can ensure easier access between the divided areas.

North-South cooperation

In addition to the existing divisions between people within Northern Ireland, there also exists a considerable amount of distrust between people living in Northern Ireland and those living in the

Republic of Ireland. Much of the more obvious distrust emanates from the Protestant/Unionist community, members of which fear the constitutional intentions of the Republic. As cooperation between the Republic and Northern Ireland is one of the key areas for consideration in any future political settlement (Chapter 8), work has been undertaken to develop contact and cooperation work between the two parts of the island.

Much of this work has been undertaken through Cooperation Ireland,[31] a voluntary body set up with the assistance of the British and Irish governments to foster cooperation on the island, which has developed a variety of programmes to achieve their objective. Cooperation Ireland resources many hundreds of community linkages each year between youth groups, women's groups, churches, and others. It has also undertaken cultural traditions work between cultural organizations both north and south of the border, to assist the development of pluralism in both constituencies, as well as regular contacts between the media from Ireland and the UK, to address issues of common concern, particularly on the reporting of the conflict.

Prime among its work, however, have been projects concentrating on economic cooperation between the two parts of the island, and appropriate infrastructural development and marketing programmes to help develop such work. This work was significantly assisted by the support of many people from the business and commercial sectors who began during the 1990s to talk openly about the economic usefulness of a cross-border economic "corridor" which could assist economic development both north and south of the border. Subsequently, many government departments in both Dublin and Belfast began in the nineties to develop programmes to secure cooperation in certain areas that appear to be functionally useful such as tourism, agricultural, and border region programmes. Many of these programmes were eventually to develop into the work of the North-South bodies which were agreed upon in the Belfast Agreement. Funding provided by the EU after the ceasefires, to consolidate the peace, also provided for a significant increase in cross-border cooperative activities, particularly between Northern Ireland and the six counties of the Republic of Ireland which border on Northern Ireland.

Training for dialogue

There were few "neutral" facilitators to help with such difficult dialogue and cooperation work in Northern Ireland. Almost everybody came weighted with their own fears, and their own political and cultural baggage. Hence there was a need for the significant development of training work to help people to develop the confidence and the skills to undertake what was often extremely difficult and sometimes dangerous work. The wide scope of such training work, developed to prepare people for many of the activities outlined above, is described in Chapter 9 of this book.

Conclusion

The work on developing contact possibilities, and on increasing the quality of that contact so that it can survive and productively deal with differences, is now well developed in Northern Ireland. As the violence diminishes, the hope and the belief is that those structures that have been carefully put in place to ensure that such contact and cooperation can develop in Northern Ireland, can develop further and ensure the greater sustainability of future political solutions. Since 1990, there has been a significant increase in the number of groups from the most ghettoized areas in Northern Ireland who are willing to come out of their ghettoes and attempt to make some new and substantial contacts with groups from other backgrounds and traditions (CRC, 2000) and to involve them in dialogue on difficult and divisive issues. Now, as the Belfast Agreement is gradually being implemented, many of these groups are turning to pick up the pieces that can ensure that the work that needs to be now undertaken as violent conflict diminishes will be successful. There is a need for ex-prisoners to be integrated back successfully into society, and this work has been developed through many community groups addressing issues such as increasing the employment skills of such prisoners, helping them to bond successfully back into their families and their communities, and engaging many of them constructively, and on a cross-community basis, in sustaining the political thrust towards peace. There are also now many groups dedicated to supporting the victims of the conflict in having their voices heard as they seek to have their physical and mental injuries recognized, as well as their need for truth and justice. Many victim groups are also now being enabled, through community work, to address their continuing needs on a joint basis, which helps to diminish the bitterness of the past. Still other community groups are working with those "dissenter" groups who are still protesting about the Agreement, and trying to engage them in sufficient dialogue to ensure their cooption to the Agreement, or at least their concurrence in refraining from further violence.

There has been a great deal of work invested into promoting dialogue and cooperative processes in Northern Ireland. Most of these processes have now been mainstreamed into the structures and programmes of many of the main institutions in the region, and will be further absorbed into many more as the EU Peace II programme comes on stream in 2001[32] and the new legal requirement to promote such good relations is implemented. In further developing such work, many of these institutions have significantly benefited from the experiences of the organizations whose structure and functions have been outlined in the chapter above.

4

The next generation

Beginnings

In the early years of the conflict, efforts at bringing children and youth together were mainly confined to voluntary organizations, such as the Peace People and other reconciliation groups which concentrated on facilitating holidays away from Northern Ireland for children and youth from differing communities. Unfortunately, whilst such holidays did provide a first opportunity for contact for most children and, particularly in the early 1970s, a welcome break from streets frequently filled with rioting, such contacts did not often last the return journeys. Participants moved back into their divided society, and often back into the mainly closed attitudes of their communities.

Increasingly such organizations began to review their practice, in the light of evaluations that questioned their effectiveness. Most of them began to increase the quality of the preparation for such contact on the part of participants, organisers and facilitators in order to ensure more effective work. Many of them began to include parents as part of their work. They also began to develop programmes to include cultural confidence work, which affirms the validity of the participants' cultural and historical identities, allied with sharing between such groups about the differences between them, and ensuring respect for such differences. For older age groups, such work also included opportunities for participants to participate in political and other contentious discussions.

Schools work

Despite their energy and goodwill, it was realized that the efforts of voluntary groups were inevitably limited, both by the scope of their own resources (a mixture of fairly minor government money and some charity trust funding) and by the limited range of their power to affect infrastructures. By the late 1980s, agreement was reached by a group of educationalists drawn from both sides of the community divide, and with educational policy makers, that in order for such work to be effective it had to encompass the vast majority of children and youth, and not just the few who could be facilitated by voluntary groups. Their conclusion was that the existing educational system (despite its segregated nature) should be used to facilitate understanding and respect between children and youth from divided communities. They agreed upon the following programmes which are now, since 1993, being implemented in all schools whether they are Catholic, Protestant, or one of the very few integrated schools.

- Education for Mutual Understanding (EMU) programmes and Cultural Heritage programmes. These were designed to ensure that pupils learn about each other's traditions, history and culture. These programmes are now an obligatory part of all schooling in Northern Ireland. In the first instance they address the need for children to feel confident in their own identities, and also to learn about the religious and political beliefs of the other communities in Northern Ireland. These programmes also include information about the increasing number of ethnic minority groups who are settling in Northern Ireland, as well as the main traditional groups. Although there have been critiques about these programmes (Smith, 1999), such criticisms centred on the need to deepen and broaden their scope, as well as recommending a coherent strategy of training to implement these programmes rather than decrease them.
- Where schools and parents agree, contact programmes are organized between Catholic, Protestant, and state (mainly Protestant) schools, and grants are made available by the government for expenses incurred in developing them. Such contact can be

joint activities (often related to curriculum demands) such as visits to historical sites and museums, allied with discussions and projects on differing identities. Some segregated schools now try to share study facilities so as to ensure contact for their pupils, particularly in their later years at school. Others have ongoing arrangements for visits to each other's schools, for debates, and for joint sporting activities. To facilitate such contact the government has provided for the development of purpose-built venues, often based near existing cultural and historical centres, to enable schools to develop residential contact programmes. Levels of participation have increased annually in such contact initiatives, and by 1999, the figures showed that almost a third of primary schools and over a half of post-primary schools were involved in some form of inter-school contact between Protestants and Catholics.

- By the late eighties, thanks to the efforts of a group of dedicated educationalists drawn from all sides of the community, an agreed history curriculum for all schools in Northern Ireland had been devised. Previously, Catholic schools had learnt a version of Irish history that often dwelt heavily on the negative role of the British in Ireland, and included very little about the perspective of the Protestant community. State schools concentrated almost solely on British history, and generally ignored the history of the island of Ireland. However this newly agreed history curriculum has become an important factor in removing the negative capacity of one-sided histories from the classrooms.

- Following the development and implementation of the agreed history curriculum, the churches, faced with the criticisms of many people who believed that the segregated system of education was a major cause of the continuing division in Northern Ireland, eventually agreed to devise a common core curriculum for the teaching of the Christian religion. This curriculum is gradually being adopted (not without some difficulties) by many schools. Although this has so far included mainly peripheral references to religions other than Christianity, it is a substantial breakthrough for a divided society where religion is such a pertinent, and often dividing, factor.

- As teachers themselves come with their own religious and political perspectives, resources have been put into the necessary training to enable them to handle such programmes with fairness and confidence, and although current evaluations show that there is a need for further development, such training work has been a significant factor in changing teachers, schools, and parental perspectives (Smyth, 2000).

- As yet, most teacher training is still carried out in a segregated manner, with Catholic and state (mainly Protestant) teacher training colleges refusing to amalgamate their training. However, they have recently agreed to share some training programmes among and between their students, and are increasingly sensitive to criticism that they should be training their teachers to be more proactive in addressing issues of sectarianism. In 2000, the Catholic training college based in west Belfast began to develop programmes for their students, and their surrounding communities, on Conflict Resolution.

- Particular projects such as the Speak Your Piece project (1996–99) have developed innovative methodologies to engage young people in addressing contentious issues in the areas of culture and politics. Such projects have significantly assisted the development of very focused and direct ways for young people from all communities to engage with each other on issues around which they have traditionally remained silent, or taken to the streets.

Most of these initiatives have only seriously begun over the last decade. The EMU and Cultural Heritage programmes have only become a mandatory part of schools curricula since 1993. So far, however, if further developed, they auger well for their objectives of increasing understanding between communities (Smyth, 2000).

Integrated schools

Few possibilities have ever existed in Northern Ireland for children to be educated together. When asked, parents from both communities usually indicate a surprisingly high desire for such integrated education to be available – approximately 70 per cent overall, with a slightly higher proportion of Catholics in favour of it. The churches in Northern Ireland, and the Catholic church in particular, have generally been opposed to such integration, fearing the loss of faith of their communities. Despite such opposition, important progress has been made in Northern Ireland for the development of integrated schools, mainly through the commitment of parents themselves.

In 1994, a group called All Children Together (ACT) composed of parents who were in favour of children being educated together began to campaign for integrated education, and the first intentionally integrated school, Lagan College, in Belfast, was opened in 1981. Its constitution provided for an ethos of tolerance, and practice was focused on ensuring such tolerance and respect. Its management board, its teaching staff, and its pupils were all drawn from both communities, and its curriculum reflected the history, languages, sports, and cultural rituals of both communities. Between 1981 and 2000, 45 integrated schools serving pupils at the primary and secondary stage of their education were opened in Northern Ireland, and many more are under consideration. While they still serve only a tiny proportion of the school sector (5 per cent), it means that choices are increasingly becoming available for parents who are committed to an upbringing for their children that challenges the prevailing segregation. The Northern Ireland Council for Integrated Education, which received much of its founding money from independent trust funds, has substantially facilitated their development.

In 1989, the government agreed to make state funding available for the establishment of new integrated schools and this has made the task of their development much easier. Further legislation followed which was designed to assist existing schools to transform themselves into integrated schools, through the incentive of additional funding for such transformation. The further development of integrated schools has been included as part of the Belfast Agreement of 1998. Evidence on the longest established of these inte-

grated schools appears to indicate that such education is of significance in ensuring positive attitudes and behaviour between pupils
from differing communities.

Youth sector

Outside the formal educational institutions, it has been much
harder to ensure quality contact between youth, but such contact,
organized on an ongoing rather than sporadic basis, has been recognized as having a potential to contribute significantly to the lessening of tension between young people. This is of particular importance given that the late teenage years are the years when young
men are most vulnerable to being recruited into sectarian hostilities,
and into paramilitaries.

A substantial amount of work is therefore being undertaken –
sometimes through the formalized youth clubs (CRC, 1999), and
through the work of such organizations as Youth Action, which
have produced policy and practice guidelines for cross-community
and anti-sectarian work with youth (Doherty and Dickson, 1993).
In addition the more traditionally segregated groups such as the
Girl Guides and the Boy Scouts are being encouraged to be more
inclusive in their membership, and in providing contact opportunities between their members. Crime prevention and rehabilita-
tion agencies, which often focus their work upon youth, have also
undertaken some significant projects, sometimes in interface areas,
aimed at ensuring contact and understanding between the different
peer groups, at what is a particularly vulnerable and potentially
hostile age.

In addition, all of the Education and Library Boards, who have
prime responsibility for educational developments, have now incorporated youth cross-community work into their programmes and
their training. Structural work for the continuation of contact has
also developed in some cases through setting up new, mixed youth
clubs, in relatively neutral areas, and in some cases through opening
up existing clubs so as to ensure more inclusiveness. It is notable

that many of the young people who have participated in such work subsequently move on to facilitating it themselves.

Further education

Research on further education has shown that even within mixed further education structures, mixing between the communities is limited, with students generally continuing to mix with their own side. Universities and Further Education colleges have frequently been riven with sectarian divisions. In the mid-nineties, the Union of Students for Ireland developed a strategy to tackle sectarianism, and improve community relations, which was aimed at addressing issues of division among students. The Union has also developed a cross-community leadership and political participation programme to ensure the more constructive involvement of students into politics, as well as some very creative programmes aimed at tackling sectarianism and bigotry among students.

Pre-school children

Pre-school opportunities for children in Northern Ireland are also generally segregated, and research undertaken in the early nineties showed that even pre-school children were expressing negative attitudes towards children and others from differing communities. The Northern Ireland Preschool Association subsequently began a programme of training, developed for pre-school teachers (Playboard, 1997), which would help them to challenge appropriately such stereotyping amongst the children in their care and help to counteract negative learning at an early stage of children's development (Connolly, 1998).

Conclusion

Work with children and young people is essential if the segregation and prejudices of communities are to be successfully combated. The experience in Northern Ireland has been that it is not sufficient to address such prejudices on a voluntary and ad hoc basis, but that the very structures of education and youth services must be harnessed and changed in order to deal with such needs in a sustained and focused manner. This work must not be relied upon in isolation to deliver more positive attitudes and behaviour on the part of young people and children; but as part of an overall strategy aimed at transforming a conflict, the experience of Northern Ireland is that, despite the difficulties inherent in its development, it is an essential adjunct to the necessary work of a divided society to ensure a future of sustainable peace.

5

Cultural traditions

Places apart

The traveller to Northern Ireland does not usually find it difficult to tell the identity of the community through which he or she is travelling. The outward signs of the differing histories and traditions are obvious features of life in Northern Ireland. Flags fly in abundance,[33] kerbstones are painted in British or Irish colours. Pubs and clubs often play music that is perceived as belonging to one or other tradition. Those that are Nationalist usually play music from the Irish tradition, and those in Unionist areas usually play mainstream British music, tunes from the indigenous Orange tradition, or sometimes Scottish music.

Marches are a frequent feature of life, particularly in the summer, which is known as "the marching season." Unionists' marches usually celebrate a particular victory that the Protestants secured over the Catholics in 1690 at the battle of the Boyne. Nationalist commemorations are usually somewhat more contemporary. The uprising in Dublin in 1916 whose aim was to achieve independence from Britain is a popular focus, and for the last 20 years many Nationalists have commemorated internment, the period from 1971 to 1975 when many hundreds of Catholics were interned without trial by the British government. Marches provide frequent occasions for street rioting and clashes, often requiring a massive security force presence to ensure the relative safety of both marchers and spectators alike.

Even decisions about which language to use have been problematic throughout the history of the region. Whilst in the eighteenth century most Catholics used Irish as their first language, by the end of the nineteenth century all but a few people (approximately 6 per cent) spoke English; it continues to be the sole language for official use in Northern Ireland. But, although the majority of Nationalists neither normally read nor speak the language, most nevertheless wish to see it freely used without legal restrictions, and also to see official financial support given for schools teaching through the medium of the language. The resistance of the broadcasting media to its use has also been a source of contention; the Irish language was excluded from radio and television for almost the first 50 years of the Northern Ireland state.

A major difficulty has been that most of these expressions of culture, and the differences they exemplify, provided, and in some cases continue to provide, considerable grounds for community tension and hostility and sometimes for outbreaks of violence. Legislation passed to deal with these issues often provoked tension rather than eased it. For example, several legislative Acts (1951 and 1954) outlawed the flying of the Irish flag, and allowed the police to take action against any use of symbols that was likely to cause a breach of the peace. This legislation effectively prohibited the use of symbols that demonstrated Nationalist allegiance by the minority Catholic population. Both sides frequently used these laws to provoke tension. In the case of the Nationalists, it became an act of rebellion to fly a Tricolour, while the Unionists for their part insisted that the full rigour of the law should be brought to bear upon such displays, thus ensuring continuing conflict between the communities and the police.

The laws that restricted the use of the Irish language by forbidding the use of Irish language street signs (1949) or the use of any language other than English in court (1739) and the customs for the use of the English language in all official transactions also became issues for continuing acts of rebellion. By 1992 over 550 Irish language street signs had been erected in Nationalist areas in clear defiance of the law. In addition, throughout the 1980s, some within the Nationalist community began to use the Irish language and its lack of official support as a cultural weapon with which to challenge the authorities; signs appeared in Catholic west Belfast which read "British soldiers speak English, what language do you speak?" in an effort to encourage people to speak Irish as a political gesture.

Cultural Traditions Group 1988

In order to address these divisions, in 1988, the Cultural Traditions Group (CTG, now a sub-group of the Community Relations Council) was set up with the assistance of government and funding from the European Community, to address productive ways forward in dealing with cultural differences. This group consisted of approximately 20 people, from both Protestant and Catholic backgrounds, who were active in the development of cultural aspects of Northern Ireland life. They were drawn from universities, museums, Irish-language and other cultural bodies, and whilst not without their political and theological differences they were committed to attempt an open appreciation of each other's culture, and to a willingness to see that culture is reflected in the structures and legislation of the state (Ryder, 1994).

Despite some tentative signs of tolerance of pluralism such as the BBC's willingness to broadcast some Irish-language programmes, the group faced an uphill task. The use of the Irish language continued in many cases to cause hostility, marching continued to need considerable security force protection, and displays of emblems and flags continued to provoke aggression.

Identity affirmation work

The first efforts of the CTG were aimed at affirming the validity of differing identities. There was agreement amongst the group that those aspects of culture that were mainly Catholic had been discriminated against both in their coverage by the media and in their support by the state. But, as such affirmation could be seen as threatening to many Unionists who feared it as a manifestation of political assertion, it was also deemed necessary to assist the development of cultural confidence (and not triumphalism or majoritarianism) among those who were Unionist.

Single-identity work on the part of both communities was therefore encouraged in the first instance, and many single-identity projects were resourced and funded. Sometimes these were historical projects; World War I and World War II projects were particularly popular among Unionists who felt that their role and loyalty in these wars had been significantly overlooked. The Orange Order, an institution feared and reviled by most Catholics, received funding to make a video of its work and history. In the case of Nationalists, extra or new funding was given to projects that endorsed and developed Irish language and culture.

The CTG group also resourced and funded a proliferation of published cultural materials, which addressed existing gaps in such materials and encouraged new thinking around the various traditions. The group also assisted broadcast media productions that would similarly exemplify cultural variety, and they helped to ensure local programming which exemplified an ethos of diversity.

Local history work

The CTG group also helped to develop the growth in local history societies in many areas, particularly through helping to resource groups such as the Ulster Federation for Local Studies. The local history societies provided for two necessary factors. In the first instance they provided for many people a place of cultural affirmation, a chance to recall their roots, and to feel proud of their areas. Such groups were also encouraged by the quality of the work itself to address their past in all of its complexity, and not just to focus on the simplicities that could confirm rather than decrease divisions. Increasingly, these groups also in many cases provided and continue to provide an excellent vehicle for encouraging cross-community contact. Many are now succeeding in crossing the political and social boundaries, and some are beginning to share history and cultural sessions on a regular basis.

Cultural fairs and exhibitions

In 1991 the CTG organized the first ever Cultural Traditions Fair in Belfast. Through it they brought together about 40 groups with very different cultural and historical perspectives for a few days to provide an open exhibition for each other and for the public. It was a unique and challenging undertaking as it brought together groups that had been in the main suspicious, hostile and often violent to one another for most of the life of the state. This was the first time ever in the history of Northern Ireland that such groups had found themselves together in the one building – and within a context where such differences were suggested by the CTG group to be positive, as opposed to dangerous. Thousands of people attended the fair, which was subsequently repeated at many locations such as libraries and local district council offices over the following two years throughout Northern Ireland. The fairs provided not only an opportunity for each group to interact, however tentatively, but also an opportunity for teachers and those interested in local studies to acquire information from a wide variety of sources for their burgeoning cultural traditions work. The fairs also provided visible evidence that differing traditions need not be perceived as necessarily hostile, but could together provide a richness that was greater than any single identity.

In addition to the cultural fairs the CTG also organized a symbols exhibition, which was been displayed in most of the local district councils. This was a very colourful exposition of the hundreds of artefacts from all traditions which are displayed in homes and halls and streets and on lapels in the island of Ireland, usually to proclaim a particular loyalty, and often relating to particular institutions. In many cases these symbols can give offence or cause hostility (McCartney, 1994b). Such cultural displays can, however, accustom people to being in the proximity of symbols with which they usually feel uncomfortable or hostile, and tentatively point to a richness of political diversity that is available to be creatively harnessed rather than used destructively. The fact that the first exhibition was held in the City Hall in Belfast, traditionally associated with Protestant hegemony, was also of useful significance.

Music and dance

Ireland (particularly what is perceived as the Nationalist tradition) is extremely rich in its musical tradition. Its instrumental compositions are based on flute, tin whistle, violin, bodhran (an Irish drum) and, in some cases, accordion music. Unaccompanied singing, local folk compositions, and the music of such groups as the Chieftains, who have gained an international reputation, add to the variety. In addition there is a vast repertoire of dance music for traditional Irish dancing. Unfortunately, although the tradition has always had some participants from the Protestant community, it has usually been seen as Catholic. Hence it has sometimes attracted both the verbal and physical hostility of Loyalists, and pubs have been attacked because of their custom of playing such music.

By the provision of opportunities for music groups to consolidate and develop an existing interest on the part of some Protestants, threats have now for the most part been averted. In addition, by encouraging the Scottish musical tradition, a tradition that is part of the heritage of many Unionists and that historically has had very strong links (both in music and in dance) with the Irish tradition, it has been possible to widen the appreciation that now exists of both Irish and Scottish music and dance in both communities. Work has also been undertaken, by a group called the Different Drums, on combining the main drums (the Irish bodhran and the lambeg, the traditional Unionist drum) in some exciting instrumental compositions, thus displaying their capacity for interaction and harmony. Such work began in 1989, and within the last decade has provided for a much less threatening musical interface between the communities. In addition it has spurred an interest in new blends that can combine the best of both traditions.

Marching traditions

In early summer in Northern Ireland you are very likely, whether in village, town, or city, to encounter the sound and sight of marching bands practising their tunes and their marches along the country lanes and city streets (Jarman, 1999). While the majority of these bands are Protestant, some are Catholic. For both sides they provide an opportunity for the youth to learn a musical instrument and participate in a group activity in their local area. Unfortunately, when they engage in seasonal marching, they can in some cases provide an opportunity for hostility. Marching is a common activity in Northern Ireland; there are over 3,000 parades each year, most of them Protestant/Orange Order parades.

Marches can appear hostile just because they are identified as belonging to one or other community. The very fact that people participating march in groups can make them appear threatening even if this is not intended. And in some cases, especially where such marching takes place through territory that does not belong to their own community a threat can indeed be implied. This is particularly a problem in relationship to some Protestant marches, where demography has changed the sectarian landscape but marchers refuse to recognize and take account of this and insist on marching traditional routes which now go through Catholic or mixed territory. Where this happens, a large police presence is often necessary to keep the peace and such incidents can generate a good deal of tension between communities. In addition, a minority of bands are particularly provocative and increase hostilities through sectarian singing and chanting.

Work to address such tensions has begun in a variety of ways. In the first instance, particularly where there has been a history of hostility, it has sometimes been necessary for the police to reroute some marches. A Parades Commission was set up in 1997 to adjudicate on these marches, and, where hostility is feared, local mediators have been used with some success, both as intermediaries between communities and the police, and as observers who closely monitor the progress of such marches (Kelly, 1997). Although tensions can still arise because of the volatile nature of the political process in Northern Ireland, many conflicts over parading have been significantly averted through such measures over the past few years. Despite successes, there are still some parades such as the Garvaghy Road march in Portadown, a town about 30 miles south of Belfast, that have the power to bring the region to a complete standstill through communal disruption, and considerable efforts will need to be directed at such remaining black spots of parading tension.

The Irish language

Towards the late eighties, and particularly under the influence of the CTG, it was recognized by many that the negative government response to the Irish language had been both short-sighted and unnecessary, particularly in view of the fact that in other parts the regional language of Welsh and Scots Gaelic had each received significant support for their retention and development. The refusal of the Unionist government to provide any support for the Irish language had provided a significant bone of contention for Nationalists who added that refusal to their list of discriminations.

The newfound assertive capacities of the Nationalist community however began to achieve some successes in the early seventies when the BBC was persuaded to introduce occasional programmes on the Irish language to its radio audiences. Although there was considerable resistance from many Unionists, the BBC persisted with the experiment, and was eventually persuaded to introduce a regular Irish-language programme in 1981, followed by some schools broadcasting in 1985. In 1991 the BBC broadcast its first television production in Irish. And throughout the 1990s, it became increasingly possible for people in Northern Ireland to receive televisions transmissions from Radio Telefis Eireann, the state-funded broadcasting body in the Republic of Ireland, which helped to broaden access for all communities in Northern Ireland to differing cultural and political perspectives.

However, it was agreed by the CTG that more needed to be done. In 1990 the British government helped to set up and fund the Ultacht Trust, a group established on a non-sectarian basis to develop and fund the Irish language, and which included on its management committee members from the Unionist tradition. In addition, the government began to fund those schools that taught through the medium of Irish on the same basis as other schools, and to assist with the funding of a daily newspaper in Irish. In 1992 the Secretary of State for Northern Ireland announced that where there is a local demand, street names in Irish can be erected alongside the English name.

The struggle to gain full parity with the Scots Gaelic and Welsh languages is still continuing. Correspondence in Irish will now be dealt with by the government, but as yet there is no official policy on publishing documents in Irish, although this does happen on an occasional and as requested basis. The fact that only about 10 per cent of the population claims to have a knowledge of the language (Census Report, 1990) is probably likely to prevent it ever reaching parity with the English language.

Irish has significantly receded as a problem of political contention (although there are still minor skirmishes in some district councils about its use) and in some cases the language is even being used to cement cross-community interaction. More Protestants feel free to learn it now that its use for political provocation has been reduced. There are several Irish classes taking place in areas that are significantly Protestant such as the Shankill area. Such groups are using their new-found interest in the Irish language as a reason to undertake visits to language centres in nearby Catholic areas, many of which they have previously feared to visit. Some Protestants, desirous of revisiting what they see as their own cultural roots, have begun to learn Scots Gaelic; as Scots and Irish Gaelic have much in common, this study is also providing for interesting cross-community sharing and comparison.

Ulster Scots language/dialect[34]

A more recent public variant in the identity debate in Northern Ireland has been the emergence of the Ulster Scots language[35] as a factor for consideration as an identity marker for those Protestants who travelled from the lowlands of Scotland to Northern Ireland in the seventeenth and eighteenth centuries. This language was protected, often through rural isolation, as a living, spoken language throughout many parts of Northern Ireland. With the advent of a more regional and international media, it seemed to be dying a natural death, until its revival by the development of an Ulster Scots Society in 1992. It became important, primarily as a cultural and political identifier for some Protestants, as had the Irish language in the eighties for many Catholics. The need for its support has been documented as part of the Agreement, and it is one of the recognized languages of the new political Assembly.

The Belfast Agreement encourages the support of the Irish language, along with the Ulster Scots language/dialect, and a cross-border Northern Ireland/Republic of Ireland language body has been set up as part of the Agreement to foster both languages, and to encourage the development of programmes for the development of both of these languages throughout the whole of the island.

Drama

Northern Ireland has always had a vibrant dramatic tradition – not just on the stages of its major city, Belfast, but also throughout its villages and towns where local drama has had a significant place in the life of the community. In some cases, this involvement has proved to be of importance both in affirming a culture and in questioning its simplifications. A report released in 1994 (Grant, 1994) showed how the work of local dramatists working in tandem with local dramatic groups can have a very significant effect in facilitating discussion about problematic issues both within and between communities. Drama can help to pose fundamental questions about issues such as identity, social concern and political possibilities which beset the conflict. In particular, when drama picks up and deals with the very complex emotions surrounding local community dilemmas, for example, over paramilitary activity, dissatisfaction with policing, social and cultural marginalization, it has an extremely engaging capacity which can be more powerful than many seminars and workshops. There are now many groups of drama facilitators who are working specifically with local groups to develop dramas that are particular to their needs and to their context in the conflict. When these groups work together on a cross-community basis, and engage in performances with both communities, their capacity for dealing with complexity, and for addressing their communities' fears and concerns, is very powerful indeed. They are able to create significant degrees of empathy across the community divide.

Increasingly multicultural

Like many European countries, until recently Northern Ireland was predominantly white and Christian. When the conflict erupted in 1969, during most of the subsequent years, people of a different colour or religion were seen as aberrant to the political situation, and jokes abounded about how those few minorities living in the country were forced to define themselves as "Catholic" Chinese, or "Protestant" Chinese and pressurised to take sides in the all-consuming loyalty game that is continuously played in Northern Ireland. By the year 2001, however, their numbers had increased to approximately 20,000. There are over 50 nationalities currently living in Northern Ireland, although by far the biggest group are the Chinese. Their increasing visibility within the community, and the growth of such organizations as the Multicultural Centre, and the Chinese Welfare Association, and their involvement in such issues as racism awareness training for the police and other institutions, has gradually helped the development of a less parochial attitude to issues of identity in Northern Ireland. In the Forum elections in 1996, one of the smaller Loyalist parties, the PUP, found that in order to gain seats in the Assembly in what was a very marginal voting constituency, they needed to get the votes of the local Chinese community. They decided to translate some of their election literature into Chinese – a clear case of the old binational world of Irish history meeting the increasingly globalized and pluralist world of the twenty-first century.

Conclusion

In Catholic west Belfast, summers over the past 20 years have frequently been hot and riotous, particularly when marked with marches and demonstrations commemorating the wrongs the community believes it has suffered in the past, and in particular what the local people see as the injustice of internment in 1971.[36] The introduction of a local summer cultural festival has, within the last few years, transformed such summers. Now many of these streets are filled with music, dramas, and historical tours. The advent of the west Belfast festival has transformed what could be merely contentious commemorations into both affirming and at times questioning occasions, filled with colour, fun, and political and cultural debate. In recent years, furthermore, the community, proud of its own capacity to develop such a festival, has begun to expand its horizons and to extend its festival invitations to try and encourage creative interaction between its own ghettoized community and those from other traditions. In 1994, community workers and others in the Protestant Shankill area began to develop a similar idea in order to explore its own and other emerging traditions in a creative and productive manner and one that can also lead them, through greater confidence, into more cross-community interaction.

A similar phenomenon has been occurring in Derry/Londonderry where enormous energy has been put in over the last few years by various cultural groups, and by the city council itself, into exploring issues of culture and identity through drama, music, and debate. Such work has helped to increase significantly the vibrancy and hopefulness of a city that had appeared, until the mid-eighties, to be sunk in a depression of bombed out buildings, dreary paramilitary activity, high unemployment rates, and prevailing divisions. Newfound vigour, much of it energized through such cultural activity, now appears also to be contributing to the city's capacity to develop economically and socially.

The 1990s were a particularly vibrant time for all kinds of cultural activity in Northern Ireland, a surprise for many visitors to the region. Much of the vibrancy came from the developing capacity of local communities to engage in their own questioning with each other, and eventually with their conflicting neighbours through the medium of culture. The strategy of facilitating such cultural pluralism has not been without its critics, some of whom are concerned with its possible capacity to increase ghettoization, or with its implications for political pluralism, a fate that is feared, in particular, by some Unionists.

However, following the Belfast Agreement in 1998 a new Ministry, the Department for Culture Arts and Leisure (DCAL), was set up and began to take particular responsibility for issues of culture and diversity. The first minister to head this body was a Unionist. DCAL set up a programme called "Diversity 21"[37] as a joint venture between the CRC and DCAL. The avowed aim of DCAL is to ensure that cultural diversity is regarded as a positive, not a negative force in Northern Ireland, and its aims are to facilitate support mechanisms relevant to cultural diversity, and to examine existing legislation, policies, and projects to ensure that they all assist the development of a culturally pluralist society. The mainstreaming of cultural pluralism as an aspiration to be supported and resourced, within a governmental department of Northern Ireland which is headed by a Unionist, is an indication of how far the programme of cultural diversity has developed. What was once illegal has now become an essential part of government policy designed to ensure a sustainable peace.

6

Policing the conflict

Forces for peace?

The major task of the control of civil unrest will inevitably, in a democracy, fall upon an existing state force, whether police or army. By the time the Belfast Agreement was reached, Northern Ireland had developed a police force of approximately 12,000,[38] which was about two and a half times the size of its normal counterpart in the United Kingdom, and an army presence that averaged about 18,000 personnel. There is little doubt that the success of such security personnel through policing, surveillance activities, and intelligence gathering has succeeded in preventing and containing paramilitary violence. The successful conviction of paramilitaries was a significant factor in ensuring that the IRA eventually realized by the late 1980s that its political struggle could never be won solely by the use of force. Such a realization assisted its decision to seek an alternative political strategy, which was to lead to the ceasefires of 1994, and eventual political agreement.[39]

The corollary, however, was that the security forces also conceded that they would never, through the use of force alone, be able to end completely the paramilitary campaigns of violence. Whilst this was partly due to the nature of the guerrilla tactics used by the IRA, it was also true, throughout the course of the conflict, that the use of the security forces to contain and resolve the conflict in Northern Ireland has been a problematic one.

The successful use of state force to contain a conflict in a democracy will depend upon a variety of factors including the degree of consensus among the people about the legitimacy of such force, the representative nature of the force, the scale of the civil unrest, and the tactics used by state forces to control and stop the conflict. In Northern Ireland, both the nature of the history of the forces in Northern Ireland and the tactics they used meant that in many cases the forces were themselves perceived by substantial sections of the community, most generally in Nationalist areas, to be part of the problem (Hillyard, 1983).

When civil unrest broke out in Northern Ireland in 1969, the fault lines within the existing police force were to render it, in many cases, counterproductive and inflammatory to the conflict. The force itself was mostly Protestant, and therefore seen as largely sympathetic to the Unionists. In 1969, it had a participation rate of 10 per cent by Catholics, which subsequently dropped to 7 per cent during the conflict.

When the troubles broke out it quickly became evident that the police were unable to react to the emerging law-and-order needs in a way that was professional and unbiased. Throughout the civil rights marches, the frequent demonstrations and the inter-communal street rioting, the police in most cases showed themselves to be clearly fearful of the Catholic demands for civil rights and in many cases they were seen to react in what were often critical and heated situations in a biased and hostile way. The Cameron Commission, set up by the British government in 1969 to examine the causes of the troubles, implicated the police as a major problematic factor in the conflict and in particular police acts of misconduct, assault and battery, and use of provocative sectarian and political slogans (Cameron Report, 1969). Both the Cameron Commission and the Scarman Tribunal (Scarman, 1972) were particularly critical of the actions of the B Specials, a section of the police force with a notable history of bigotry towards Catholics (Ryder, 1991).

Consequently, the reform of policing formed one of the main objectives of the British government. It was recommended that the B

Specials be disbanded and that a new part-time force be established, the Royal Ulster Constabulary (RUC) were to be disarmed, a police authority was to be set up to provide a buffer between the police and the Unionist government, and a complaints system was to be developed. These recommendations provoked strong condemnations within the Unionist community, including rioting in Protestant areas in Belfast, and the shooting dead of a policeman.

Although Catholics generally welcomed the recommendations, they were in the main offset by the introduction of internment in 1971 that resulted in the imprisonment without trial of over 1,500 people, almost all Catholics. The majority of those interned (most of whom were subsequently released without charge) had been imprisoned on the ill-informed advice of the police (Bardon, 1992).

During the late 1970s, however, there was a gradual professionalization of the police, which helped to upgrade standards in policing. Their increasing impartiality was exemplified in the way in which the police have on many occasions since the seventies found themselves in open opposition to many Protestants when trying to uphold controversial decisions. These included subduing the rioting that occurred in many Protestant areas after the imposition of the Anglo-Irish Agreement in 1985, during which protests many police were attacked and driven out from their homes by Protestants who resented the Agreement. In addition, there were frequent clashes between the police and Protestant communities because of the actions which they have undertaken in order to secure convictions among Loyalist paramilitaries. Throughout the nineties in particular, police came under frequent attacks from Protestants as they attempted to police the rerouting of contentious Orange Order marches when Protestants were forbidden to march down roads whose residents were mainly Catholic.

In addition, the police carried out many thousands of acts of personal and collective bravery aimed at averting the deaths of both Catholics and Protestants through their vigilance in preventing bombings, finding caches of arms, and through intelligence warnings to suspected victims from all sections of the community. Nevertheless, they are still viewed suspiciously by a sizeable element within the Catholic community partly because of historical attitudes and a perceived bias in their daily interactions with local communities.

A foreign army?

Following the outbreak of violence in 1969, when it became evident that the police were neither able to contain the rioting, nor in some cases willing to protect the Catholic population, the British government decided to send the army into Northern Ireland to maintain law and order. At the time of the decision it was agreed that this should be a limited operation, and that they would be withdrawn as soon as possible. The Catholic population, who had felt besieged and unprotected by the police, initially greeted the army with relief and gratitude and for about six months they succeeded in maintaining the confidence of the Catholic community. However, a combination of factors converted what had been a fairly supportive Catholic population into one that became openly hostile to the presence of the army; the determination of the rapidly growing more powerful IRA to provoke confrontation with the army, whom they saw as representing the traditional enemy, and an overzealous use of search tactics during army operations in Catholic areas.

From 1970, the army became the enemy for most Nationalists, an attitude that was increasingly confirmed by tactics that appeared to border on a direct policy of killing suspected terrorists with little apparent effort being made in many cases to detain them. Among such incidents were the killing of eight IRA men who were involved in attacking a rural police station in Loughgall in Co. Armagh in 1987, the killing of three IRA members in Gibraltar in 1988, and the killing of three IRA men who were about to begin a murder operation against Protestant workmen in Coagh in Co. Tyrone in 1991. The army had a particular problem in maintaining its credibility as an impartial force because of the existence of the Ulster Defence Regiment (UDR) that had been established in 1970 to replace the discredited B specials. Most of its members were indigenous and Protestant; they were part-time and hence often did not receive the training that accompanied full-time army career development. A disproportionate number of their ranks were found guilty of serious crimes of a sectarian nature, the force was on occasions infiltrated by Loyalist paramilitaries, and it developed a particularly harsh reputation for harassing Catholics in the course of its duties (Ryder, 1991). From the mid-eighties there was evidence that some soldiers, and in particular soldiers from the UDR, released files on suspected IRA activists to Loyalist paramilitaries, in order to facilitate their murder.

Secret services

The work in Northern Ireland of the intelligence forces, whose task it is to work at an undercover level detecting and preventing terrorist crime where possible, is in general, highly secretive. What is known about it reveals a variety of often competitive groups at work who, despite their undoubted successes in preventing and detecting crime, have frequently themselves come under criticism for what are believed by some to be questionable and counterproductive methods. Specialist units within the police and army carried out most of the intelligence work. Within the police RUC Special Branch officers worked in conjunction with the Army Intelligence Corps. There were also firearms specialist squads that include the Mobile Support Units of the RUC and the Special Air Service (SAS) who appear to have been particularly actively involved in the seventies and early eighties in Northern Ireland, and to whom the murders of about 30 IRA activists have been attributed (Urban, 1992). Both police and army run "agents" upon whom they depend to secure accurate information, particularly from within the ranks of the paramilitaries. But for various reasons, including a succession of "supergrass" trials[40] during the eighties which fell apart because of their reliance on informers controlled by these intelligence sections, repeated allegations of assault during interrogations, and alleged patterns of duress imposed in attempts to obtain information, the credibility of many of these services was seriously undermined, and by the mid-nineties many such counterproductive methods had been abandoned.

Legal security measures

From 1921 until direct rule was introduced in 1972, the Unionist government regulated internal security by what was known as the Special Powers Act. This Act gave the Unionist government the power to introduce internment, and any other measures it saw fit, to control what it perceived as subversive groups. This capacity was renewed under the Emergency Provisions Act in 1973, and the Prevention of Terrorism Act was introduced in 1974, initiated by the British government as part of their direct rule of the state. This latter Act allows the police to hold suspects for questioning for seven days, and to exclude those whom they suspect of involvement in supporting paramilitary activities from entry into Great Britain. In addition, the right to jury trial for "scheduled" offences (that is paramilitary offences) was replaced in 1973 by non-jury courts in order to try to address the problem of jury intimidation by defendants.

Most of these measures were consistently criticized by many human rights organizations, including the European Court of Human Rights, and by the main opposition party in Britain during this period, the Labour Party. The question of achieving a balance between the need to provide adequate protection from the effects of paramilitarism and the need to uphold the civil rights of the citizens of the region remains a contentious one. Subsequent to the ceasefires of 1994, the Special Powers Act was repealed.

Casualties and cause

The security forces themselves have suffered significantly at the hands of the paramilitaries, in particular because of the strategy of the IRA, for whom the security forces were prime targets. It has been estimated that over 1,000 deaths, about 31.5 per cent of the casualties of the war, have been those of members of the security forces (9 per cent police and the rest the army and other security forces). During the course of their work, it has been estimated that the security forces (mainly the army) have been responsible for killing at least 382 people in the course of the conflict, which is about

10 per cent of all the deaths that have occurred.[41] About half of these deaths appear to have been targeted, or have happened as the result of gun battles with the paramilitaries and almost one third of these deaths have occurred as a result of the involvement of the security forces in managing riot situations.

Improving the security interface

Northern Ireland is not unique in discovering the difficulty of effectively policing a conflict whose combatants are using guerrilla methods of warfare, and in some cases receiving protection or at least acquiescence from many in their communities, without further alienating that community and increasing support for its cause. The British army had recognized by the late eighties that it would be unable to achieve a complete military victory against the paramilitaries in Northern Ireland, and that its main task was to contain the violence until a political settlement could be reached between the communities. In achieving such a long-term solution the security forces increasingly realized that their own occasionally hostile interface with the communities (mainly Catholic, but occasionally Protestant) and the tactics that they sometimes employed, became a problematic of the conflict itself, and were used by their enemies to exacerbate and prolong the conflict. By the early nineties, both sections of the security forces began to address this problem much more seriously, and, in conjunction with some community conflict resolution groups, developed more adequate ways to address such difficulties of the interface.

The main source of irritation and resentment about the security forces was often the quality of the interface between them and the public, when conducting for example vehicle checkpoints, foot patrols, or house searches (Hamilton, 1995). The number of such interactions taking place was estimated to be about 40,000 per day. The most widespread complaint about such interaction was that of rudeness by the security forces, followed by concern about their use of abusive and sectarian language, very frequent street searches, prolonged car searches, aggressive house and body searches and interference with Nationalist emblems and symbols. Beatings and scuffles were sometimes reported, particularly between young men and the security forces. Sometimes death threats were made either against the person being searched or against a relative. It has been further proved that in some cases threats were made to pass on information to Loyalists. Attempts to harass or blackmail people into giving information were also a source for frequent complaint (CAJ, 1992).

There are a variety of reasons why such interactions occurred. Undoubtedly there was stereotyping and bigotry, based either on perceived ethnic or class bias. In addition however there was the anger that can be felt by the security forces after a murder of one of their colleagues. The fact that securing a conviction was very difficult meant that the security forces were often interacting with people whom they believed to be suspects for murders or bombings, but against whom evidence could not be secured for a conviction, thus rendering such interactions very contentious. In addition there was sometimes deliberate provocation by those being searched in order to create an incident and use it for propaganda purposes.

Given the above scenario, fraught as the context was with the ongoing murders and bombings by the paramilitaries, thought was given by the security bodies themselves, in conjunction with the Community Relations Council and other conflict resolution bodies such as Mediation Network, and the Peace and Reconciliation Group in Derry/Londonderry to the possible interventions that could ensure that the interface itself did not continue to be a problem in fuelling resentment and diminishing cooperation with the security forces.[42]

Selection and training

Both the RUC and the army took steps to increase the quality of their recruits, and selection programmes were introduced to try to identify bias on the part of would-be trainees. Both sections of the security forces intensified their training to include a much greater emphasis on social skills and interaction work. The army prepared its staff better for coming to Northern Ireland through an intensive regime which included an understanding of the history of the region, cultural awareness work, video training on interface work of a positive quality, and in some cases talks with community workers from both of the main traditions about ways to improve the interactions between the army and the community. The army also introduced very strict rules governing the expected quality of soldiers' interactions on the streets, with strict disciplinary measures if these were transgressed.

In 1993, the RUC, in cooperation with the CRC and NGO conflict resolution bodies began to develop its own programmes to deal with issues of sectarianism among the force, and to promote and encourage a greater respect and understanding among its staff for the differing cultural and political traditions in Northern Ireland. Such training is now an integral part of the initial training of all recruits entering the force, and has also been introduced as part of the in-service training of established police personnel. In the late nineties learning from other divided societies such as South Africa, the United States and Belgium also began to play a part in shaping the training of the RUC. In addition, during the nineties, the RUC began to undertake some shared training with the Gardai, the police force in the Republic of Ireland, which was a historic undertaking for forces that had long distrusted each other.

Reviewing complaints

Traditionally, the police had handled complaints internally, but in 1977, an independent Police Complaints Board was established with responsibility for reviewing the handling of complaints against the police. Its record of disciplinary charges was deemed unsatisfactory, and hoping to boost public confidence in the complaints system, the government replaced it by an independent Police Complaints Commission in 1988. This had some limited success in that it has succeeded in attracting Nationalist representation on to the Commission. Since the Belfast Agreement, a totally independent Police Ombudsman, with considerable enforcement powers, has now replaced the Police Complaints Commission. The Ombudsman has the power to not merely react to specific complaints received, but to initiate inquiries or investigations even if no specific complaint has been received.

The Army introduced a system whereby an identity card was immediately available from an army patrol in the event of any negative incident occurring that caused hostility, and the government also set up an independent commissioner to monitor the effectiveness of the Army complaints procedure.

In addition, both sections of the security forces increased the rapidity with which they could identify any hostile interface patterns that were emerging in a particular area, or by a particular regiment. Such methods meant that they could more speedily intervene to curtail any negative patterns identified.

After a critical report in 1979 by an English Crown Court judge, a video monitoring system was introduced to monitor interviews and complaints about intimidation. Many of the police were trained in mediation techniques and more informal dispute resolution practices were introduced into their repertoire of skills.

Limiting collusion

Several disturbing reports (Stevens, 1990) showed that collusion between some of the security forces and the Loyalist paramilitaries, while neither widespread nor structurally endorsed, had been happening. Such collusion was mostly attributed to members of the UDR, although individual lapses by some police were also alleged. Files and photomontages of Republican suspects were passed on to some Loyalist paramilitaries for use in targeting IRA suspects. Such practices proved to be difficult to detect and to limit. Where possible, new technology has been brought into use, making access by police and soldiers to computer files extremely difficult. In addition the use of specially secured photocopiers meant that the replication of information such as photographs and address lists likely to be of use to paramilitaries was made almost impossible. Such techniques have significantly restricted a practice that, although limited in extent, seriously undermined the confidence of the Nationalist community in the security forces.

The end of the UDR

The rate of complaints of suspected killings and harassments against the UDR was significantly higher than other sections of the security forces (Ryder, 1991). In addition, proven collusion (Stevens, 1990) between members of the UDR and Loyalist paramilitary forces seriously damaged the reputation of the force, and in particular its credibility with the Nationalist community. In 1992 it was decided to disband the force, and merge their members with an Irish regiment of the British army, some of whose members come from the Republic of Ireland.[43] The new regiment was called the Royal Irish Regiment. In the process, the number of part-time members serving in the force was substantially reduced and this move was successful in diminishing the number of complaints against its soldiers.

Catholic participation

Catholic participation in the police throughout the conflict was estimated to be around 7 per cent, despite widespread campaigns to try and increase their recruitment. Several factors had contributed to such a low participation rate. The first is that the Catholic population in general remains suspicious of the perceived bias of the police, and the second is that the IRA were particularly likely to target Catholic policemen, branding them as traitors to their community. In addition, however, there is the factor that within the police force itself, Catholics can be culturally alienated when surrounded by an ethos that is primarily British and Protestant. In order to address this the RUC, as part of their cultural awareness training, began to look at some possibilities for ensuring that their own organization becomes more culturally neutral where possible so as to diminish any feelings of alienation on the part of the minority. As violence ends, such efforts on the part of the RUC are likely to result in an increased number of Catholics joining the police force over the coming years. Within six months of the ceasefire of 1994 it was interesting to note that the number of applications from Catholics wishing to join the police had increased to 23 per cent. The reforms introduced as a result of the Patten Report, which resulted from the Belfast Agreement of 1998 (see below) have further increased the number of Catholics willing to join the reformed police service.

Community liaison groups

The Police Authority for Northern Ireland, which was set up in the 1970s to administer the police in a more neutral fashion, set up police liaison committees to try to ensure greater communication and cooperation between the communities and the police. However, as the main Nationalist party, the SDLP, refused to join these because of its members' overall suspicion of the police, they proved to be mainly Protestant. During the nineties, however, there was an increase in the number of community-based liaison groups such as the Derry Peace and Reconciliation Group (PRG), the Drumcree Faith and Justice Group in Portadown, and the North Belfast Community Development Centre, which developed a productive role with the police in ensuring a more positive interface in those areas where they function. Such groups, which operated on a cross-community basis, engaged the communities in expressing their concerns to the police, and shared their ideas about more positive policing methods. These groups will be replaced with the new district policing Partnership Boards which will be eventually introduced as part of the reforms recommended by the Patten Report on Policing.

Belfast Agreement and policing

Given the historic problems with policing in Northern Ireland, it was not surprising that policing and the necessity for its reform was to play a significant part in the Belfast Agreement. The signatories to the Agreement said that they believed the agreement provides the opportunity for a new beginning to policing in Northern Ireland with a police service capable of attracting and sustaining support from the community as a whole. They believed that the Agreement offers a unique opportunity to bring about a new political dispensation, which would recognize the full and equal legitimacy, the identities, allegiances, and ethos of all sections of the community in Northern Ireland. This approach should inform and underpin the development of a police service representative in terms of the make-up of the community as a whole. They also suggested that an unarmed police should be the ideal. The Agreement recommended that an independent commission should be established to make recommendations for future policing arrangements in Northern Ireland including means of encouraging widespread community support for these arrangements.

The Patten Commission[44]

In 1999, the Patten Commission recommended the following points for action:

(a) There should be a comprehensive programme of action to focus policing in Northern Ireland on a human rights-based approach, including a new oath, code of ethics, and training in the principles and standards of human rights and the practical implications for policing.

(b) An entirely new Policing Board should be created to hold the Chief Constable and the police service publicly to account. The Board should have 19 members, 10 of whom should be Assembly members drawn from the parties of the new Northern Ireland Executive, and the nine independent members should be selected from a range of different fields — including business, trade unions, voluntary organizations, community groups, and the legal profession.

(c) Each District Council should establish a District Policing Partnership Board (DPPB) to provide a local advisory service for the police.

(d) The three contentious holding centres at Castlereagh, Gough Barracks, and Strand Road should be closed and all suspects should in future be detained in custody suites in police stations.

(e) Provided the peace process did not collapse and the security situation did not deteriorate the size of the police service over the next 10 years should be reduced by about one third.

(f) All community leaders, particularly Catholic leaders from political parties, local councils, churches, schools, etc. should take steps to remove all discouragement to members of their communities applying to join the police, and make it a priority to encourage them to apply, and an equal number of Protestants and Catholics should be drawn from the pool of qualified candidates.

(g) The recruitment agency should identify Northern Ireland Catholic officers in other police services, including the Republic of Ireland, and encourage them to apply for positions in the Northern Ireland police.

(h) Community awareness training for police recruits should be developed to include representatives of all the main political and religious traditions in Northern Ireland. Community awareness training should be integrated into all aspects of training.

(i) While the RUC should not be disbanded, it should be named the Northern Ireland Police Service; the new Police Service should adopt a new badge and symbols, entirely free from any association with either the British or Irish states, and the Union flag should no longer be flown from police buildings.

The summer of 2000 was spent in the lengthy and often contentious implementation of the Patten Report. Particular difficulties for the Unionists were recommendations about the need for neutral, as opposed to British, symbols for the police, and a new name for the service. Eventually, however, after almost a year of wrangling, almost all of the Patten recommendations were implemented, although there still remained some disagreement about the nature of the powers of the Secretary of State for Northern Ireland. The name of the service was changed from the RUC to PSNI (Police Service for Northern Ireland). A new Policing Board was set up to represent the overall community, and, for the first time in the history of Northern Ireland, it had members drawn from a Nationalist party, the SDLP, although Sinn Fein refused to take up their seats until final agreement had been reached on the remainder of the Patten reforms. A recruitment process to recruit significant numbers of Catholics to the reformed force was successfully begun, and in November 2001 the first recruits, drawn 50 per cent from each of the main communities, began their training. Policing, provided the peace process prevailed, looked set to become, in future years, an acceptable force for the majority of both communities in Northern Ireland.

7

Challenging the armed struggle

Traditions of violence

The use of illegal force to achieve political leverage has been a consistent factor in politics in the island of Ireland. Both Republican and Loyalist paramilitaries, throughout the history of the island, have long continued to use violence to exert political leverage either in favour of, or against, a political option.[45] Despite the small numbers of active members – there were believed to be about 500 militarily active Republican and Loyalist paramilitaries in total during the course of the conflict – they have provided for most of the horrific headlines of bombings, shootings, kidnappings, racketeering, and intimidation which have characterized the last 30 years of the conflict in Northern Ireland. Their re-emergence in the 1960s (see Chapter 1) was to add a bloody and bitter layer to the conflict, which was to leave over 3,400 people dead by the time of the Irish Republican Army (IRA) and the Combined Loyalist Military Command (CLMC) ceasefires of 1994, and another 200 hundred dead by the time of the Belfast Agreement in 1998.

Republican paramilitaries

There has been a physical force tradition in nationalism stretching back two centuries. The IRA was born out of the Easter rising of 1916 in Dublin. This was a rebellion against British rule by Republicans, which failed in the short term, but assisted in bringing an end to British rule in most of Ireland by 1921. The IRA claimed to be a direct descendant group from the rebellion. The military group, except for a brief campaign of violence in the 1950s, had effectively lain dormant since the civil war that had followed its opposition to the acceptance of the partition of the island.[46] However, when the civil unrest erupted in 1969, Republican paramilitary violence was to develop significantly. Although the IRA had played no major part in fomenting the civil unrest in 1969 (Bishop and Mallie, 1987), some Catholics, fearful for their safety in the riots that followed the civil rights marches, began to take up IRA offers of protection.

By the end of 1969, the IRA had begun to regroup, and by early 1970 its members were confronting British troops who had arrived on the island to assist with riot control.[47] By December 1970, it was estimated that the IRA had recruited many hundreds of activists, and during the following months the violence of the IRA grew into extensive bombing campaigns directed against civilian, public utility, and military targets. In August 1971, in an attempt to curb the escalating violence, internment (imprisonment) without trial was introduced. Thousands of soldiers locked up hundreds of Catholics/ Nationalists[48] whom they suspected were involved in provoking or carrying out violence. No attempt was made to intern any Loyalist suspects, despite the record of Loyalist violence. The information on which the authorities were acting was seriously ill informed and out of date (Bardon, 1992: 682).

Increased violence followed internment. On the day following its introduction, 11 people were killed in Belfast alone; barricades were put up in the Creggan and Bogside areas of Derry/Londonderry; and thousands of people were forced to flee their homes because of intimidation. Although most of those detained under internment were later released, internment helped to strengthen significantly the support for the Republican paramilitaries. In January 1972, support for the IRA was further increased when British soldiers opened fire on a demonstration by Nationalists in Derry/Londonderry killing 13 men. While the official inquiry that followed concluded that the shooting had bordered on the reckless, it did not affirm the innocence of those who died.[49] For many Catholics, the incident marked the end of their hopes of achieving their rights through the existing state structures and the issue of the conflict now became "a United Ireland or nothing."[50]

By the end of the seventies, the IRA realized it needed to build up a mass political base if its campaign was to succeed. Following a successful hunger strike campaign by some of its imprisoned members, in which one of the hunger strikers, Bobby Sands, was elected a member of parliament, the IRA devised the strategy of "the ballot box in one hand and the armalite in the other." This strategy meant that it agreed to combine both political and paramilitary pressure to achieve its aims. Sinn Fein, the political wing of the IRA, fought in the local and regional elections, and in 1983 and 1987 they won over 11 per cent of the Northern Ireland vote, a percentage that increased to 16 per cent in the Assembly elections of 1998, after the ceasefires. For most of the conflict their vote in the Republic of Ireland remained around 2 per cent, although this too has increased since the ceasefires. The number of active paramilitaries who are Republican was estimated to be about 200–300 (RISCT, 1991) although obviously many more supporters assisted the military campaign by providing safe houses, hiding weapons, and providing finance.

Following the ceasefires of 1994 and 1996 two IRA splinter groups emerged. In 1995, after the first IRA ceasefire, the Continuity IRA emerged as a result of dissatisfaction with the peace process within the IRA, and in 1998, the Real IRA emerged, again as a result of dissatisfaction with the peace process by those who felt the IRA were "selling out" on the cause of a united Ireland. Both of these groups were to challenge the actions of Sinn Fein/IRA in ending the paramilitary war against the British without having achieved their objectives of a united Ireland and "Brits Out."

Loyalist paramilitaries

The historical counterpart to the IRA on the Protestant side was the Ulster Volunteer Force (UVF). This force was established in 1912 to fight the threat of independence for Ireland in the earlier part of the century when the British offered it. It was in the sixties that Loyalist paramilitaries began to re-emerge. They were worried by the tentative civil rights reforms suggested by the Prime Minister of Northern Ireland, Terence O'Neill, which were seen as threatening Protestant hegemony in Northern Ireland, and in 1966 they began to engage in sporadic acts of violence.

With the rise of the IRA they became a more significant paramilitary force and recruitment to the ranks of the Loyalist paramilitaries was substantially increased when violence erupted on to the streets in 1969. There was rioting between Catholic and Protestant working-class areas of Belfast almost every night, and bombings almost every day by the IRA, often of pubs frequented by Protestants, or in the city centre. There was frequent sniper fire from Protestant areas into Catholic areas and vice versa. In almost all the working class areas of Belfast the men, both Catholic and Protestant, formed themselves into vigilante groups in order to protect their streets; many of these vigilantes subsequently joined the paramilitaries. In 1972, angered at the imposition of direct rule from Westminster, when local political control of Northern Ireland was abrogated in favour of direct control from London by the British government, many of the Protestant groups merged to form the Ulster Defence Association (UDA), whose specifically military wing called itself the Ulster Freedom Fighters (UFF). Their programmes mainly consisted of bombing Catholic pubs and targeting Catholics for murder. They usually justified their killings on the basis that their targets were actively involved in the IRA, although these claims were rarely substantiated. In 1974 the Loyalist paramilitaries, as part of the Ulster Workers Council, played a significant part in overthrowing a political agreement reached by the main political parties to share power. Their opposition was based on their rejection of the proposed co-operative structures with Dublin to be set up as part of the Agreement. The Loyalists blocked petrol and electricity supplies, closed the ports to the import of food, fuel, and agricultural feed, and killed 32 people through indiscriminate bombings in the Republic of Ireland. These actions forced the demise of the most promising political agreement reached by all the constitutional political parties in Northern Ireland in the decades preceding the Belfast Agreement.

Throughout the course of the war, both the UDA and the UVF appear to have operated under a variety of names, e.g. the Ulster Freedom Fighters (UFF) for the UDA, and the Protestant Action Force (PAF) for the UVF. Other Loyalist groupings have included the Red Hand Commandos, Tara, and in the latter years of the nineties the Loyalist Volunteer Force (LVF). The number of active Loyalists is estimated to be around 150–200 (RISCT, 1992), although they too have active and passive support from many more people in their communities.

Community support

Although it is possible for a few hundred paramilitaries to continue a guerrilla-type war for many years without defeat, their survival as an action group will usually depend upon a degree of communal support for their activities. How much they will get will obviously depend upon the circumstances prevailing, such as how much communities feel under threat and in need of their protection, whether or not they feel fairly treated the government and the security forces, and how "justified" they believe the kind of activities they see their paramilitaries involved in, as both Loyalist and Republican paramilitaries know that they can lose substantial support through, for example, the multiple murders of civilians. However, most paramilitaries know that lurking beneath the surface for many in the most marginalized communities in Northern Ireland lies a sense of fear about the safety and survival of their community, and such fear engenders passive, if not always active, support for them.

Most obvious support for paramilitaries will be voiced in the more socially marginalized areas. It is also however probably true to say that even among the middle classes in Northern Ireland, there are some who have felt that their preferred constitutional options are being upheld by those involved in violence, although most would avoid or even deny any open support for such violence. Exact figures for support of the paramilitaries are difficult to ascertain. While the percentage of those who vote for Sinn Fein, the political wing of the IRA, is sometimes quoted as the number of those who support the use and continuance of such violence, such a vote is often estimated to be more a social and political protest vote, rather than actual support for the IRA campaign. It is notable that after the ceasefires of the nineties, the voting support for Sinn Fein in Northern Ireland rose to 16 per cent. Most of those who vote (and work) for Sinn Fein are unemployed. Support for Loyalist violence is also higher in those areas that are more socially marginalized, as many alienated Protestant areas share the same suspicion of the authorities as those in Catholic neighbourhoods.

Paramilitary backgrounds

Surveys have revealed that, in general, paramilitaries in Northern Ireland are not very different in personality, background, or intelligence from other people. The thesis that they are monsters or thugs, committing mindless violence, has not been borne out by the evidence available. Studies have shown that Republican political prisoners were more likely to be slightly more intelligent than others from their neighbourhoods who were not involved in violent political leverage (Elliott and Lockhart, 1980). A study undertaken in 1993 (Shara, 1994) studied the backgrounds, employment, and criminal records of both Republican and Loyalist paramilitaries. Most activists had become involved for the first time as teenagers or in their early twenties. Most were single, and most were still living in their parental home at the time of their arrest – a fact not surprising in view of the Northern Ireland culture in which it is unusual for young people, particularly those from working-class areas, to leave home before they are married. Most of those arrested had left school at 16 with no formal qualifications, and none had gone on to higher education. The vast majority were working class. About 36 per cent were actually in employment at the time of their arrest, and approximately 26 per cent had had a previous criminal record, mostly for property-related offences. Only 6 per cent of those convicted for offences committed in consequence of their alleged political convictions were women. The surveys show, therefore, that those involved in paramilitary violence are mostly male, young and working class, and not atypical of their peers. My own research appears to show that paramilitaries were motivated by a variety of reasons. For many in the IRA, historical family allegiances played a large part in their choice to join the IRA. Others were motivated by a desire to challenge perceived injustices or by a desire to avenge violence by the security forces or by other paramilitary forces. For yet others, it was the identity and meaning that was provided by paramilitary membership that was important, particularly to young men from socially marginalized areas (Fitzduff, 1989b).

Intimidation

The use of intimidation by paramilitaries within their own communities, in order to punish informers, to enforce support for their activities, or to socially control, has been a common phenomenon for the last two decades (CIRAC, 1993) and has continued despite the Belfast Agreement. Punishments are also meted out to those who fail to conform to the requirements of the cause such as giving to fund raising, or putting out flags and emblems as required. People are often afraid to question paramilitary actions lest such questioning will lead in turn to their own intimidation. Internal law and order within a community is often "upheld" by paramilitaries, for example where the youth have been involved in thieving, or in stealing cars, or otherwise being a social nuisance, the paramilitaries will frequently intervene to impose punishment. It has been estimated that 60 per cent of teenagers in government care during the 1990s were placed there by parents and social workers to protect them from punishment by the paramilitaries. Such punishments can range from beatings to kneecapping (shooting a bullet through the knee) to spine shooting (called 50/50 because it has a 50 per cent chance of causing paralysis) to expulsion, or ultimately to murder. Over 100 such incidents are usually reported each year.

Such internal punishment is usually confined to working-class areas, where unemployment and social marginalization is high, and in some areas the nuisance caused by many petty criminals is seen by some in the community as enough to warrant the arbitrary punishments meted out to them by the paramilitaries. Acceptance of such arbitrary anti-crime activity is particularly common in communities where people are often unwilling to involve the police in dealing with social or criminal problems. The activity of "informing" on one's neighbour to the police, particularly in relation to political crimes, is also traditionally held in contempt in many communities and punishment by expulsion or murder is common.

Intimidation is also common in situations where communities are mixed and where people are driven out of their houses because of the fact that they are from a different community. In some cases, such as the border areas of Northern Ireland, it appears that the IRA concentrated on murdering the elder sons of isolated Protestants so as to ensure that such farms would eventually pass into Catholic hands, a claim denied by the IRA, who say such men were murdered because of their connections with the security forces. Whatever the motives, the result has been a form of ethnic cleansing, as many Protestants have moved from their land and into nearby towns for safety. Cities have also been significantly divided by the actual or perceived threat of paramilitaries and their supporters, and the two largest cities, Belfast and Derry/Londonderry, have ghettoized significantly during the course of the conflict.

Intimidation in workplaces – not necessarily by paramilitaries – has also been a common factor of Northern Ireland life. Sometimes this takes the form of subtle or cruel sectarian jokes, death threats, and in some cases, has resulted in actual physical intimidation and murder. Groups such as Counteract, specifically set up to address sectarianism in the workplace, have significantly succeeding in addressing such intimidation through a combination of employer and employee programmes.

Violent tactics

Throughout the 30 years of the conflict, the paramilitaries from both sides have wreaked offence and vengeance in varying measures and against varying targets. Crowded pubs were often blown up, and some days were characterized by multiple explosions. On one day in 1972 (known as Bloody Friday) 26 explosions were carried out by the IRA in Belfast; 11 people were killed and 130 people were injured. 1972 saw the highest casualty rate in Northern Ireland with a total of 467 people killed. Mass killings have included the murder of a Catholic show band, the murder of a busload of Protestant workers, setting explosives to kill guests at a hotel dance, the killing of people gathered to pray in a Remembrance Day ceremony in 1987, the killing of nine people in a fish shop on the Protestant Shankill in 1993 followed by a gun attack on a pub by Loyalists in Greysteele, which killed seven people; in the summer of 1994, another pub attack by Loyalists killed six people who were watching a world cup football match. Although such activities have decreased significantly since the Belfast Agreement, in 1998 a group of 29 Protestant and Catholic shoppers in the town of Omagh in Co. Tyrone were killed by the dissident Republican group, the Real IRA. In addition to police and army stations, public installations such as water or electricity stations were frequently blown up. A favourite target of the IRA was the train between Dublin and Belfast, which was rather ironic in view of their stated desire for a united Ireland. Such activities led to hugely fortified towns and villages, and innumerable military checkpoints that made everyday life extremely difficult for all communities.

Resourcing the paramilitaries

In order to pay for their campaign, and in particular for their weapons, the paramilitaries have required substantial funds. In 1993, the Northern Ireland Office estimated that the paramilitaries had an annual income of over £10 million a year (RUC, 1993; Horgan and Taylor, 1999). Such funds were acquired through a range of means, which varied according to time and opportunity. Whilst the amounts coming from the USA to supporters of the IRA was thought to be substantial in the seventies and early eighties, this decreased in the mid-1980s. The majority of the funding for both

Republicans and Loyalists since the eighties has come through tax frauds, legitimate businesses, drinking clubs and gaming machines, pirated videos, smuggling, armed bank robberies and extortion, particularly of businessmen and builders under threat of harassment or destruction if such protection monies are not paid. Some paramilitaries, particularly Loyalist paramilitaries, are also believed to be involved in drug trafficking.

There is evidence that Loyalist paramilitaries have acquired some of their weaponry through South African channels, but evidence of any other external assistance is thought to be minimal (RISCT, 1991). Much of the financing and a substantial amount of the weaponry of the Republicans appears to have come from abroad. Financing and arms supply for the first two decades of the conflict appear to have come from Colonel Quadafi of Libya. In the nineties much of their munitions came from Eastern Europe, and there is clear evidence that they attempted to purchase US weaponry, such as stinger missiles (RISCT, 1991). However, the majority of the most deadly explosives of both Republican and Loyalist paramilitaries have been home-made devices such as petrol bombs and mortars constructed from hardware store materials. By the end of the conflict, the IRA in particular were extremely well equipped with arms and explosives, and the decommissioning of these proved to be a substantial problem in the wake of the ceasefires.

Containing the armed struggle

Containing and challenging those who choose to use violent political leverage, particularly through the use of guerrilla tactics, is an extremely difficult task in any situation. The tactics used by paramilitaries have the capacity for flexibility and surprise, and the anonymous nature of the way in which the paramilitaries conduct their campaigns can make it extremely difficult to protect targets without enormously restricting civil liberties. The tacit, if not active, acceptance of their activities by many within some communities can also make their conviction extremely difficult. However, Northern Ireland has not been lacking in attempting such challenges, and there is some evidence that many of the activities of the more intelligent and sensitive civil servants, of local communities, and of the security forces have contained the level of violence in Northern Ireland.

Decreasing unemployment and social exclusion

There appears to be an obvious, though by no means total, correlation between levels of unemployment, membership of the paramilitaries and voting patterns for parties apparently supporting violence, including Sinn Fein. Unemployment, variously reckoned to be between 18 and 20 per cent overall during the conflict, depending upon the calculation methods used, has been consistently higher in Northern Ireland than in any other region of the United Kingdom. Areas that recruit the most paramilitaries (and which usually suffer most from the conflict through sectarian killings) are those with the highest levels of unemployment – in some areas such unemployment has been almost 60 per cent and those unemployed were mostly males.

Recognizing the correlation between unemployment and support for violence the government (belatedly some would say) involved itself in various initiatives designed to reduce unemployment such as the Making Belfast Work initiative developed in the early nineties (Fitzduff, 2000) and a variety of funding packages for private enterprise projects.

Two other factors are seen to have assisted support for Republican paramilitaries in the community. The first has been the existence of major inequalities that have existed between the communities since the foundation of the state, and which have seriously fuelled Catholic anger and alienation, and subsequent support for the IRA. Such equity issues, and ways of addressing them, were detailed in Chapter 5. The elimination of many of these inequities has removed a substantial amount of the anger on the part of Catholic communities. The other major issue has been the lack of ownership, and subsequent lack of responsibility, felt or taken by many Catholics in regard to the institutions of the state. While this has most seriously affected their attitude towards the security forces, it has also under-mined their capacity to support their local councils, universities, health boards, and other institutions associated with the state in a positive way. However, the substantial emergence of a Catholic middle class, many of them professionals, and their increasing in-volvement in positions of responsibility within their organizations, is gradually increasing the Catholic sense of ownership towards such bodies, and their revulsion at their destruction through the contin-uance of paramilitarism.

Force and legal process

The first option in challenging the armed struggle is usually to use the state police or army to contain it by undertaking surveillance work aimed at preventing atrocities, through securing people or weapons and, in the case of Northern Ireland, where the existing law generally prevails, by using the legal processes to restrain those who choose to use illegal paramilitary force. While all of these have been possible in Northern Ireland (Chapter 6) they have their limitations both in terms of their effectiveness and, in some cases, because of their counterproductive nature in increasing the hostility of a sub-stantial section of the community to the presence of the security forces, therefore lessening their cooperation.

In substantiating this it may be sufficient to point out that an average of 16,000 soldiers and a level of policing almost three times that required in the rest of the UK have failed to do more than limit the force of the paramilitaries. Since the eighties it has been con-ceded by the British army that it will never defeat the paramilitaries by means of force alone and increasingly the state has used other means to counteract paramilitarism.

Limiting funds and weapons

The option of cutting off supplies of weapons and funding to the paramilitaries is one that received increasing attention over the last decade of the conflict, with some degrees of success. By the nineties, the amount of money coming from the pro-IRA organization NORAID (Northern Aid committee) in the USA was estimated to be approximately one third of what it was 10 years previously. Several factors assisted this. One was the setting up of alternative groups, such as the International Fund and the Ireland Fund, which draw upon the pro-Irish sentiment in the USA to put resources into assisting economic and community development for Northern Ireland rather than paramilitary activity. The other factor has been the discussion work undertaken by the Social Democratic and Labour Party (SDLP) and the British government in the USA and elsewhere pleading for constructive and non-violent support only to be given to the region by those interested in its progress.

In 1988 a special anti-racketeering coordinating task force, consisting of the police, the tax authorities, Customs and Excise, and the intelligence services was set up to combat the flow of funds to paramilitaries through illegitimate businesses and extortion, particularly of businessmen. New legislative powers were enacted by the British government to enable the courts to confiscate the assets of anyone who has benefited from terrorist activities and the Irish government also passed emergency legislation to seize funds that it believed had been obtained by the IRA under threat of kidnap and murder.

A special confidential telephone line was set up to help business people and others who were threatened by racketeering paramilitaries, although its success was somewhat limited by the fact that the police felt unable in many cases to provide sufficient protection for victims to feel safe in coming forward and giving evidence. Police had some considerable success however, in detecting illegal business activities such as pirated videos and smuggling activities.

The politicization of the IRA

On 1 November 1981, Sinn Fein met for its annual conference in Dublin, where Danny Morrison, their director of publicity asked the question: "Who here really believes that we can win the war through the ballot box? But will anyone here object if through the ballot box in this hand and an armalite in this hand we take power in Ireland?"

Thus began Sinn Fein's new strategy of jointly contesting elections and at the same time continuing to support the campaign of violence. There is some evidence that where they were successful, and achieved governance through elections, the support for the use of IRA violence was diminished, e.g. there has been almost negligible bombing during the 1990s in the city of Derry/Londonderry, when the Nationalists (SDLP and Sinn Fein) had the majority of political power, compared to the seventies and eighties when much of the town was destroyed. Obviously, having responsibility for the running and development of a town did not sit easily with a parallel support for its destruction through explosives! It is also believed that Sinn Fein's increasing confidence in using the regular democratic process of district councils increased its capacity to move away from the need to use paramilitary violence (Bean, 1994).

After the ceasefires of 1994, many people who had been active within the IRA were incorporated into the political activities of Sinn Fein. Such incorporation seems to have been a definite policy to constructively engage the energy of former combatants in politics at both a regional and local level in order to ensure that the ceasefires, and political progress, were to last. There was also a need to portray such involvement in political power as a "victory" in the face of claims from many within the Republican community that the war had been ended without gain. This strategy eventually saw a major IRA figure such as Martin McGuinness as the new Minister for Education, following the Assembly elections of 1998. Although such moves were repugnant to many Unionists, and Nationalists who had not supported the IRA, there is little doubt that they helped to secure the success of the Agreement.

Political Education Group

As the political momentum that followed the ceasefires increased, Loyalist figures also began to involve themselves more significantly in politics. Such involvement was helped by the activities of the Political Education Group (PEG), a small group set up by the author and a few others following the 1994 ceasefires to provide financial support and training, which would help the paramilitary-related parties, particularly the Loyalists, to move into the democratic process and build up their political infrastructure. This group functioned from 1995 to 1999 (ceasefires to post Agreement) to assist emerging political activists to enhance their skills in effective political discussion and debate, negotiation, use of the media, lobbying skills etc. and in training people in running electoral and political campaigns.

In the years in which the group functioned, the equilibrium between politics and violence was very uncertain. I remember a phone call one day from a small Republican party, which was seen as a political front for a splinter paramilitary group which was not on ceasefire, but which was interested in possibly receiving support from PEG. Their main questions were around whether or not they could achieve greater power for their group in the future through politics, or through their continuing usage of violence. Such were the questions facing all of those who had been involved in paramilitary leverage, sometimes for decades, and who were now rethinking their future, as politics became the increasingly dominant mode for power in Northern Ireland.

And indeed, developing and sustaining alternatives modes of engagement for former combatants, at various levels of community or electoral politics, is now known to be a critical ingredient for the successful development of a peace process (Darby and MacGinty 2000). It was noticeable that the Loyalist party, the Progressive Unionist Party (PUP), which eventually gained two seats in the Assembly elections in 1998, remained much more strongly in favour of the Agreement, and sustaining the peace, than did their Loyalist competitors, the Ulster Democratic Party (UDP), who failed to gain seats in the elections. In years subsequent to the Agreement, in 1999–2001, the paramilitary wing of the UDP, the Ulster Defence Association, and its various aliases, continued to provoke a considerable amount of violence on the streets after the ceasefires, not only against Catholics, but also against other Loyalists, mostly associated with the PUP, whom they perceived had been successful at the new order of politics, where they themselves had failed.

Community challenge to paramilitarism

There were many peacemakers within the communities who attempted to challenge and persuade the paramilitaries to cease the use of violence. Experience has shown, however, that it is often easier to mobilize support for violence than for peacemaking, and developing a community challenge to paramilitarism has not been an easy task. In the first instance, the level of open support for the political objectives of the paramilitaries is as broad as the communities themselves, as evidenced in various voting patterns of the communities. The level of support, whether active or tacit, for the use of violence to achieve such political ends is obviously much lower, and varies from area to area and according to the particular context. In addition, the custom of silence, often maintained through fear, ensures that open discussion about the use of such violence, and opposition to it, can be difficult to generate and organize.

Achieving consensus on how groups opposed to violence can mount a successful challenge to its use by paramilitaries has also been difficult because of differing perspectives on the practicality (or in some cases what some people saw as the ethical dilemma) of talking – either at community or governmental level – with those who are using violence for political leverage. Many people did not wish to accord a legitimacy to such groups by engaging them in talks, pointing to the existence of a democratic process through which they could – but chose not to – pursue their goals. Many, particularly those who have suffered directly through the violence of the paramilitaries, understandably recoiled from engaging with those who were responsible for their suffering. Others pointed to the uselessness of using talk to persuade the paramilitaries to desist, and often called instead for much tougher security measures to destroy them.

Other groups however, were convinced that trying to persuade those involved in violence to end their military activities was likely to be more effective in achieving such change than merely condemning them from a distance. What little evidence there is about paramilitaries who decide to give up violence appears to indicate that challenge, of an emotional and intellectual kind, and persuasion that takes place at a personal or group level are both needed to ensure such a cessation. This is because the paramilitaries themselves have personality variables that respond to different levels of pressure, and because of the diversity within the local communities from which they come (Fitzduff, 1989b).

Moral and intellectual challenge

There is often a need felt for an emotional and collective public challenge to the paramilitary campaigns of violence, particularly in the wake of atrocities, if only to validate the moral outrage felt by many in the wake of killings. Many such demonstrations organized by the trade unions and others have temporarily united the communities against the use of violence. However, years of moral challenge to the paramilitaries in Northern Ireland from a Christian or other perspective have shown that such pressure will have little effect if not linked in some way to the paramilitaries' own sense of ethical code and to their alleged objectives.

Most paramilitary groups have devised their own code of "honour" about such things as legitimate targets for murder, despite the obvious fact that such factions often display extreme recklessness in their campaigns, with consequent loss of civilian life. It has been shown (Darby, 1993) that the IRA goes to great lengths in its weekly newspaper *An Phoblacht* to justify its choice of particular targets, usually security forces, those civilians carrying out some work for them, or Loyalist paramilitaries. The abandonment of kidnapping as a legitimate tactic by the IRA in 1983, after the public outrage that followed such an incident, and the damage done to their support by their killing of a policeman from the Republic of Ireland in 1996, shows the sensitivity of the paramilitaries to extensive public pressure. Bruce (1992) has shown that Loyalists too feel that the support they gain within their own communities is diminished by people's perceptions of their murders as purely sectarian – which explains why they frequently follow their murders by allegations (often disproved) that their victims were members of the IRA. Apologies from both factions have happened on occasions when a "mistake" has obviously been made, and those killed are seen to be the "wrong" or illegitimate target.

Condemnation of murders from significant people in both communities, including Catholic communities after the murders of security force members, and cross-community attendance at the funerals of such victims, significantly increased in the 1990s. Since 1993, one of the region's main newspapers, *The Newsletter*, read mostly by Protestants, refused to carry the allegations made by paramilitaries that their victims were paramilitary members from the other side. They also treated all deaths as equal, and to be equally condemned because of their perpetration without trial or justice. Since the mid-nineties, *The Irish News*, the Nationalist newspaper, also refused to carry IRA death notices. Such shifts towards principled, rather than loyalty-based, condemnations of murders, provided a way of ensuring that paramilitaries were left in little doubt about the decreasing support for their actions by the community as a whole.

Actions by local communities

The most effective and the most difficult place from which to challenge the actions of paramilitaries is usually from within the local communities themselves. It is far easier to condemn from afar. Within a community you may be faced with someone whose actions you suspect to be murderous but who is a neighbour, possibly someone who was a schoolmate, whose children play with your children, and who drinks in the same pub as you on a Saturday night. This difficulty is in addition to the ambiguity that many people in such communities have about the paramilitaries, and their possible need for their protection.

Women, and in particular women whose own families have suffered through the conflict, and who have gained a credibility for commitment to their community through community development work, have been particularly effective at such challenges, whether in public, over the airwaves, or through community group meetings. They are particularly effective on issues of intimidation that are happening within the community. Groups such as the Drumcree Faith and Justice group carried out community surveys to show that there was little support for the Republican paramilitaries punishing anti-social activity through kneecapping and managed to achieve the near cessation of such activities in their community in Portadown. Community pastors and priests set up community meetings aimed at challenging paramilitary actions. Although in some cases these had to be abandoned because of threats from the paramilitaries, they often effected at least a temporary cessation in such activity. Behaviour such as those of the Families Against Intimidation and Terror (FAIT) group, who publicly protested outside the offices of the political wings of Republican and Loyalist groups, and shared demonstrations between communities after an outrage by the paramilitaries, have also helped, as did the (eventual) condemnation by Amnesty International of such activities.[51]

There is little doubt that such activities provided a check to those who would continue to assert a mandate from the people for their actions. The very fact that many involved in such campaigns were themselves victims of paramilitary acts of violence is an indication that they posed a challenge to the continuance of such activities.

Victims and post-crisis work

It is hard to overestimate the levels of anger and tension that can accrue after a killing in Northern Ireland, and in particular after an incident that has involved the deaths of a group of people. In the confusion and fury that follow, it has been all too easy for retaliation to loom large in the minds of the victim community, and for the anger of the community to spill over into communal violence. Unless such destructive energies can be controlled, the spiral of violence can continue to rise. The experience of the peacemakers, and in particular the work of many of the reconciliation organizations, has increasingly ensured that such retaliatory actions are contained. Since the late 1980s many such groups have ensured that each killing elicited a wave of sympathy from communities right across the social spectrum. Flowers were frequently sent across community dividing lines by courier, if people were fearful of personally venturing into a territory that would be tense after any such atrocities. Letters and cards of condolences also cross the communities, and, where groups are organized and have had the courage, for example, the Women Together group, they have personally crossed the barriers bringing with them flowers and food for the "wake" of the victim.[52]

One particular incident will demonstrate how such actions can ease the aftermath of a killing. In 1992 a young policeman was killed in Armagh. His father had pleaded for no retaliation for his killing on the television just a few days later at the funeral service. He told of the anger that he and his family, and their close community had felt in the days that followed the killing. His family was a very traditional family, and had rarely met or known many Catholics. Like many others Protestants, he presumed that most Catholics tacitly supported the IRA. However, the avalanche of sympathy cards and letters that he had received from Catholics following his son's death had convinced him that this killing had not been carried out with the consent of the Catholic community; hence his plea for no retaliation. His was just one of many such stories about the kind of work that has seriously limited the amount of tension in the community in the last few years of the conflict.

In developing such work, the churches too have played an increasingly positive role. By 1993 almost all funerals resulting from a conflict-related killing were attended by clergy on a cross-community basis, which attendance also helped to sustain community stability in a time of possible retaliatory aggression.

Victim support

It has been estimated that each victim affects at least 30 people in his or her immediate circle, so it is probable that more than half the total population of roughly 1.5 million has been directly affected by the violence. The relatives of victims who have been murdered, in particular, are often in tremendous need of support and counselling. Such support is not only needed by the bereaved, but is also necessary for society if anger at the actions of the paramilitaries is not to turn to bitterness and be energized into a desire for revenge.

The work of supporting the relatives of victims, preferably by those who have also been bereaved, has been the focus of the work of some reconciliation groups such as Corrymeela, and of groups specifically dedicated to it such as Widows and Widowers Against Violence (WAVE). In the aftermath of a death, such groups will sensitively contact the murdered person's family in order to see if they can be of assistance. Not only have such groups provided tremendous individual support to each other, but as their members come from right across the community divide, and include the wives of murdered security force personnel, they have also provided a stabilizing cross-community network which limits the amount of communal tension that can quickly gather after a murder if work is not undertaken to prevent it.

Since the Belfast Agreement such work with victims has increased significantly as people begin to use the safety of the cessation of violence to talk about the tragedies that have hit so many because of the conflict. Many groups have now formed to deal with the issues of victims, and the European Community has given a substantial amount of money for such victims (McGowan and Patterson, 2001). Although many of these groups are still single identity in nature, representing for example victims of security forces, or victims of the IRA, it has been noticeable how many of these groups have succeeded in developing a cross-community remit through which Protestant and Catholic victims can share their perceptions of the conflict, and, in some cases, mourn their losses together.

Anti-intimidation work

By its nature, anti-intimidation work is extremely difficult, and often fraught with danger for those involved in it. Nevertheless, it is work that has been more effectively developing in recent years. In 1992, the CRC brought together 15 agencies involved in dealing with the victims of intimidation – mostly intra-community intimidation – and those interested in challenging it. Such groups included the Housing Executive and other housing organizations, the Probation Board, the Health and Social Services Boards, the advice agencies, the police, and various community and reconciliation organizations that had been involved in challenging the activities of Republican and Loyalist paramilitaries. Some of these – such as Base 2 and the Derry Peace and Reconciliation group – had been involved in particular in trying to prevent intimidatory actions against young people who were being faced with arbitrary punishment or forced emigration to London or Dublin. They assisted these young people through negotiation with the paramilitaries to have their sentences lifted. Where this failed, they helped with the necessary assistance for emigration.

Other groups, such as FAIT, brought together many of the families of the victims of paramilitary violence to highlight their anger at atrocities as they occurred. Others, such as the housing organizations, were involved in trying to deal with the many victims, often of mixed marriages, or from mixed areas, who had been forced out of their homes. From this group, an anti-intimidation network was formed, which concentrated on sharing information about best and effective practice both in dealing with the victims of intimidation and in challenging the practice. As such work has been both difficult and potentially dangerous, requiring both knowledge and courage, training was provided for people involved in it.

Advice was offered to all citizens through the local advice agencies about possible avenues for potential or threatened victims, and a unit specifically aimed at the problem was established in conjunction with an organization called Counteract, set up by the trade unions in 1990 specifically to deal with workplace intimidation. They carried out substantial training with all their shop stewards (who come from both sections of the community) on how to deal with, and eliminate, intimidation among their workforces. Their work has in many cases successfully diminished such workplace intimidation, and has significantly increased the possibilities for safe and integrated workplaces.

Persuading the paramilitaries

Down through the years of violence there have been various attempts to engage the paramilitaries in dialogue with the aim of persuading them to desist from violence. These attempts have been made both at informal community level and at governmental level. Community workers in particular, have frequently maintained and cultivated some connections with those involved in violence, and many frequently used these connections to try to limit the paramilitaries' activities. In the 1990s negotiations with Loyalists were carried out by some Protestant clergy, mainly directed at persuading them to stop their murder campaign, and there is evidence that such clergy have been a significant factor in persuading the Loyalists to cease their campaign in the wake of the cessation of violence by the IRA. In assisting the IRA campaign to end, one of the main persuaders/negotiators was a Catholic priest, who provided a conduit between Sinn Fein and the Irish government, in a series of dialogues that led to the ceasefire of 1994. Politicians have also from time to time become persuaders. Most notable of such persuaders was John Hume, the SDLP politician, who had been meeting Sinn Fein since early 1993 in an effort to persuade the party to enter the democratic process. And in 1994, some Unionist politicians began to engage in dialogue with Loyalist paramilitaries in order to persuade them to end their campaigns. All such contacts were to prove significant in securing the ceasefire of 1994.

Governments and paramilitaries

During the conflict there have always been some informal mediators with a capacity for movement who have ensured that government officials, ministers, and paramilitaries have been able to keep each other informed about any developing possibilities for moving out of the conflict. Sometimes such mediators have come from reconciliation groups such as the Derry Peace and Reconciliation group, or from the Quakers and others committed to keep open any useful lines of communication between the parties. Organized mediation between the government and the paramilitaries have been far less common. One such meeting was that between the British government and the IRA in 1972, when a team of IRA negotiators was flown to London to talk to then Prime Minister. These talks failed to reach any agreement. Secret peace talks were again held in 1974 with the IRA, this time mediated by Protestant clergy, but these also failed. At the end of 1993 it was revealed that the British government and representatives of the IRA had secretly been in contact for a period of many years to try to reach an agreement on an end to IRA violence, and the consequent inclusion of Republicans into the political process. The British mediator in this instance was a retired member of the British army. While such talks eventually broke down at the end of 1993, there is little doubt that they contributed significantly to a much greater understanding by both parties about what was necessary in terms of developing a framework document that could facilitate an end to the IRA military campaign.

During 1994, it was also revealed that the Irish government had had its own channels of communication between itself and some Loyalist paramilitaries, which were mostly mediated by a Presbyterian minister and later by a Protestant trade unionist from Dublin. These talks were also significant in achieving the cessation of the Loyalist paramilitary campaign.

Talking between paramilitaries

Occasional meetings between Republican and Loyalist paramilitaries have been organized by various community leaders, but these have rarely had any clear outcomes in terms of agreements. Part of the reason has been that the Republican paramilitaries have seen the British as their main enemy, and see Loyalist paramilitaries as only a secondary problem. In addition, Loyalist groups have often been faced with threats from their own side when such meetings have become public knowledge and this seriously limited their capacity for talking. I remember in the early 1990s offering to facilitate some dialogue meetings for John McMichael, a commander in the UDA, who jokingly said that it was his own people he was afraid of if he took up my offer – and indeed less than a year later he was murdered by his own side. From 1993 to 1994, however, there were an increasing number of meetings between activists on both sides, arranged mostly by community workers and mediators. The ceasefires of 1994 enabled a significant increase in such discussions, both at a private and a public level. In some areas, former paramilitaries began to cooperate on common social problems, as they increasingly realized their collective social disadvantage. Such discussions all served to decrease their suspicions of each other, and enabled them to talk together about each other's political aspirations and fears.

The use of external contexts

The use of visitors and facilitators from external conflict contexts has also been useful. One initiative undertaken with such groups involved the use of a visit by a group of mediators who had been working with Euskadi 'ta Askatasuna (ETA), the paramilitary group fighting in the Basque country for independence from Spain. When the visit took place in 1992, these mediators had been trying, with some apparent success, to channel the energy of ETA into constitutional politics, and in particular into the development of a pan-Nationalist non-violent alliance in the Basque country. As there are many significant similarities between the methods and aspirations of ETA and those of the IRA the visit provided a useful opportunity for Loyalists and Republicans to reflect (separately) upon possible alternatives to the armed struggle. Interestingly, the development of just such a pan-Nationalist alliance was the major focus for Sinn Fein during the two years before the IRA in its campaign, and is believed to have provided it with its major escape route for ending a military campaign that was obviously not going to achieve its stated goals, and had ceased to have any substantial support at the community level.[53]

Many people involved in the peacemaking process in South Africa also visited Northern Ireland to meet with reconciliation workers, with some politicians, and with those who were close to paramilitary activists, thus enabling wider frameworks for the resolution of the Northern Ireland conflict to be considered. Emulation of the ANC by Sinn Fein was of significant help in encouraging the organization to move away from the use of military violence to political activity.

In addition, the leverage of many businessmen, congressmen, and others from the United States, in some cases acting under the auspices of the American president Bill Clinton, was very helpful in ensuring the ceasefires of 1994 by the Republicans, and in positively liaising with Sinn Fein/IRA to ensure their eventual involvement more fully into politics, and away from violence (Arthur, 2000).

Work with prisoners

In formulating paramilitary policy, paramilitary prisoners in Northern Ireland have played a significant part. Prison often provided the first opportunity for many people to think through their objectives in a thoughtful manner (Fitzduff, 1989b). Such thinking was assisted by the range of educational courses (including Open University courses) that were made available for prisoners during their confinement. Through such courses many of the inmates have come into contact not only with each other, but with political, sociological, and social-psychological ideas that have challenged some of their assumptions and beliefs. Work had also been going on since 1993 with Loyalist and Republican prisoners within the prisons through organizations such as the Mediation Network, looking at issues of sectarianism, political options, and conflict resolution. The reasoning behind such work is that prisoners, both while in prison, and when released, can and do often substantially influence the continuance or otherwise of the military campaigns of the various factions. Subsequent to the ceasefires, many ex-prisoners became involved in work aimed at reintegrating prisoners back into their communities, and also into community development work aimed at the social and economic development of their communities (Gormley, 2000; Shirlow, 2001).

Governments talking

While many people and groups contributed to the development of what became known as the "peace process" over the latter part of 1993 and most of 1994, undoubtedly the work of the Irish and British governments (and in particular their officials) in developing strategies for paramilitary inclusion in the democratic process, and frameworks for political development was of the utmost importance. The Anglo-Irish Agreement, signed in 1985 despite the full opposition of Unionists, provided all the necessary official machinery through which later agreements could be reached. The result of two governments' energetic cooperation throughout the latter half of 1993 was the Downing Street Declaration. This document spelt out the willingness of the British government to leave Northern Ireland if and when the majority of people within the region wished it to go. And in February 1995, the Framework Document, developed and agreed by the two governments (Chapter 8) significantly confirmed such "neutrality" on the part of the British government, and pointed to the need for Nationalists to persuade Unionists (rather than the British government) of the merits of a united Ireland. Such an agreement rendered pointless the continuance of a military offensive by the IRA designed to persuade the British to leave Northern Ireland.

The IRA and CLMC ceasefires of 1994

By the end of 1993, the IRA was faced with a considerable degree of unity and cooperation between the Irish and British governments, the realization that they could not win the war militarily, a decreasing amount of support for their military campaign in Nationalist areas, a society that was proving to be more equitable now towards Catholics (thus contradicting the assertions of Sinn Fein that only a united Ireland could deliver on such equality), a security force interface that was, in general, decreasingly problematic, structures that were proving themselves able to accommodate Nationalist as well as Unionist culture, a Unionist community that was more determined than ever to resist a united Ireland, and a better-organized and more effective Loyalist campaign of violence.

The IRA was also facing the possibility that the next round of political discussions, based on the framework agreed in the Downing Street Declaration might actually succeed, thus leaving Republicans completely marginalized if they failed to take up the invitation to them to renounce the armed struggle and join the democratic process.

Hence, the IRA's decision to cease violence on 1 September 1994 was not totally unexpected. Although the IRA knew that the conflict could be continued with as little as a few dozen committed militarists, and it continued to have a store of arms that could last for many more years of conflict, the conflict would no longer have been seen as a campaign for its people, and it faced a future as a marginalized group.

The Loyalist groups were thus faced with a dilemma. Their concerns had always been expressed as twofold. In the first instance they were worried about a diminution of the union with Britain, and they also saw themselves as the main defenders of their people against the threat of the IRA. They received reassurance from the British Prime Minister that, as agreed in the Downing Street Declaration, the Union would be maintained as long as the majority in Northern Ireland so wished. With the threat of the IRA no longer in place, they had little reason to sustain their campaign, and hence they too declared a ceasefire on 13 October 1994.

Conclusion

The campaign to defeat the support for paramilitary violence as a means of achieving political leverage has been complex and difficult, and the programmes outlined in this chapter are a testimony to the variety of approaches that are necessary, and that have had varying degrees of success. In particular this chapter points to the necessity to look beyond the mere use of security measures, which, if used in isolation from an understanding of the need to change the social, cultural, and political contexts, can be counterproductive, and in some cases, may actually increase the support for political violence. The programmes outlined above do indeed testify to the many attempts that have been made to think beyond such security approaches, particularly by policy makers and legislators. They are also a testimony to an extraordinary amount of courage shown by many people in the community, some of whom have found their own lives at constant risk because of their opposition to such violence. While this chapter may provide some reassurance to those now working in the midst of violence that at least some alleviation of communal fracture is almost always possible, even in the worst of circumstances, it should also provide a warning about the need for preventive work, particularly in the areas of social and communal justice, that can stop the scourge of violence emerging in a situation of conflict. As we know, to our terrible cost here in Northern Ireland, containing paramilitary violence, once it has developed, is an extremely complex process that can take many years to be successful.

8

Political initiatives – Tracks One and Two

The difficulties of dialogue

It would be very difficult to overestimate how problematic it was to have conversations between enemies during the conflict in Northern Ireland. Those who tried to facilitate such conversations frequently found themselves in danger from one or both sides to the conflict. This was brought home to me in the early 1990s, when a journalist made it clear that he was going to write about a suspected "channel" of dialogue between Republican groups and the British government. Fearing the consequences of such exposure, this particular person came looking for assistance to try to prevent it. We failed to avert the publication of the journalist's suspicions, and the inevitable happened – the person was threatened by both Loyalists and Republicans, and eventually found it expedient to leave Northern Ireland for his own safety and that of his family.

The difficulty in part comes from the fact that Northern Ireland is a very small region – the population is roughly 1.5 million, which is about one fifth of that of London. Its very smallness, and the tight knit nature of many of its neighbourhoods, makes dialogue more, and not less difficult. Even where territorial divisions are not total, and work or social events permit contact (more often in the predominately middle-class mixed urban areas or those villages and towns that do remain shared) communities have developed very effective ways of relating to each other so as to ensure that even where structural barriers have become porous, very effective mental barriers are available to replace them. The rules of engagement for mixing, the "telling" that people undertake of each other prior to engaging in any interaction are usually learnt by the age of 11 when children have begun to be competent in the clues that will enable them to know which "side" they are talking to (Cairns, 1987).

People have also developed very effective barriers that come into play when meetings do happen, which will further diminish the possibilities of dialogue taking place at any meaningful level. What will often inform such relationships, when they happen at an individual level, will not in fact be hostility, but politeness. This is because of the peculiar schizoid sense which often characterizes relationships in Northern Ireland (Jackson, 1971); people at a private individual level will rarely show other than concern and hospitality to each other, while at a general and public level both verbal and sometimes physical expressions of hostility are permitted. This apparently disjunctive level of behaviour can easily be understood if one accepts that prejudice and discrimination between the two communities come not from the nature of the individuals but from the nature of their relationships with other groups (Hewstone and Browne, 1986).

In private, every effort will also be made by both parties to avoid any references to, and above all any discussion on, a topic on which they are likely to have differing political or religious views. An extra complication, which makes both talking and mediation to assist such talking even more difficult, is the fact that straight talking, even within communities, is not the normal mode of communication in Northern Ireland; traditional private styles of communication, particularly in a conflict situation, often tend to be subtle and non-direct. For these reasons, it is difficult in communities from differing backgrounds to engage in dialogue of any extent or depth despite the small territorial and population size of the region.

What follows from the above is that it is even more difficult for those who are most at the political interface, such as politicians (or suspected paramilitaries), to involve themselves in personal dialogue with each other, as they are even more closely watched and therefore more open to cries of betrayal. In fact, during the course of the conflict, political dialogue between politicians from opposing groups rarely happened on a private level, only at a public level. And at the public level, it was usually addressed to two audiences – primarily to one's own constituency who many politicians fear are watching, listening, and waiting lest they betray any of the community's presumed beliefs, and only secondarily to one's political opponents.

Added to the above is the difficulty that circumstances will often dictate to whom one is "permitted" by one's constituencies to talk to, and the decades in Northern Ireland have shown a consistent pattern of such refusals. At various times, Unionists have refused to talk to the British government; the Social Democratic and Labour Party (SDLP) has refused to talk formally with others in the Assembly (1982–86); churches, government ministers and others have refused to talk to Sinn Fein; Sinn Fein have consistently refused to talk with the police; the Orange Order refuse to talk to the Catholic residents who live on the routes down which they wish to march, etc. Fashions for such permissions changed over the years in the light of paramilitary atrocities, or political developments. Added to this the fact that Northern Ireland is such a small place it can almost be guaranteed that such talking cannot be done with any degree of privacy and will often incur threats from one's own community who fear such dialogue and see it as betrayal.

It can therefore be seen why political dialogue and negotiation are difficult. Nevertheless, despite such difficulties, it has been through a long and protracted series of both public and private dialogue initiatives that a modicum of agreement and settlement has been reached.

Track One initiatives

What are normally called Track One initiatives, that is initiatives that primarily involve governmental and political representatives, have abounded throughout the decades of the conflict. The fact that almost all of them are seen to have ended in "failure," until the Agreement of 1998, probably misrepresents their usefulness. Many of them in fact built on the often minor understandings achieved through previous talks – a process of organic development that we now know is characteristic of many peace processes.[54] Indeed, it is noticeable that many of the agreements reached in the power-sharing agreement of 1974, which fell apart within six months, were echoed many years later in the 1998 Agreement which looks set to be successful, thus testifying to the concept of "ripeness" so aptly described by Zartman (1989; see also Mitchell, 1995).

1974: Power sharing-assembly

In 1972 the British government dismissed the Stormont government because of its perceived inability to handle the aftermath of the civil rights movement. But in 1974 the government did negotiate an agreement among the main constitutional parties to a form of power sharing in government. It set up a devolved parliamentary body to rule in Northern Ireland, and in addition it achieved agreement that there was to be a Council of Ireland which was to be a cross-border body drawn from the Republic of Ireland and Northern Ireland. While the Unionists involved in the agreement had hoped to persuade their voters of the merits of these new arrangements, the old suspicions surfaced, and eventually, after five months of the executive (which achieved a surprising amount of cooperation among all the parties involved), tensions among some Unionists rose to such a height that they called a general strike against the agreement. This strike, organized by Protestant workers and in which the Ulster Defence Association (UDA) Loyalist paramilitaries played a substantial part, eventually led to the overthrow of the executive and the return to direct rule by the British government.[55]

1982: Assembly

In 1982, the government announced another political initiative; a new assembly was to be set up, provided it received broad cross-community support. Power was to be devolved incrementally, as and when the parties could agree on such devolution. This offer of an assembly was however rejected by the SDLP on the basis that power sharing within it was not mandatory, and it excluded an Irish dimension to the solution. For some time the assembly existed as a talking shop for Unionists but it was wound up by the British government in 1986, mainly because the Unionists began to use it as a platform from which to condemn the Anglo-Irish Agreement, which had been signed by the British and Irish governments.

1985: Anglo-Irish Agreement

In 1983 the government of the Republic of Ireland set up a forum – the New Ireland Forum – which deliberated on possible ways forward for Northern Ireland. This suggested four possible courses: a unitary Irish state, a federal Ireland, joint British and Irish authority over Northern Ireland, or, if these could not be agreed, continued discussions on ideas for progress. The then British Prime Minister, Mrs. Thatcher, dismissed the first three options but took up the fourth, and in 1985 the two governments signed the Anglo-Irish Agreement. The Agreement recognized that any change in the status of Northern Ireland could only come about with the consent of the majority of people in Northern Ireland and established an intergovernmental conference where both governments could discuss matters of policy affecting Northern Ireland; the governments committed themselves to resolve any differences between them through the intergovernmental conference. The Agreement was widely backed in Britain and in the Republic of Ireland, but the Unionists, who saw it as diluting the union with Britain, rejected it. Although welcomed by the SDLP, Sinn Fein saw it as confirming partition and rejected it.

Despite the widespread opposition of Unionists to the Agreement it was to prove to be one of the most important elements in eventually securing the Belfast Agreement. It functioned as a useful vehicle through which concerted efforts, and assorted disagreements, were dealt with by both governments. It was the first formalization of interstate cooperation since the creation of Northern Ireland, and as such constituted a substantial shift on the part of the British, who had hitherto insisted on treating Northern Ireland as a totally internal problem. For the first time, a voice was provided for the Irish government in the affairs of Northern Ireland and the Agreement served to significantly change and harmonize their perspective on Northern Ireland, which considerably increased the capacity of both governments to address the conflict as a joint problem.

1990–92: Inter-party talks

In 1989 the then Secretary of State for Northern Ireland, Peter Brooke, began a series of meetings with all political parties (except Sinn Fein which was excluded because of its refusal to condemn the use of violence to effect political leverage) to see if any agreement could be reached between them about possible political ways forward. It was negotiated by all parties that there should be three strands to the talks, which were internal structures for Northern Ireland, possibilities for the all-Ireland context, and the issue of the British–Irish relationship. These talks were agreed by most of the parties to have been a useful exercise, in that they provided them with a practical framework for a possible political solution, as well as an opportunity for constructive political dialogue. However, in the end the differences between the parties proved too difficult to surmount and the talks ended in summer 1992.

1993: Downing Street Declaration

None of the above initiatives had included Sinn Fein, who were thought to be too closely aligned to the violence of the IRA. In 1988, in what can now be seen as the beginning of the structured peace process, the SDLP and Sinn Fein held a series of meetings to see if they could resolve their differences, particularly over Sinn Fein's support for the use of violence. In March 1993, following the breakdown of the inter-party talks in 1992, John Hume, the leader of the SDLP, and Gerry Adams, the leader of Sinn Fein, restarted their series of talks to see if they could achieve a breakthrough in the stalemate that saw violence continue and no political solution in sight.

It had been obvious for some time that many people within Sinn Fein no longer had faith that a military offensive on their part would achieve a British withdrawal, and who felt the need to engage in a "peace process" which I define as beginning when both sides realize that they cannot achieve a unilateral victory, and realize that they must look to a compromise with the other side. To that end, Sinn Fein had begun to explore the option of creating a much more widely based Nationalist front in order to progress their aim of achieving their goal of a united Ireland. They began to change the nature of their demands, softening their statements on the need for a stated time frame for a withdrawal by the British, recognizing the need for Unionists to consent to a united Ireland, and asking the British government to be persuaders to that consent. Sinn Fein also appeared to recognize that Britain was no longer staying because it was in its interest to do so, but out of a sense of duty to the majority in Northern Ireland who felt they were facing betrayal, and also out of a legitimate fear that such a declaration of intent to withdraw could provoke a civil war.

Discussions between John Hume and Gerry Adams continued for most of 1993, and they eventually agreed upon a series of principles, which they hoped would make it possible for Sinn Fein/IRA to end the violence with some sense of success. And, towards the end of 1993, it was revealed that, although they initially denied it, the British government, through some intermediaries, had been having talks with intermediaries of Sinn Fein/IRA in secret, directed at ending the violence. These talks had focused on how such an ending could be progressed, and how Sinn Fein could be included in open political discussions with the other political parties on the future for Northern Ireland, once they had renounced violence.

In the end, most of the principles agreed by Hume and Adams appear to have been incorporated into a Declaration issued by both governments in December 1993 in the hope that such a document would provide a sufficient excuse for the IRA to end its campaign. The Downing Street Declaration once again reiterated the commitment of the British government to maintain the union until the greater number of the people in Northern Ireland decided otherwise. This decision could be ratified by referenda both north and south of the border, thus allowing for the "self-determination by the people of the island of Ireland" that Sinn Fein had said was necessary if the violence of the IRA was to cease. The declaration also announced the setting up of a Forum for Reconciliation by the Irish government, which would provide a vehicle for dialogue among all the political parties in the island, including Sinn Fein when it renounced violence. It also provided for North-South cooperation on a variety of issues, and, once again, it provided for a devolved government in Northern Ireland.

In August 1994, the IRA declared a ceasefire, followed six weeks later by a similar declaration by the Combined Military Loyalist Command.

1995: Framework Document

In February 1995 the British and Irish governments produced a document which outlined the British government's perspective on a framework for internal government in Northern Ireland, and the two governments' joint thinking on a framework for a political agreement between them, as well as cooperation on an island-wide basis. The section of the Framework Agreement concerned with an internal government suggested the formation of an assembly in Northern Ireland elected by proportional representation, a system of assembly committees, constituted broadly in proportion to party strengths; a panel of three elected people to complement the work of the assembly, and a system of detailed checks and balances intended to ensure an element of power sharing among the parties.

The section of the document concerned with the relationship between the Republic of Ireland and Northern Ireland reiterated the commitment of both governments to sustain the region within the United Kingdom for as long as the majority voted for the continuance of the link. In addition it suggested the formation of a North-South body, comprising elected representatives from, and accountable to, a Northern Ireland assembly and the Irish parliament, to deal with matters designated to it by the two governments in agreement with the parties. It suggested the formation of a parliamentary forum for representatives from North and South, and an intergovernmental conference, which would consider matters of mutual interest, but not those transferred to any new political institutions in Northern Ireland. The document also committed both governments to protect specified civil, political, and cultural rights.

The proposals, and in particular those concerned with North-South cooperation, were greeted with resistance and anger by many Unionists, who felt they represented just one more step on what many of them saw as an inevitable road to a united Ireland. Paramilitaries on both sides, however, reiterated their commitment to maintaining the ceasefires, and committed themselves to pursue political progress through democratic means. In early 1995, talks began between the civil servants of the British government and Sinn Fein, and with parties representing the Loyalist paramilitaries, which explored some possibilities for involving them in political dialogue with other political parties. In March 1995, the government entered into ministerial talks with the Loyalist paramilitaries having received some reassurances from them about their commitment to decommissioning arms, and in May 1995, the government entered into ministerial dialogue with Sinn Fein, which also committed itself to discussing arms decommissioning along with other matters of political interest. In the meanwhile, all other political parties were invited by the government to re-enter into political dialogue with the governments about possible ways forward for the political future of Northern Ireland.

1995–96: Decommissioning talks

The issue of decommissioning, however, began to threaten the process significantly. In March 1995, the British government made paramilitary decommissioning a requirement for entry into political talks. The IRA felt it was sufficient that they had called a ceasefire, and that this should suffice for entry into the talks. They believed that discussions about decommissioning should be part of the process of dialogue and not precede it. In an attempt to resolve the issue, an International Body on Decommissioning was set up, chaired by US senator George Mitchell. It reported in January 1996, advocating a set of six principles that should underline the process of political dialogue. These included a commitment to exclusively peaceful means for resolving political issues, the total disarmament of all paramilitary organizations, an agreement that such disarmament should be verifiable, opposing the use of force by any party and abiding by the terms of any agreement reached in all-party negotiations, and a commitment to try to stop the "punishment" beatings that were being inflicted by the paramilitaries for social control reasons at local community level.

In response to these principles, the IRA called an end to their ceasefire in February 1996, accusing the British government of wasting the opportunity for peace. It then exploded a huge bomb in London's Canary Wharf, a flagship project at the heart of the redevelopment of the London docklands. The Loyalists maintained their ceasefires.

1996: Forum for political dialogue

The British and Irish governments announced the setting up of a forum for political dialogue, from which Sinn Fein were excluded because of the breakdown of the ceasefire. The Loyalist political parties, the Progressive Unionist Party (PUP), associated with the Ulster Volunteer Force (UVF) and the Ulster Democratic Party (UDP), associated with the Ulster Freedom Fighters (UFF) and the Ulster Defence Association (UDA) who were associated with the paramilitaries were included, due to their maintenance of the ceasefire. The Forum was useful as a dialogue process, and as a means of bringing several new parties into the political dialogue process who provided some new political thinking – most notably the Loyalists and the Northern Ireland Women's Coalition, a cross-community women's party. However, without the involvement of Sinn Fein/IRA, there was a feeling that the peace process could not develop further.[56]

1997: New British Labour government

It had been fairly obvious for some time that the Conservative British government, led by John Major, was unable to progress the peace process, as it was limited by its dependence on Unionist support for its political survival. In addition, a vociferous minority within the Conservatives were totally opposed to the peace process, which they saw as appeasement to terrorists. However, in May 1997, a new Labour government, led by Tony Blair, achieved a massive parliamentary majority, which gave them more room to manoeuvre on further developing the peace process. It quickly set about drawing Sinn Fein into the negotiations. The British government gave commitments to Sinn Fein on policing reform, employment equality, action to address contentious parading by Protestant Orangemen through Catholic areas, and the transfer of Republican prisoners from jails in England to jails in the Republic of Ireland. Crucially, the Labour government announced that decommissioning was secondary to actually getting people into talks and the demand for decommissioning prior to entry into the talks was dropped. The IRA declared another ceasefire in July 1997.

1997/1998: Inclusive political talks

For the first time ever, talks which included almost all the parties to the conflict including the two governments, most of the major political parties, and parties representing the main paramilitary organizations, started and were chaired by Senator George Mitchell.[57] Despite many difficult days, including periods when both Sinn Fein and the UDP were expelled from the talks for limited periods because of continuing violence by the parties with which they were associated, the talks continued. In April 1998, after 48 hours of intensive non-stop negotiations, all parties finally accepted the Belfast Agreement.

1998: The Belfast Agreement

The Agreement had the following main constitutional provisions:[58]

(a) A united Ireland would only come about if majorities in both Northern Ireland and the Republic of Ireland voted for it.

(b) However, Northern Ireland's current constitutional status was within the United Kingdom.

(c) Citizens of Northern Ireland would have the right to an identity that was British, or Irish, or both, including holding passports associated with such identities.

(d) The Irish state would drop its territorial claim on Northern Ireland.

In addition, there would be:

(a) A power-sharing assembly within which the parties would allocate chairs and vice chairs on an agreed basis, and the necessity for a cross-community consensus on issues of major relevance to both communities.

(b) A North-South ministerial body would be set up, dealing with issues of common concern.

(c) A British-Irish Council would be established, which would draw members from the newly devolved Welsh and Scottish Assemblies, as well as from the Northern Ireland Assembly, and the British and Irish governments.

A number of other issues were also addressed in the Agreement, for example the setting up of a Human Rights Commission, the development of social, economic, and cultural inclusion policies, the necessity to recognize the needs of victims, the acceleration of paramilitary prisoner releases, the normalization of security arrangements as the threat of violence diminished, and the setting up of independent commissions for the criminal justice system and policing.

It was also decided that the Agreement would need the ratification of the majority of people on the island of Ireland, both North and South. A copy of the Good Friday Agreement was sent to every household and the Agreement was put to a referendum. Despite the reluctance of many Unionists who saw the Agreement as a sell-out to terrorism, and the reluctance of some Republicans, who saw it as a sell-out on their goals of a united Ireland, the referendum was passed with a Yes vote by over 71 per cent of the people of Northern Ireland, and 94 per cent in the Republic of Ireland.

1998–2001: Implementation of the Agreement

Following the Agreement, Northern Ireland had a long and difficult summer. There were significant tensions between what came to be known as the "Yes" camp who were those in favour of the Agreement, and the "No" camp who were those against the Agreement. In August 1998, a bomb exploded in the market town of Omagh, in Co. Tyrone, which killed 29 people, both Protestant and Catholic. The bomb was the work of a dissenting Republican group. The shock of the attack was such that it had a sobering affect on the political leaders, and in September 1998, David Trimble, the leader of the Ulster Unionist party and now first minister designate in the new assembly, met Gerry Adams, the leader of Sinn Fein, for their first ever face-to-face meeting. Gradually, the various aspects of the Agreement began to be implemented.

The main sticking point continued to be decommissioning, and in the face of the refusal of Sinn Fein/IRA to accept any definite date for a start, the UUP abstained from the establishment of the power-sharing executive in July 1999. There was much frustration, with all parties blaming each other for intransigence. The political parties and the governments again asked Senator George Mitchell to conduct a review of the decommissioning process in September 1999. This review reported in November 1999, and in December 1999, the IRA confirmed that it would appoint a representative to the Independent Commission on Decommissioning. This representative was appointed, and the power-sharing executive set up simultaneously on 2 December 1999 with its full quota of ministers and committees. The work of the assembly continued to be hampered by a series of rows over the slow progress of decommissioning, which also impeded the developing work of the cross-border bodies and eventually, Trimble resigned as First Minister over the issue in July 2001. Subsequently, the fall-out of the 11 September 2001 destruction of the World Trade Center towers led to increasing pressure by the US and others on Sinn Fein/IRA to disarm, and in October 2001, the IRA announced that it had begun to decommission its weapons. Trimble then resumed his post as First Minister, where he was joined as Deputy First Minister by John Hume's successor, Mark Durcan, who was newly appointed to the post by the SDLP, and the work of the power-sharing assembly continued.

Track Two talking

Many of the above initiatives were achieved through the efforts of governments, politicians and civil servants, assisted in some cases by members of civic society. But, in addition, there were a variety of second-track mediation initiatives that significantly assisted first-track processes. Many of these concentrated on trying to develop fruitful contact between the politicians, between the paramilitaries and governments, and between politicians and civic society.

The role of community mediators

Throughout the conflict there have been many hundreds of initiatives aimed at achieving contact, or shuttle diplomacy, between the participants to the conflict.[59] Indigenous mediators undertook most of these initiatives, although there were some very useful interventions by people from outside of Northern Ireland and particularly by some who came from a Quaker or Mennonite tradition. Such mediators tried to provide safe and unthreatening opportunities for politicians to look at issues of mutual concern such as social issues, or the economy, or conflicts elsewhere. Such processes were designed to increase the trust that could develop between them, without necessarily burdening them by initiating direct mediation. Direct mediation on political possibilities, by politicians, was often deemed by them to be more appropriately the concern of Track One initiatives.

In addition, there were also thousands of people involved in community initiatives aimed at achieving political dialogue between communities and in the early nineties these numbers increased significantly. Such work was often called 'sub-political' or 'pre-political' dialogue, and was based on the belief that not only should communities be involved in dialogue on issues of political choices, but that such dialogue was also necessary if communities were to understand what compromises were possible or necessary to achieving agreement by the politicians. Training for dialogue was developed by many organizations, such as the CRC and the Workers Education Association (WEA), and hundreds of local workshops took place which brought together people from all sections of the community to look at a variety of issues, including political options for their future together.[60] Many other initiatives, which aimed to stimulate dialogue through drama, music, and art initiatives, for example, also proliferated (CRC, 1990–98). It is noticeable that the years preceding the Agreement were marked by a large increase in cross-community attendance at the funerals of victims of political and sectarian assassinations, and huge public demonstrations, organized by trade unionists and others against continuing violence. Such initiatives contributed significantly to the development of a context that made it possible to achieve readiness in the community on the part of both paramilitaries and politicians for a political agreement.

Academics

Although many within the academic community stayed aloof from the conflict, there were a few who were committed to very constructive dialogue processes. One such initiative was undertaken by academics who were located at the University of Ulster, and which facilitated a collective look between the parties at the development of a Northern Ireland Centre in Brussels in the early nineties.[61] Because the parties were able to focus on common issues of concern, the centre was successfully established under the auspices of both the political parties and the business community, and enabled some levels of knowledge and trust to be developed between them.

During the nineties academics and others were also very useful in organizing workshops for politicians and others to meet in places like the USA or South Africa in order to address issues of conflict resolution. These conferences often provided opportunities for relationships to form between the politicians, which were difficult in Northern Ireland given the restricted nature of society and the watchful eye of the media. Some academics also became official or unofficial "advisors" to political parties and although this meant that they in many cases seen as no longer "impartial," many of them did help to bring a capacity for strategy and analysis to some of the parties, which helped the political dialogue. In addition, there were other academics who assisted local communities to study their social needs in such a way as to facilitate cross-community dialogue on issues of common concern. The EDI (Equity, Diversity, Interdependence) initiative, a training initiative which involved many people from the communities, as well as many civil servants and local councillors, was developed by a group of academics and others based in the University of Ulster. In addition, the Institute for Irish studies, based at the Queen's University, often provided a safe space for cultural and political analysis, which was lacking throughout most of Northern Ireland.

Initiative 92 – community consultation

In 1992 a major programme, called Initiative 92, funded mainly by the Quakers, asked local communities and other interested bodies and individuals to express their views about ways forward for the future of Northern Ireland on a political, economic, and social level. Although condemned by most politicians (who initially saw it as irrelevant or threatening) the initiative was a significant success in achieving its objective of stimulating discussion. It received over 500 submissions from people and groups in Northern Ireland, many of which had been developed on a cross-community basis. It held public workshops at which various contributors were given an opportunity to expand on their ideas and it also provided for private submissions, and anonymous submissions, aware that speaking frankly in public was very difficult for many individuals and communities in a context where intimidation often prevailed. The submissions were eventually contained in a huge ideas book for Northern Ireland called the Opsahl Report (Pollak, 1993). Many of these ideas were to prove very fruitful in eventually generating the Agreement.

Role of the churches

Although the churches themselves had in the main contributed little to dialogue processes (Morrow, 1994) there were some exceptions. In addition to the work by some members of the Catholic clergy in opening up and developing dialogue with Sinn Fein in order to end violence, confidential workshops were held over a period of several years in the mid-nineties between Sinn Fein and members of the Protestant/Unionist clergy. Although there was significant hostility to such dialogue by many within the Unionist community, when they were eventually disclosed, they provided a very useful context within which Sinn Fein could address the reality of the perceptions and fears of that community, and take them into account in developing their strategies.

Business community

A late, but very effective, newcomer to the peace process was the business community, who began in the mid-nineties to cooperate with each other and with the trade unions, to see if a more strategic approach could be put in place which would put pressure on both Republican and Loyalist paramilitaries to end their campaign of violence (International Alert, 2000). They also publicly encouraged all parties to get involved in political negotiations, and privately chided them for not committing themselves more wholeheartedly to the search for a political settlement. Groups such as the Chamber of Commerce, the Confederation of British Industry, the Institute of

Directors, and the trade unions involved themselves in dialogue with Sinn Fein and the Loyalist parties, often on issues of the economy. Their influence was very helpful, particularly as it attempted to put pressure on the political parties to enter into serious dialogue.

United States of America

For the first few decades of the conflict, those people in the USA who were interested in the conflict in Northern Ireland, and whose families had usually some Irish background connections, had primarily appeared to be sympathetic to the politics of the Nationalist community in Northern Ireland. Much of the funding for the campaigns of the IRA in the 1970s and 1980s came from the United States, through NORAID. The US government, however, perceived itself as having a "special relationship" with the UK government, particularly in matters of security cooperation, and was reluctant to disrupt this relationship. Subsequently, during the 1990s, various congressmen, senators, and business people from the USA, with a particular concern for Irish politics, began to look for the development of an inclusive process of political dialogue, involving both Republicans and Loyalists, that could end the violence. In addition, the American Consulate in Belfast helped by its many informal gatherings to extend and develop contact between differing sectors of both communities. This search was aided by the advent of Bill Clinton as president who, not least for constituency reasons, was very open to constructively assisting with the development of peace in Northern Ireland. Various congressman, businessmen, and others eventually brought significant pressure to bear upon Sinn Fein to end violence, enter into dialogue, and engage with the Unionist community. Such dialogue efforts were significantly assisted by the maintained efforts of President Bill Clinton, and by Senator George Mitchell who became chairman for the multiparty talks that were eventually successful in reaching an inclusive agreement between the parties (Arthur, 2000). Their subsequent support, and leverage, in the years that followed the Agreement, and the leverage subsequently exerted by the Republican US government under George Bush, until the first act of actual decommissioning by the IRA in October 2001, was crucial to the maintenance of the peace process.

Conclusion

Without doubt, the major difficulty in Northern Ireland has been achieving sufficient dialogue between politicians and communities to engender enough understanding and trust to find solutions to issues of equality and political choice. Most sides felt threatened by each other, and fears turned into anger, exclusion, recrimination, and the murder of over 3,700 people. Starting and continuing the debates about the development of a shared and pluralist society has been extraordinarily difficult.

While formalized Track One political efforts are and should be pre eminent, the experience of Northern Ireland has been that such initiatives would never have succeeded without the plethora of Track Two initiatives, which developed the context for more formalized initiatives. It was Track Two initiatives that broke the logjam of non-dialogue between governments and paramilitaries. It was also the creativity and courage of many informal actors such as academics and, business and community people which developed contexts in which politicians could meet each other away from the destructive glare of the political spotlight. It was the enormous number of dialogue efforts by hundreds of community groups that enabled many of the politicians to engage in dialogue, in the knowledge that such dialogue would not be political suicide.

Relationships between the two tracks have not always been easy. Frustration with the lack of political leadership has been an abiding complaint of many involved in Track Two work. Politicians have complained about the lack of appreciation by many about how difficult their task has been. Both sides have often been reluctant to acknowledge the contribution that each has made to the development of the peace process. And such tensions continue. Since the Agreement, many within civic society who feel that they have contributed an enormous amount to the development of the peace, have felt excluded from the considerations of the newly elected assembly. Although the Agreement provided for a civic forum, where community, business, trade unions, and churches have a chance to contribute to the assembly, the newly elected politicians have, with a few exceptions, been noticeably cool about its development.[62] Politicians are now anxious to prove that they can deliver on the implementation of the Agreement and are keen to exercise their new powers.

Such tensions are understandable and need to be recognized, understood, and anticipated by those involved in the processes. But, without the courage and commitment of the many thousands of people involved in Track Two initiatives, the reality is that the Belfast Agreement would never have been reached. Given the tensions that have continued between the political parties since the Agreement was signed, it is equally unlikely that the Agreement can be sustained without a continuing commitment by politicians and civic leaders and others to the continuance of both Track One and Track Two initiatives in the difficult years ahead. Conflicts do not end – they merely change. In the new order of Northern Ireland, although the bombs and the bullets are falling increasingly silent, the need for dialogue at all levels will continue to be a priority, and will need all the complementary approaches that can be brought to bear on the continuing divisions in society if peace in the years ahead is to be secured.

9

Training for change

Neutral or partial?

The ever-changing context of violence in Northern Ireland made dialogue on differences extremely difficult. During the late 1980s, I began the development of a project aimed at increasing the capacity and skills of people to involve themselves in dialogue, even on the most contentious issues such as grievances about inequalities, the capacity of the police to serve all communities equally, and the existence, or otherwise, of the state (Fitzduff, 1988). I believed such work to be important, on the understanding that the capacity to discuss differences and articulate grievances and have them addressed through dialogue and politics was probably the most effective antidote to violence. Such processes were not easy. I remember one particular incident during a dialogue workshop in the early 1990s, where, during the first coffee break, I was approached by a young man who had just realized that the brother of one of the participants in the workshop was in jail for having murdered his brother, and he was, obviously, having great difficulty in dealing with this. He said he could think of nothing except planning to kill him in return and avenge his brother, and felt he needed to go home quickly before he lost control. As the dialogue work increased, such difficult meetings multiplied, and often posed great problems for the facilitators. Another major problem was the fact that such work often took place against a background of ongoing violence, and it was not unusual for incidents, such as IRA bombings or security force killings or other very contentious issues, to significantly increase the level of anger and fear at such workshops. Developing people who were confident of handling such situations, and managing the levels of emotions which often attended such discussions, so as to progress the participants towards dialogue that focused on future options for agreement between the communities, was not an easy task.

This question, of how to secure or develop change agents, at individual or organizational level, that are capable of positively progressing conflict resolution work is one of the most important issues for conflict strategists. In most situations of conflict, as is the case of Northern Ireland, almost all the citizens, and most organizations, are either partial, or perceived as partial, in the conflict. Those of us who work in conflict situations are familiar with the search for supposedly "neutral" change agents. Finding such "neutrals" has not proved to be absolutely impossible in Northern Ireland, and mention has been made previously of the services offered by facilitators such as the Quakers in their various guises, and of individual academics who have undertaken some interesting work in mediation. Our experience has been, however, that to depend primarily upon people and agencies deemed to be "neutral" because of their non-involvement in the conflict would be impossible in Northern Ireland. There are very few who would be accorded the status of "neutral" by all parties, and the work to be undertaken is too extensive to allow of such a limitation. The problem of neutrality is particularly pertinent when it comes to the preparation of specific people such as trainers, facilitators, and development workers who are working to address the many conflict resolution needs at the local and regional level. This is because of the close scrutiny under which such people work, often within a context that may be hostile to them because of perceived identity.

The lack of such perceived "neutrals," initially seen as a problem, has engendered a completely different way of working in the situation. There is now a fairly universal acceptance that few are "neutral," that almost all are "partial" and that this factor need not necessarily exclude the undertaking of excellent change work.

In the early years of the conflict, the initial temptation for many groups seeking conflict resolvers was to look outside Northern Ireland for such assistance, on the basis that only outsiders to the conflict could be truly neutral. During the seventies and eighties what little training there was often happened under the auspices of international as opposed to indigenous facilitators. Although some of these experiences were creative and empowering, a few workshops proved to be so destructive as to be counterproductive (Doob and Foltz, 1974). The hiatus in the development of such training work between the middle seventies and middle eighties in Northern Ireland was deemed by many to have been the result of a few such bad experiences.

By the late eighties, however, there was a renewed interest in training that could be pertinent to the needs for conflict resolution in Northern Ireland (Fitzduff, 1988) and as the requests for training increased, it was obvious that to continue to "import" facilitators would be unfeasible in terms of the amount of work that needed to be done.

There was also the difficulty that while it might be easier at some level to import mediators who had no particular political convictions about Northern Ireland, it also meant that the facilitators, by very virtue of their supposed neutrality, could escape from having themselves to deal with the very nuanced difficulties with which many of the participants were struggling. Hence the challenge of dealing with such nuances, forming as they did an almost indigenous language on the part of the participants, and needing to be included as part of the process.

After much thought and discussion, among and with groups, several ways were eventually found to deal with the problem of the supposed need for neutrality. The first was the recognition that the commitment required from facilitators was not that of an absence of a particular political preference, but that of a positive commitment to certain principles about the process of the training or group work. Such principles included a firm and prior commitment to the process of the group itself, and the equal participation of all in it; to respect for all feelings, fears, claims about rights and history, as articulated by the participants; and to the achievement of ground rules agreed by all about how such discussions could be most productively undertaken. Facilitators were not asked to give up their personal political preferences, but merely to suspend them for the duration of a group or training process, unless it had been previously agreed that to articulate such preferences would actually be productive in terms of the objectives set for the work (Fitzduff, 1988). Such a "temporary" commitment to the process enabled many who would have shied away from assisting with such training, because of their personal political preferences, to increasingly offer their talents.

The very fact that they commited themselves and their groups to a process that involved listening and respecting other viewpoints as part of the work, to be, at least temporarily, what Ury (1999) calls the "third side" means that almost inevitably their own simplifications are challenged, and their own perspectives were coloured by listening to other needs, fears, and reasoned political preferences. Their preferences, even if retained, are enlightened by the knowledge of the need to take account of those of their neighbours. Eventually, many of these facilitators mirrored in themselves the kinds of changes and developments that happened within the groups to which they were committed, and this increased the richness of such facilitation work.

Co-facilitation by "partials"

The second useful addition to the above process was the gradual introduction of training, carried out by co-facilitators, each broadly representing a different aspect of the political divide. Such facilitation is now increasingly recognized internationally as a useful model and facilitators have acquired the term "insider-partials" (Lederach, 1991). Insider-partials are able to "model" openness about their own upbringings, their fears and their political convictions, while at the same time ensuring a productive process for discussion. Such a modelling provides for adequacy in terms both of depth of understanding, and in displaying an alternative to the aggression (or silence) that so markedly characterizes most difficult discussions in

Northern Ireland. The use of the insider-partials model is the one now most commonly used for training where time and resources allow for it.

The use of partial co-facilitators in conflict resolution work has also significantly increased the capacity of the work to involve many of those closest to the conflict, including the paramilitaries themselves. This was brought home to me by a taxi ride I took in 1993 from a Belfast railway station to the city centre. I noticed that the driver was reading a historical pamphlet frequently read by Loyalists. In Belfast, taxi businesses were commonly believed to be used to subsidise the various paramilitaries, and indeed to provide day jobs for some such militarists, a belief that had made their drivers a frequent target for assassination over the years. I assumed I was in a Loyalist cab, and began a conversation about the book. In fact it turned out my driver was a former Republican paramilitary prisoner who was reading such literature to understand the Loyalist position. He also informed me that he had been on a Community Relations Council (CRC) training course and had recently set up business with a Loyalist former paramilitary prisoner in order to provide co-facilitation for political discussion work in hard line Loyalist and Republican areas, despite the threats that the work had entailed for them. He assured me that because neither of them had abandoned their political aspirations, and had indeed served jail time for their convictions, they were much more able to promote discussion in such hard line areas, focusing on respecting their political differences, rather than abandoning them, in any new political accommodation.

Such ex-paramilitaries, and there were others like the above, have played a very significant part in the development of many of the conflict resolution programmes in Northern Ireland, bringing as they did to the process their own particular credibility, knowledge, and partiality.

The experience of the last few years in Northern Ireland suggests that the use and development of partials (whether agencies or individuals) has been extremely significant in ensuring the development of conflict resolution work. In addition, it has resulted in the parallel transformation of bodies and people like these into increasingly positive change agents, capable of successfully developing models of inclusion and conflict resolution that are integrated into their own personal skills and those of their agencies. While it may initially have been more difficult to secure such a development, given the immense and often difficult learning that was needed by "partials" in such a process, there is little doubt that the many instances of its achievements auger well for the future sustainability of the work and its continued development.

Training for change

The CRC defines training as "the acquisition of knowledge and skills, in a structured context, which has immediate application to the conflict resolution work in hand." It believes that this preparation of people and groups to deal more confidently and effectively in the prevention, management, and resolution of conflict will usually require two overlapping elements: the acquisition of knowledge, and the development of extra skills. The knowledge requirement for such intervention is usually for new ways of analysing and understanding the dynamics of conflict that can circumvent older and more destructive ways of resolving it, for example the need to devise win/win solutions to the conflict as opposed to win/lose scenarios, or the concept of conflict phases necessitating different intervention functions. An understanding of the various biological and sociopsychological theories that are used to suggest some of the root causes of conflict may also be helpful, as can some understanding of the particular history of individual conflict situations.

The understanding and the acquisition of new knowledge, while it may be a necessary preliminary foundation, will usually need to be enhanced by the acquisition of extra skills for intervention that focus on increasing the possibilities for individuals or groups to intervene productively in a conflict situation.

While the term "training" is one that is in common use in relation to preparation that includes such knowledge acquisition and skill development, the term occasionally carries overtones of order and skills transfer that do not necessarily echo the existing reality. Certainly in Northern Ireland, preparation for dealing with the different dimensions of conflict has proceeded very much on an experimental basis, beset, or energized, by unfolding challenges. Not the least of these challenges was the ongoing violent context in which the training has occurred, and the emotional and almost constant engagement of both participants and facilitators alike in the difficult context of violence. Nevertheless, despite or because of this context, the amount of training work for addressing conflict in Northern Ireland has substantially increased since 1990.

Delivery

The CRC quickly recognized that with training, as with all community relations work, it was extremely important to make the best use of existing agencies in terms of dissemination. The CRC, therefore, developed a policy of gradually engaging with an increasing number of people and organizations willing to add such training to their existing programmes. Organizations like the Health and Social Services boards, the Education and Library boards, the Sports Council and the Training and Employment Agency, businesses and student bodies, were encouraged to train their own personnel to undertake the anti-intimidation, anti-sectarian, or community relations training work that was needed to address the particular issues relevant to them.

Other groups such as the trade unions had been involved in developing this work since 1990 and were one of the first major groups to develop in-house training with shop stewards and managers. Their work (through their organization Counteract) has been developed in often difficult and dangerous circumstances, but they have succeeded in almost eliminating much of the intimidatory behaviour, based on sectarianism, that has unfortunately marked so many workplaces in Northern Ireland for so many decades (Counteract, 1993).

Gradually during the nineties, training for such work has become incorporated as part of an overall training strategy and it is increasingly being undertaken by in-house trainers. Thus the training skills available throughout Northern Ireland have multiplied and their effectiveness has been substantially enhanced.

It should be noted that this development, in its initial stages, was often met with resistance on the part of many organizations and groups, and in many cases with open hostility on the part of those who were either fearful of its capacity to further increase divisions, or those who saw it as counterproductive to their own political preference. Careful entry strategies, which involve securing the consent and support of those responsible for policy making and resource allocation, were required with all groups and organizations in order to ensure that the work could proceed effectively.

Focus and structures

A major problem facing training work was that of the appropriate focus for the work. A conflict throws up so many necessities that the problem of being overwhelmed by obvious needs is substantial and not necessarily conducive to accurate prioritizing. In one particular week, trying to arrange for a containment or cessation of violence may have been the most pressing priority. On the other hand the more long-term work of trying to deconstruct the structures that continued the violence, such as structures of inequitable patterns of housing or work or divided educational systems, needs to be undertaken so as to ensure an eventual diminution of the circumstances that spawned the occurrence of violence. Gradually, within Northern Ireland (which has had the luxury of occasional spaces from the kind of communal violence that has beset many other conflict areas), a variety of approaches was developed to take account of parallel needs, locational needs, and short-term, medium-term, and long-term needs.

Four different kinds of training for conflict resolution work are generally on offer. The first is a modular approach that offers training for particular needs that have been identified, or pilot testing of training for emerging needs. The second approach is to offer training through more intensive action learning programmes for those often involved full time in conflict resolution work. The third approach has been to develop customized programmes in conjunction with other organizations (public, statutory, voluntary, community, or business) which are based on more precise identification of their needs for conflict resolution. The fourth and most recent approach has been to organize such training on a locality/area base, so as to ensure that the conflict resolution needs of a particular place – village, town, rural ward or city estate, or hostile sectarian interface – are addressed in a more effective manner.

Modular work

These training modules are run on a one or two-day basis, addressing particular areas of difficulty or need. They are offered so as to provide a repertoire of skills for use in various conflict situations, and the participants usually come from a variety of backgrounds, community workers, trade union representatives, local council political representatives, youth workers, and others. The following are some examples of such work, which have been tailored to address particular problems pertaining in Northern Ireland.

Contact facilitation skills

This work addresses the fact that Northern Ireland is a divided society, where most people live, work, pray, and play separately. It includes ideas about how to network with other organizations willing to participate in such work, creative ideas about how to organize qualitative contact, and arranging for longer-term sustainable opportunities for continuing contact, thus ensuring its effectiveness.

Prejudice reduction work

Ignorance, prejudice, and stereotyping often prevent constructive dialogue; work to address such issues includes the acknowledgement

and identification of prejudice and stereotyping, accurate information sharing between communities about each other's hopes, fears
and beliefs and, where possible, alliance building between groups
and communities.

Political dialogue and cooperation skills

Where interaction on contentious issues occurs, it is often characterized by politeness, silence, defensiveness, and fear of discussing
issues of conflict. Training for political dialogue includes practice
in listening and clarification skills, and constructive discussions on
differing political choices and preferences by the participants. Such
workshops have increasingly included politicians and people from
the security forces.

Cultural traditions work

Cultural expressions – of music, language, dancing, commemorations, marching – are often divisive or threatening to the other
community. Training to deal with this includes work that facilitates
the sharing of cultural expression in a non-contentious way through
shared fairs, festivals, and workshops. It also includes training for
single-identity work (see below) on issues such as how to facilitate
non-threatening discussion about identity and loyalty choices within
a community.

Cross-community justice and rights work

In Northern Ireland, issues of justice such as emergency legislation,
bills of rights, and security practice are often contentious. Cross-
community justice work includes training to ensure that groups address issues on a principled basis rather than a loyalty basis, and such
training can enable discussion on such issues as a bill of rights, equity policing.

Single-identity work

Communities, particularly those most ghettoized through history and locality, frequently lack confidence, and can be too defensive and aggressive to engage in successful contact work. Single-identity work looks at ways to enable communities to look undefensively at the validity and worth of their own history and culture. It also includes work that enables groups to begin to identify issues on which they feel they can safely meet and cooperate with people from different communities.

Anti-sectarian work

Many organizations and groups often consciously or unwittingly exclude people from other communities. Training to address such segregation assists people in conducting community and organizational audits to assess their sectarian nature, and subsequently work on developing programmes to increase their inclusive capacity through mixed management committees and shared work on social issues.

Security interface work

The history of the police in Northern Ireland, and the task of the containment of paramilitarism by both police and army can produce an interface between the security forces and the communities that is hostile and counterproductive. Work on improving this interface includes the identification of factors and patterns of hostility, and programmes to change these patterns, including the development of effective community liaison work.

Anti-intimidation work

The existence of both intra-community and inter-community intimidation includes verbal and physical intimidation, and sometimes murder. Addressing such intimidation is both difficult and dangerous, and training for the work includes acknowledging and identifying the fears and dangers associated with it, but also becoming aware of what resources are available either to eliminate the problem or deal with the victims. It also includes assistance with drawing up organizational and community strategies to deal with the problem.

Mediation skills

The need for mediation within and between communities, between politicians and between paramilitaries is vitally necessary, because of divisions that preclude easy contact and dialogue. Such training includes standard mediation practice skills, and political discussion and agreement skills. Much of this work has been facilitated through the development and the work of the Mediation Network which now provides official mediators for many governmental bodies.

Mainstreaming work

This work helps organizations to look at their responsibilities in a divided society, and their necessities for redirection and training to address this responsibility. Such work can include customer audits, cultural diversity assessments, and training for staff in organizations to deal more constructively with issues of conflict and division.

Victims work

Dealing with the anger of victims, so as to ensure that it does not exacerbate the cycle of violence but could act as a positive catalyst to conflict resolution work has always been an important part of the work in Northern Ireland. It has become even more important since the ceasefires of 1994, as victims felt it safer to express their anger about what had happened to them. Such work often happens in community-based groups, but also, increasingly, since the Belfast

Agreement of 1998, some groups are undertaking victims work on a cross-community basis, which of course significantly increases the capacity of the work to assist long-term peace-building.

Action Learning Programme

As the interest in and resources for community relations work developed in the early nineties, so too did the number of people involved in full-time community relations work. What had once been a voluntary, often part-time activity began to develop into a full-time, quasi-professional occupation. It was in response to such developments that the CRC initiated an Action Learning Programme for those involved in full-time community relations work. The programme took place over a period of six months, consisting of three residential workshops, and six working days. As part of the course, participants initiated, developed and evaluated a conflict resolution project in their own area of work, which was written up and evaluated. The course was particularly geared to local conflict resolution strategy identification and practice. The programme also provided the individual with increased skills in intensive group work, political discussion, prejudice reduction work, and conflict mediation skills. These kinds of action learning programmes have been replicated many times, and for many sectors of society, and there is now an accredited course for the Open College Network, a UK accrediting institute.

Customized programmes

As the training programmes developed, the importance of tailoring such training to be both relevant and effective for particular organizational needs became more apparent, and as reflected in the development of many more customized programmes undertaken with many institutions and agencies. Such programmes are probably now the most common form of training in Northern Ireland. The programmes are tailored to suit the needs of particular groups to deal with issues arising from the conflict. They are drawn up in consultation with an organization, and if possible or appropriate, such work will try to involve its training or personnel officer. Organizations already involved have included education groups, the Sports Council, the security forces, groups working with prisoners, all the main churches, local councillors, health boards, social services, community relations officers, and many others.

Localized programmes

As the number of people willing to be involved in reconciliation work has increased, networks in particular areas began to develop collective programmes to address particular area needs, and training to address these locality needs. In Derry/Londonderry, for example, many groups from differing areas of the city, and from varying areas of interest such as human rights and church work, began to address collectively the major exodus of Protestants from the west bank of the city to the east bank of the city. In north Belfast, the Community Development Centre put in place a collective strategy to address the conflict needs of a very tense and divided area which has had the highest murder rate in Northern Ireland during the conflict.

Methodology

The methodology used in the above training varies, but usually consists of a combination of inputs, for example on conflict resolution theory, cultural/political information sharing and practice, live facilitations of contentious discussions, mediation exercises, case study analysis and strategy development. Some experiential personal work is often included in order to elicit an acknowledgement of the emotional forces present in prejudice and sustaining the conflict. Methodology has to be very carefully tailored to the culture and capacity of the groups involved; customized programmes usually have to take account of what can be usefully used in developing such work, and are careful to take into account the culture of the organizations they are working with. If methodologies are not carefully thought through they can elicit fear, defensiveness, or rejection by particular groups, particularly on issues of equality, rights, and political and constitutional choices. Organizations that are used to more input-based methodologies such as the civil service, or the security forces, can find it difficult to adjust to experiential work and care must be taken to ensure the work is not rejected because of culturally inappropriate methods.

Support structures

The need for support in developing or facilitating training in Northern Ireland has proved to be substantial. Workshops are often fraught with denial, or with anger and tension. Participants are drawn from widely differing perspectives, and few participants have been untouched by the violence. Workshops can include relatives of people who have been killed by the security forces, and relatives of people who have been killed by the paramilitaries. Dealing with such issues can be extremely demanding and the need for support and for casework sharing is vital. To meet such a need there is a training network, the Conflict Resolution Training Learning Consortium (CRTLC) that enables trainers to meet on a regular basis. The network considers issues such as the trainers' development needs, and new issues emerging in the field. The network also provides an opportunity for people involved in facilitation to provide and receive support for their work, and it provides a valuable resource for skills sharing, arranging "apprenticeships" for learners, and choosing co-facilitators for the work. It also provides space for people to evaluate their work in terms of its overall effectiveness, and provides funding for the further development of training.

Conclusion

Most of the conflict resolution work currently being undertaken in Northern Ireland is being undertaken by local and regional agencies. There has been little other choice, given the extensive need. For the most part, it has been acknowledged that there are few agencies, even those seen as most biased by the other side (for example, the security forces, the Catholic Church, and the ex-prisoners groups) who have not been able, with sufficient and sensitive work that takes account of both their defensiveness and their capacity, to be engaged at some level in outreach work with their enemies. While the results have often varied in the level of their success, there are now many examples of agencies who have gradually transformed themselves through such work from exclusive, ghettoized, or uninterested organizations into bodies that are proud of their newly developed conflict resolution capacities.

It is not easy to prepare people to involve themselves constructively in conflict intervention, particularly in intervention in their own conflict. The initial development of such training was fraught with difficulties, compounded by fear, despair, and a lack of both good examples of practice and of theoretical frameworks within which to develop the work. Increasingly, however, interveners in the conflict have found themselves substantially more confident about their capacity to work constructively with groups, even in the most difficult of areas, and on the most difficult of issues. Such increasing success is a testimony to the extensive energy that has been put into developing the field of preparation and training for the resolution of conflict, and inspires the hope that developing such skills may be increasingly useful in what may yet prove to be difficult years ahead.

10

Peace by piece?

One of the most difficult questions facing those involved in conflict resolution work is whether and how their work is actually contributing to the development of an eventual agreement. This was brought home to me with particular force, one bright spring day in the centre of Belfast, in 1994. My offices were just a few hundred yards from the centre of the city – tucked away behind some old cinemas which have usually protected them from the worst of the blasts that have so frequently rocked the city centre during the conflict. Like many others, I was hurrying down the main street, taking advantage of the lunchtime hour to do some shopping. I had just turned the first corner when the shots rang out, just a few yards away, from under an awning across the street. In the midst of the confusion – the ambulance, the army – the story came through. The victim was a young construction worker, killed by the Irish Republican Army (IRA) because they believed him to be a part-time member of the security forces.

Just half an hour later, on my way back to the office, and just 100 yards away from the recent murder, I was rocked back on my heels by the blast from a nearby explosion. This subsequently turned out to be a Loyalist attack on the City Hall room of Sinn Fein councillors, set off in the hope of murdering some Republican councillors or their supporters.

In a sombre mood, I returned to the office.[63] The blast had been a small one, and there were no broken windows in the office this time. Work was going on as usual, with hardly a comment passed. Bombs, and refugees from other offices more exposed than ours to bomb blasts, were just a weekly hazard of the city. Being back at my desk and coming fresh from that violence made me throw a particularly questioning light upon the validity of the work that was being undertaken by so many groups in attempting to end it.

Yet, despite my questioning mood, I remember that afternoon as one full of hope, as the staff came in and out with the tales of their various tasks. A request had been received from a group in one of the "harder" Catholic areas – who wanted to meet and work with some Protestants in an equally "hard" area across the peace walls. The last remaining district council had agreed to implement a community relations programme. A group of Loyalists had phoned the office looking for "political" skills so that they could talk more confidently with Catholics. Another of the major churches had agreed to undertake anti-sectarian work as part of its training for clergy. A meeting with Catholic and Protestant community workers from the 13 interface (and most violent) areas of Belfast had gone well, and the workers had requested more such meetings. And a group of Protestant women from the Shankill wanted assistance to go away with some Catholic women – to Donegal, to learn some Irish, traditionally for them perceived as a hostile language.

The question was – how was the work adding up to eventual peace? It was easier to believe that it was than to prove that it was, particularly if a cessation of violence was the only marker by which to measure such success. Although the task has not been easy, trying to find a variety of ways by which to distinguish the various intermediary markers on the road to the cessation of violence has been an important process in maintaining and developing the work of peace-building.[64]

A jigsaw of peace creation

Constructing peace in Northern Ireland has had many of the characteristics of a doing a difficult jigsaw. The board is full of broken pieces – pieces of inequity, shattered and discordant relationships, frequent flashes of destruction and violence. Such horrors have not of course been the whole story. Here and there, the pieces have interlocked – a community agreed, work shared well or a relationship sustained, although relationships were often hard to sustain in the midst of the continuing violence and political discordance.

Faced with such a jigsaw, it can be easy to despair, particularly when, as in Northern Ireland, the conflict had developed an apparently intransigent character, and its continuance had drained so many observers of their hope and their belief in its resolution. Measuring, and being confident about the success of the many strands outlined in this book has not been an easy task. It is one of the difficulties for those involved in conflict management that they can be demoralized by the need for final solutions (understandably when lives are being lost) and fail to recognize the smaller, but significant shifts that may be taking place because of their many and combined efforts (Ross, 2000), and the often piecemeal nature of the work, as represented by Rothman's phrase 'pieces of peace' (Rothman, 1992). It is easy to lose sight of the fact that, with a conflict that has continued for so long (25 years, or 800 years, according to your perspective) dramatic changes in group relations, and agreements about political sharing, are unlikely to come easily. This is particularly true where the violence has meant that over 50 per cent of the population has been affected.

But changes do come, and the evidence in Northern Ireland is that a combination of approaches addressing both the hard structural changes in equality and legislation, allied with the psycho-cultural work of addressing dialogue, communication, and cooperation began to accrue some significant shifts in both behavioural and attitudinal terms throughout the community. Without such changes, the ceasefires of 1994 would have been unlikely, and the Belfast Agreement of 1998 impossible.

Positive trends

In order to assess some of these changes, and in the absence of many approaches to the satisfactory evaluation of conflict interventions, the concept of Trend Based Criteria as used by the United Nations to measure performance and success is a useful one (Kendall and Mac-Donald, 1992). The emphasis in such a trend-based approach is on a comparison between objective realities over time; analysis is based on empirically based evidence rather than solely on evidence that is subjective. The following are some of the positive trends that have been taking place in Northern Ireland, some of which began as early as the 1970s, with many more of a recent nature.

Equality issues

Most of the major issues of inequality between Catholics and Protestants, which provoked the civil rights movement in the late sixties, have all been substantially addressed. Such issues included the unfair voting process, rigged electoral boundaries, biased housing allocation, and unequal educational funding. While some unemployment differentials continue to remain a problem, as does representation at the highest levels of the civil service, there is evidence that this problem is being satisfactorily addressed through a combination of the existing and developing legislative, educational, and social need programmes. Such work has ensured that many of the major inequitable factors in Northern Ireland life have been addressed, and do not provide the impetus for anger that they did throughout the years of the violence. Such work has seriously changed an inequitable context, which provided for the sustenance of support for Republican paramilitarism, and thus has ensured that the maintenance of political agreement between the parties is much more likely to be durable.

District councils

Work at local district council level has proved to be increasingly productive, a surprise to many in view of the fact that for over 70 years the councils have generally been seen to be discriminatory and sectarian. Most councils now exercise voluntary sharing and this example has been extremely important, not only for cooperative work at a local level, but because through their work they constructed a model that was useful in developing the Belfast Agreement, setting up the regional power-sharing assembly in 1999. All councils are now conducting community relations programmes in their areas, and the initial hostilities and suspicion with which these were conducted in many councils in the first year of their existence has disappeared in almost all cases. Surveys have shown that where there has been an active local council community relations programme in place for one or two years, relationships between the communities are seen to be more positive than in areas where such programmes have just started. The Partnership Boards, set up to distribute European Union Peace money in 1996, have had active participation from the district councils, who now work alongside businesses, trade unions, and the community and voluntary sector in developing and delivering programmes to consolidate the peace.

Mainstreaming

The number of organizations adopting community relations programmes as part of their strategic/operational plans and voluntarily implementing them as part of their work has been, since 1990, an increasing phenomenon. Such organizations include the trade unions, security force personnel, sporting bodies, higher education bodies, farmers' organizations, health and education boards, museums and other cultural bodies, training and employment agencies, major voluntary bodies, many community groups, and all government departments. As section 75 of the Belfast Agreement includes the necessity for almost all public bodies, including district councils, to promote policies that ensure not only equality but also the requirement to promote and foster good "good relations" between the communities, this should significantly change the way in which public sector business is carried out in what is still in many ways a divided society.

Workplaces

Workplaces are slowly but increasingly becoming more integrated places, as the legislation on monitoring and discrimination becomes more effective. In addition, the anti-sectarian and anti-intimidation work on the part of groups like Counteract has ensured that the amount of tension and violence in workplaces, which used to result in harassment, and sometimes in murder, has substantially decreased. The evidence is that mixed workplaces, and flag flying and poster displays are no longer as contentious as they have often been in the past, because of the efforts of many institutions to find compromise solutions to the conflict that such symbols can provoke. In addition, the use of mediators, as opposed to sectarian violence, is much more likely to be used to resolve remaining differences over cultural and political tensions.

Increasing cooperation

Because of the extreme community violence in the 1970s, which resulted in very significant ethnic segregation, and because of the continuing violence from 1969 to 1994, cooperation between the communities had obviously decreased significantly from what was possible in the uneasy decades of peace that existed before 1969. However, in response to such violence and estrangement, conscious cross-community projects, undertaken on a voluntary and organized basis have also substantially increased, particularly since the early nineties. The Community Relations Council (CRC) alone has resourced over 1,600 such projects since 1990 with groups such as trade unions, local community groups, interface area groups, sporting bodies, higher education, farmers' groups, cultural groups. Such work has begun to break down the barriers to dialogue which have traditionally always existed between such groups, and between whom dialogue and cooperation were made extremely difficult (and in some cases dangerous) because of the ongoing violence. Other organizations, such as the district councils' community relations programmes and some of the many reconciliation groups (Hinds, 1994) have also provided hundreds of such opportunities, as have community educational organizations like the Interface project of the Workers Education Association (WEA), and many other groups.

Such activities have increased significantly, particularly in the wake of the ceasefires (Hughes and Knox, 1997). The funding from the European Union to consolidate the peace has provided the impetus for a huge increase in cooperative projects between the communities, both within Northern Ireland and across the border (CRC, 1998). Two important trends in the development of this work have also been identified. The first is the increased willingness of groups to move more quickly and confidently into addressing issues of difference and contention. The second trend is for groups to apply concepts of conflict resolution to practical problems of shared and contested areas such as village development, cultural celebrations, and problems of intimidation in areas such as Derry/Londonderry, and in north Belfast, which is infamously noted for having the highest conflict-related murder rate in Northern Ireland (Jarman and O'Halloran, 2000). Although there still remain significant tensions, at community level, particularly in areas such as north Belfast where Protestants feel they are losing out demographically to Catholics,[65] what is noticeable is the number of community mediators who now customarily cross the community divide to solve such differences, and who are joined by an increasing number of politicians who are (finally) beginning to work together at local levels on resolving such tensions.

Churches moving

Some churches which have been traditionally hostile to community relations work (in some cases because of their theological suspicions) are now actually employing people to help develop it. They include the Presbyterian church, and the Evangelical Conference of Northern Ireland. All the main churches are now sponsoring a cross-community approach to youth work, and have agreed to include training to address sectarianism and practice in community relations both at a personal and community level as part of their ongoing development work for trainees and for incumbent clergy. Most important, many more clergy have been crossing territorial lines to attend funerals and wakes where political or sectarian murders have occurred, and offering public sympathy both in their churches and through the media to the families of such victims. Such actions and statements are now the norm rather than the exception they would have been for most of the 1970s and 1980s (McMaster and Higgins, 2000).

Positively plural

The Irish language, which used to be deemed illegal in some instances, is now being promoted as part of the richness of Northern Ireland's cultural heritage, along with Ulster Scots, and the power-sharing government is now supporting events and publications in both languages. Cultural events that used to take place on a separate and divided basis, often provoking anger and sometimes violence, are now increasingly sharing their culture much more positively. Some previously hostile groups now march together on feast days and some have joint musical festivals. Local history societies now often share their meetings on a cross-community basis, and cultural resource fairs and exhibitions, for the first time ever in the history of Northern Ireland (and indeed the Republic of Ireland) include groups from both major traditions. Museums are now much more inclusive in their approach to their contents and their exhibitions, and have increasingly played a crucial part in helping people to understand their differing and their shared histories. In some cases, such as the museums in Derry/Londonderry, and in Enniskillen, the development of these museums has been undertaken collectively by the differing communities, and significantly increased communication and understanding between them (Murphy and Murray, 1998).

Media

When civil war broke out in 1969, the media in Northern Ireland was mainly representative of the Protestant community. There were no senior Catholic producers in the BBC; there were no programmes in the Irish language, nor on traditionally Irish sports. In addition, there was a great dearth of programmes on cultural and political issues. By 2001, this had all significantly changed. While there are still mainly Catholic and Protestant newspapers (except for the main evening daily which is almost reaching parity in its readers) the two main daily newspapers have since the mid-nineties begun to co-operate on many issues to try to forward the peace process together. In addition, the management of the media is much more inclusive in its approach to all sections of the communities. All television and radio providers are required to be comprehensive in their approach to programming, including programmes in the Irish language, and on culturally Irish sporting events that were previously excluded. Such work has ensured a media that is much more equitable and pluralistic in its approach to programming.

North-South cooperation

Since the ceasefires of 1994, and even before the signing of the Belfast Agreement, which validated the further development of cross-border links through the creation of six North/South bodies; economic, tourist, health, agricultural, and financial bodies were increasingly developing joint programmes together on an island-wide basis, in the belief that such cooperation could be of substantial mutual benefit. This was in marked contrast to the suspicion that greeted such work in the earlier decades of the conflict, and this work has been further consolidated since the Agreement with the political freedom for such work that has been engendered by the developing peace.

Decreasing security tension

The problems caused by a problematic security interface, with its capacity to increase resentment rather than trust, are showing signs of abating. There have been no security force-related deaths since 1992, and the use of plastic bullets (which have caused several deaths) to contain riots are now rarely deployed. Allegations of forced confessions also decreased significantly, as did complaints in general against the army. The Belfast Agreement, which provided for the setting up of the Patten Commission on policing, started a substantial change process on policing, which should ensure a more qualitative and inclusive policing service, and substantial training is already in place to ensure this. By 2001, these changes, and the first recruitment exercise of the new police service was showing significant signs of success in attracting Catholics into the force.

The next generation

The context for the children of Northern Ireland has been transformed. The number of explicitly integrated schools has risen from none to 45, most of which have been developed during the nineties. In addition, new legislation and funding are enticing many state schools to become more proactive in creating integrated schools and this should in the future significantly increase Northern Ireland's capacity for integrated education. The Education for Mutual Understanding programmes (now legally enforced in all schools since 1993) ensure that even where contact does not occur, schoolchildren learn about each other's perspectives and fears on such things as history and religion, through the study of common history and religious curricula which have now been agreed between the schools. Most segregated schools also include some contact programmes, and although these programmes are not without their limitations (see Chapter 4) they at least ensure that few children will be able to leave school without having had some cross-community experiences, which may help address their prejudices.

Power-sharing assembly

In November 2001, the leader of the SDLP received the first ever invitation to address a meeting of the Ulster Unionist Party.[66] This exemplified what was probably the main achievement to exemplify changing attitudes, which has been the capacity of the opposing political parties to work together in a power-sharing assembly, as agreed by the Belfast Agreement. Although working together in the assembly is not without its problems (Brocklehurst et al., 2000), there is significant evidence accruing that on many of the difficult day-to-day issues of responsibility, many of the assembly structures and committees are working well. It is also notable that in the 2001 elections, most of the parties campaigned on the grounds that they were making a success of working together to serve their constituencies on the many social and economic issues now facing Northern Ireland as it makes it way slowly from violence to sustainable peace. Another indication of shifting alliances was that a minor, if unseemly, physical brawl by politicians in November 2001 was not, as used to be the tradition, between Unionists and Nationalists, but one in which Nationalists sought to protect pro-agreement Unionists from physical attack by members of the DUP, who opposed the Agreement.

Attitudes

Whilst the issues above have outlined changing behavioural trends, there is clear evidence that attitudes on the part of communities towards each other are also changing positively. This has been particularly true in the nineties. In 1989, only 21 per cent of the population thought that community relations had got better in the past five years, and 28 per cent thought they had got worse. In 1996 attitude surveys show quite significant positive change with 46 per cent of people believing they had got better and only 11 per cent worse. By 1999, things had improved still further with 50 per cent believing that relationships between the community had got better, and only 7 per cent believing they had got worse, although there was some evidence that Catholics were more optimistic than Protestants about such relationships. Even more importantly, however, in looking to the future, the majority of people believed that such relationships would continue to improve for the foreseeable future.[67]

The end picture?

Conflicts do not end, but they can and do change, as the above indicators show. Whether such indicators, as they continue to develop, will definitely provide a sufficiently healthy base for sustainable political cooperation is as yet unknown. What is certain is that together they constitute, for the first time in the history of Northern Ireland, an intentional and structural commitment to the existence of pluralism in its many forms – based on equity, cultural rights, and respect for differing political aspirations. Together they represent a commitment to an "ending picture" (Lederach, 1995) which is now acknowledging the importance of the quality of the interdependent relationship between the major communities, and in which the participants are now willing to accept their need constructively to develop positive forms of cohabitation. There is an increasing acceptance that differing perspectives on rights, culture, and political options must now be dealt with rather than eliminated, and dreams of a polity that is either totally British or totally Irish in its ethos and structures have now been abandoned by almost all protagonists.

Such complexity and pluralism have been enshrined in, and are protected by, the Belfast Agreement. In addition, many of the educational, workplace, and social chasms of separateness which existed between the communities (and which were deepened further by the conflict) have now begun to be bridged by many thousands of statutory and community initiatives. Some of these initiatives are now compelled by a legislative imperative, which is helping to increasingly develop a region that in many cases has mainstreamed both equality and cooperation between the communities on many hundreds of differing levels. While such interlocking is obviously not an absolute guarantee against further conflict and violence, it is certainly likely to provide a more secure societal infrastructure than those that have preceded it.

11

Lessons learned

In the autumn of 1993, an IRA bomb planted in a shopping pre-
cinct in Warrington, England, killed two young children. There was
a surge of popular outrage in the Republic of Ireland against the
IRA, which resulted in the formation of a new peace group, called
Peace '93. As the business of the Community Relations Council is
assisting such groups to develop, either through some minor financial resources or developmental work, I was not surprised when the
office phone rang requesting some such assistance. In responding to
the call, the council was faced with a familiar dilemma.

Legitimate and heartfelt outrage at violence, creating the desire by
groups to express it, has been a frequent occurrence throughout the
years of continuing violence in Northern Ireland. The streets of both
the North and the South have often been filled with many thousands
of people demanding an end to violence by the paramilitaries. The
most prominent of these movements was that of the Peace People.
This group emerged in 1976 following the death of three children
killed by a car, whose driver had been shot dead by a British soldier,
while the car was being used by an IRA unit to attack the security
forces. For over a year the marches of the Peace People attracted
huge crowds, particularly of women, from both sides of the community. The movement raised large sums of money, and in 1977
the founders were awarded the Nobel Peace Prize. Eventually, however, the level of support for the marches dwindled away, as people
eventually lost their faith in the process of marching.

And it is indeed hard to secure the evidence that such marches, and the accompanying emotions, can, as a major tactic, actually affect the level of violence. Hence the dilemma of the CRC about whether and how to actively support such demonstrations, which are frequently organized by some of the many reconciliation and conflict resolution groups that exist in Northern Ireland and the Republic, or by groups such as the trade unions. They are usually supported because there is an immediate need for people, in the face of the latest atrocity, to express their revulsion in some explicit way. However, it was gradually realized that anger is not enough to end a conflict, and that the need is for such groups to consider developing a plan for some longer-term work, perhaps addressing some structural or political aspects of the conflict, so that newly found enthusiasm for the peace process can be further engaged and not dwindle into hopelessness or despair in the face of continuing violence. This Peace '93 eventually did. By 1994 its members were examining issues of equity, facilitating dialogue between communities north and south of the border, and organizing political discussions between politicians and spokespersons for the paramilitaries.

The progress of the development of these activities, and the many discussions that Peace '93 members have had among themselves about how to make their work more effective in achieving peace, echo the many arguments that have both challenged and enlightened the debate among conflict resolvers about how best to prioritize and resource such work in Northern Ireland. This chapter is for those who are interested in the development of that debate, and how that debate eventually informed the developing practice in conflict resolution in the region.

It has not been an easy debate. Reflection upon what worked in achieving peace is as yet problematic; some of what has been achieved may well still be fragile, and only time and further investigations will test the validity, strength, and usefulness of many of the programmes outlined in this book. In addition, as the conflict begins to make its way out of violence, revisionism is ripe on all sides about how, why, and by whom, political agreement was achieved, a necessary flexibility no doubt where so many parties, and so many institutions, now see it in their interests to espouse the tide of agreement for peace. Nevertheless, despite such reservations, it may be useful to reflect upon some of the possible lessons for conflict resolution, gradually and often painfully learned, which appear to have emerged from the experience of the conflict in Northern Ireland.

A "hard" or "soft" approach?

It has often been difficult to achieve agreement among theorists and practitioners alike over a suitable strategic framework for resolving the conflict, and prioritization of resource allocation and programme development for conflict resolution work in Northern Ireland has been at times a difficult and contentious task. A fundamental problem has been the disagreement between those who saw the problem as a structural one and those who saw it primarily as a psycho-cultural problem. These perspectives are sometimes referred to as the "hard" or "soft" approaches.

It has been suggested by Ross (1993) that structural explanations for conflict, violence, and warfare focus on how the organization of society shapes action and explains the conflict as one of incompatible interests which arise from the structure of a community, whether the community be that of a nation, a region, or a local community (LeVine and Campbell, 1972). Structural theories often seem to imply that there are incompatible claims upon power and that inequality is inherent in the existing structure.

In contrast, psycho-cultural explanations look to the actors themselves and how they interpret the world. Psycho-cultural theories of conflict place a greater emphasis on identifying the fears and misperceptions arising between communities, the lack of available trust for political negotiation work, and the need to develop, in the first instance, relationships between the conflicting parties that are conducive to negotiation, compromise, and cooperation. They also occasionally frame their theories within a context that looks at issues such as aggression, motivation, and unconscious psychoanalytic forces (Volkan, 1988; Montville, 1990/1). Because these theories attribute the primary cause of conflict to differing sources, each theory will implicitly suggest very differing approaches to the conflict.[68]

Those addressing the conflict in Northern Ireland from a structural perspective have concentrated on issues of justice and rights work, equity issues, and political and constitutional negotiation and bargaining. In some instances the structural approach in Northern Ireland has included negotiations over the very existence of the state, as there were some participants in the conflict, notably Sinn Fein/ IRA and to some extent the SDLP, who would suggest that that existence is the problem; they therefore argued for many years for a review of it.

Those approaching the conflict from a psycho-cultural point of view concentrate in the first instance on eliminating where possible the ignorance and fears that fuel the defensiveness, resentment, and aggression of communities, and make it almost impossible for negotiation to begin or to succeed. Hence they will concentrate on quality dialogue work, on opportunities for cooperation on issues of common concern, on providing communities with access to opportunities to learn about each other's history and culture, on securing opportunities for integrated schooling, working and living opportunities, and on work focusing on the deeply rooted hostility, fear, and anger existing between the communities.

In Northern Ireland those advocating the structural approach have tended to be dismissive of those who have adopted a psycho-cultural approach, and have perceived those who adopt such an approach as being reluctant to address issues of power relationships. Those advocating a psycho-cultural approach have insisted that agreement on ultimate political solutions will be difficult to sustain without prior work on relationships, both between politicians and between communities. A significant lack of understanding or respect for each other's analyses and practice has traditionally limited cooperation between the two schools of thought.

Increasingly, however, the evidence from Northern Ireland is that such approaches were eventually recognized by most people to be necessarily complementary (Bloomfield, 1997). Even the most ardent and radical advocates of structural reform began to recognize that without a context of dialogue, it was difficult to get agreement among communities about issues of rights. And those who had been most involved in psycho-cultural approaches showed an increased willingness to include discussion of structural issues as part of their programmes, and indeed as the necessary end result of their contact and cooperation work (McCartney, 1994a).

One of the most interesting and influential reframing of this dilemma was the work undertaken by the Future Ways Project, which developed a framework addressing issues of Equity, Diversity, and Interdependence (EDI). This framework emphasized the necessity for work that addressed inequality, work that validated the diverse nature of Northern Ireland, and work that recognized the need to develop positive respect and cooperation between communities. This framework has now been adopted by the many organizations as exemplifying underlying values, and the EDI framework is now significantly influencing the nature of much of the work being undertaken by the public sector in Northern Ireland (Eyben et al., 1997).

Who is the enemy?

Another major difficulty in securing an agreed focus for the work has been the difference between those parties who saw the conflict as the responsibility of an exogenous (external) party, where blame is placed upon a protagonist who was external to Northern Ireland, and those who saw the problem as an endogenous one, that is, one related to internal factors within Northern Ireland and in particular to the problematic relationships between the communities (O'Leary and McGarry, 1993).

To many Nationalists, the cause of the conflict in Northern Ireland was seen to be the continuing presence of the British government in the region. To many Unionists, the problem was the continuing desire of the Republic of Ireland to reclaim Northern Ireland as part of its territory, and they saw Republican paramilitaries as pursuing that agenda violently. Some Unionists (as exemplified by the Rev. Ian Paisley of the DUP) also perceived the

Roman Catholic Church in Ireland as working to an imperialist, expansionist agenda set by Rome. Republican parties endorsing the exogenous theory were likely to see the 'British Out' approach as the most important necessity, and Unionists who tended towards blaming 'external' forces saw it as a priority to seek to have the Republic of Ireland withdraw the articles of its constitution that laid claim to Northern Ireland.

However, a substantial school of thought focused on internal, and not external factors as the main problem. While not denying the role of external factors, they saw the main source of the problem as the inability of the communities within Northern Ireland to agree on a political solution for Northern Ireland. They believed that both the British and Irish governments were likely to accept whatever the communities agreed, and that conflict resolution work on securing an agreement between the parties and communities in Northern Ireland, on the future of Northern Ireland, should be a priority.

In 1993, the British and Irish governments agreed the Downing Street Declaration, which stated clearly that the responsibility for a political agreement rested primarily with the communities in Northern Ireland. As a result of this clarification, the focus on an external enemy as the primary cause of the conflict between the communities was gradually seen as less and less useful. Thus, the focus of the work gradually changed and the emphasis since 1993 has been increasingly on the work that needs to be undertaken between the communities of Northern Ireland in order to secure, and sustain, a political agreement. Indeed, the Belfast Agreement of 1998 was essentially an agreement between the political parties in Northern Ireland, fostered by the British and Irish governments who were in the main "neutral" on a political agreement, and willing to accept what the parties agreed between them.

A comprehensive and complementary strategy

By the end of the 1980s, the Northern Ireland conflict was beginning to be seen as not one problem, but a series of problems, demanding a variety of approaches and solutions (Fitzduff, 1989a; Darby, 1993). The confluence detectable in Northern Ireland where a number of approaches are increasingly perceived as compatible and not competitive mirrors the development of various systemic theories that are now being articulated elsewhere by, for example, Dugan (1994) and Lederach (1995). Dugan has developed what she calls a "nested paradigm" which enables both the broader contextual issues to be validated as a focus for action, while allowing for more immediate progress to be made on the presenting of issues of conflict. Dugan's approach reflects the complementary approach to conflict that has been developing in Northern Ireland, particularly over the last few years.

In a conflict, it is too easy to assume that the prime necessity is to work with those people who are apparently central to any peace process, for example the politicians, or in the case of an armed conflict, military or paramilitary leaders. To prioritize these groups for attention is the obvious strategic temptation for those wishing to see a speedy end to a conflict. In some cases such prioritization may indeed be useful, but it will often, however, prove to be insufficient as leaders will usually believe, or suggest, that their role as representatives limits their capacity to be flexible and to deliver any compromise solution that will be unacceptable to their people.

Hence in Northern Ireland, the need for such a comprehensive involvement has gradually been developing (Fitzduff, 1989a). Since the early nineties there has been some considerable success in promoting the idea of a much more comprehensively strategic approach to the major dimensions underlying the conflict, and securing an agreement that these dimensions are complementary, not contradictory, and that all were necessary in order to achieve a solution. Figure 2 illustrates the main dimensions that were generally agreed to be important in Northern Ireland in achieving a just and sustainable agreement.

Without the recognition of such complementarities, it would not have been possible to achieve progress. Economic development was necessary to ensure that work aimed at achieving equality was not seen as a win/lose situation, particularly for the Unionist commu-

Figure 2.   Complementary dimensions in peace-building in Northern Ireland

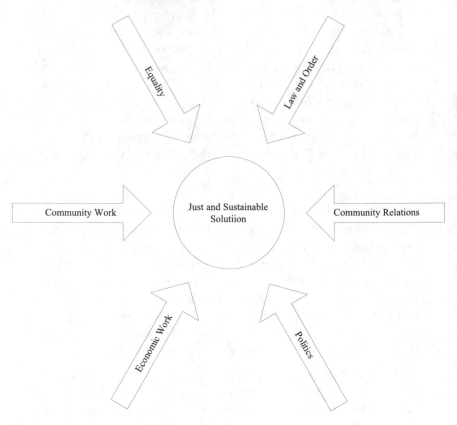

nity. Without work aimed at developing community, and the development of some new community leadership, it would have been impossible to shift the party political landscape. While the military containment of the paramilitaries was vital, without work that ensured a less contentious interface with the security forces, particularly on the part of the Nationalist communities, such contention would have assisted the continuance of violence. Without work aimed at validating cultural diversity, communities would have feared and distrusted community relations work, and seen it as an attempt at removing rather than respecting differences. Without community relations work, it would have been impossible to address the issues of justice and political choices between the communities. And without community development work, which increased the confidence of communities to address their differences, we would have lacked the addition of new political leaders from the communities who were eventually to help transform the political process, and make the Agreement possible.

Levels of engagement

In addition to addressing the need for a complementary approach to the issues that needed addressing, it was also important to ensure that such issues should be addressed at every level of society, and not just between a few main actors. Figure 3, which utilizes Lederach's approach, demonstrates the levels and kinds of engagement that have been commonly undertaken in Northern Ireland.

The work included within each level was tailored to fit the particular context of the conflict. Work at Level 1 in Northern Ireland has consisted of work with political, military, and paramilitary leaders, as well as policy advisers and administrators from both British and Irish governments. Such work has included achieving ceasefires and political reframing, political agreements and the necessary mediation work to achieve them, as well as the necessary and, where possible, sensitive military containment of the violence.

Work at Level 2 consisted of work mainly with major agencies such as statutory bodies, large community bodies, and other non-governmental organizations, the major churches and educational institutions, cultural and sporting organizations, housing and planning institutions, trade unions and business sectors, and the security forces. Such work was essentially mainstreaming work, that is, work aimed at ensuring that all such bodies took responsibility for incorporating the work necessary to successfully achieve a sustainable end to violence into their strategies and programmes.

Figure 3.   Northern Ireland variations of "Actors and
              Peacebuilding Foci across the Affected
              Population" (Lederach, 1995)

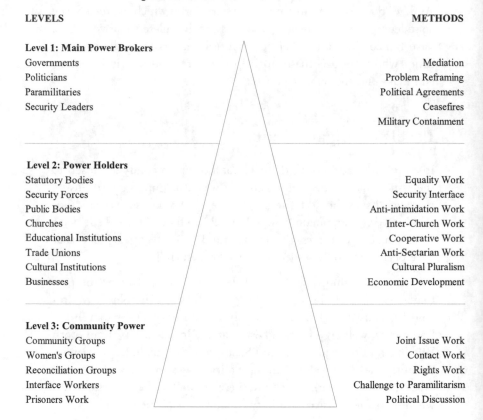

LEVELS	METHODS
Level 1: Main Power Brokers	
Governments	Mediation
Politicians	Problem Reframing
Paramilitaries	Political Agreements
Security Leaders	Ceasefires
	Military Containment
Level 2: Power Holders	
Statutory Bodies	Equality Work
Security Forces	Security Interface
Public Bodies	Anti-intimidation Work
Churches	Inter-Church Work
Educational Institutions	Cooperative Work
Trade Unions	Anti-Sectarian Work
Cultural Institutions	Cultural Pluralism
Businesses	Economic Development
Level 3: Community Power	
Community Groups	Joint Issue Work
Women's Groups	Contact Work
Reconciliation Groups	Rights Work
Interface Workers	Challenge to Paramilitarism
Prisoners Work	Political Discussion

Work at Level 3 consisted of activities with local communities,
indigenous leaders from these communities, along conflicting inter-
faces with prisoners and former paramilitaries and with community development programmes. Such work included contact and
cooperation efforts, community challenge to paramilitaries, mediation, community development and community leadership activities,
and victims and political discussion work within and between communities.

The advantage of such efforts is that it can help the development of what Lederach (1995) calls a 'peace constituency' in order to ensure ultimate success in resolving a conflict. If the ground is not right and enough support for an accommodatory solution has not been garnered, solutions that are eventually proposed, with necessary elements of compromises, may not be understood, and may well be rejected by the communities.

Crisis work versus long-term needs

A particularly useful way of approaching conflict resolution work is to recognize that approaches that focus on short-term needs are complementary to approaches of a more medium or long-term nature. Where a conflict is aggressively violent, with most people in the communities affected either as perpetrators or as possible immediate victims of the violence, the immediate need is usually for the diminution of the ongoing suffering, if possible through arranging ceasefires, and the alleviation of the victims' suffering through aid and refugee work.

While such work is vital to save lives, it may so engage the energies of all involved that they have little time even for reflection upon the necessary medium or long-term work that may be important to ensure that ceasefires can hold, and that the basic infrastructure which may be unjust, or embittered, will be transformed. In Northern Ireland, where violence is on a more sporadic basis than that of former Yugoslavia, or Rwanda, there has been some capacity and energy available, particularly on the part of policy makers, to take into account the medium and long-term needs of the conflict, and this book outlines many such examples.

Short-term work

In areas of violent conflict this work was usually aimed at limiting the continuance or the results of such violence. This meant organizing local (and sometimes regional) ceasefire arrangements and arranging for rumour clarification and control to prevent escalating violence. Frequently it meant mediating between communities, and between communities and security forces in violence-provoking situations such as marches. For many groups it also meant working with paramilitaries to achieve the release or safety of citizens who have been under threat from the gunmen. And for many community organizations it meant ensuring sufficient cross-community interaction after a murder or bombing to decrease tension and possible retribution by the victim community, and sufficient interface work to decrease rising communal tension.

Medium-term work

When time permitted, medium-term work usually concentrated on dealing with ongoing, recurring conditions that were a direct consequence of the political divisions, such as drawing up programmes to deal with intimidation and sectarianism in the workplace and in communities. In Northern Ireland this work also meant identifying and dealing with negative interfacing by the security forces with communities, assisting work to facilitate power sharing at local council level, and developing programmes to address issues of equity and rights. Training programmes that prepared communities and individuals to work with local conflicts at community and organizational level and problem-solving workshops addressing issues of political options were also part of such work.

Long-term work

In Northern Ireland, long-term work has been about the prevention of negative attitudes through educational programmes in schools, and through the building of integrated schools. It also means planning for increased contact between the communities, and developing anti-sectarian programmes with churches, prisons, security forces, sporting bodies, and government agencies. Long-term work also included the development of economic and structural infrastructures that can increase equitable employment levels, the planning of integrated housing projects, and working environments that can achieve sustained contact between communities. Of considerable importance in Northern Ireland has been the increasing development of people's capacity to involve themselves in positive political decision making through general community development and empowerment work, including leadership development and training for political activity.

Keeping in mind these time frames has also been useful in ensuring that at least some work could be continued in difficult times. Kriesberg et al. (1989), addressing the issue of intractable conflicts, has identified several strategies that may be usefully pursued in trying to free the gridlock of a conflict. One approach he suggests is to find some areas of possible settlement, and try to work to attain them in the hope that such "pieces of peace" (Rothman, 1992) will gradually be able to add to what is necessary for a sustainable peace. This has been a useful approach in Northern Ireland and it has meant consistently identifying areas where progress, with some energy and courage, appeared to be possible. Such a multifaceted approach has also meant that at difficult times, when one area of work becomes too difficult or too dangerous to progress, there are others where some success can be achieved, and thus the momentum of progress can be retained.

Of importance in furthering this work has been the recent development of typologies for conflict intervention, which point to the importance of the need to distinguish between the various phases of conflict, each of which will necessitate differing aspects of work. Thus our understanding of the need for preventive work in areas of high tension, particularly at volatile times of the year, or after particularly difficult incidents of violence, has become extremely important, as has the need for preventive anti-intimidation work within factories so as to prevent sectarian violence from occurring and possibly fuelling community aggression.

However, it is also useful to recognize that, given the level of violence and stress in our many streets, our experience has also been that practice often cannot wait on the establishment of coherent theory. Hence practice has often been characterized by innovation born out of fear, courage born out of anger, and occasionally actions attempted merely to combat despair. Given the developing state of the field however, such actions have often served to suggest or validate emerging hypotheses about the effectiveness of the work, and intuitions born out of the need for emergency action have often proceeded to inform the further effective development of the work in particular areas.

Recognise that change is possible

Inevitably, there are people for whom change is extremely difficult. Such resistance can be based upon a reluctance to lose power, while for many it is a fear of losing their identity. Some individuals and groups, whose core meaning has become bound up with their engagement in the conflict, may also resist its resolution, knowing (perhaps only at a subconscious level) that such resolution may leave them bereft in some way (Fitzduff, 1989b). However, the experience of Northern Ireland would seem to suggest that there are few organizations or people that are not at some level capable of developing positive changes in their attitudes and behaviour towards the out group, even when a conflict is in progress. The work also suggests that approaches for evoking such change must be flexible and sensitive to each group and situation. Even while such change is occurring – and not necessarily after it – most individuals and groups can also act as positive change agents with others in facilitating further developments in attitudes and behaviour that can gradually accrue and contribute to an overall shift in the conflict. The successes articulated in Chapter 10 demonstrate that with commitment and strategic thought, allied with a substantial amount of courage and political intelligence, it is possible to address the causes of a conflict, change many of the institutions that have exemplified many of the causes, and assist the development of sufficient dialogue and cooperation processes to ensure the move of a society from violence into politics.

Recognise that change is cumulative

It can be so easy to despair when involved in the tough work of peace-building. Time and again, fragile agreements are broken, partnerships are disrupted by violent events, and hopes are dashed again and again under the weight of differing loyalties, and the demands of fearful and angry communities. Yet the evidence from many parts of the world is that peace processes are cumulative, often flowing and ebbing again and again, and only gradually accruing enough agreement to enable communities to move out of violence and into political, constitutional, and other processes of conflict resolution. In addition, as agreement looms, "dealers" in a peace process often have to contend with "spoilers" to a process who increase their violence in the face of looming compromises, and significantly threaten the progress of political agreement.[69] It is also important for workers in this field to appreciate the length of time that is necessary for leaders and their communities to come to terms with just what is required of them in the way of compromise in order to achieve and implement an agreement, and to realize that communities will often struggle for years, or even decades, before coming to terms with such compromises. Patience, and understanding that such resistance is normal, and that achieving change in long-established conflicts is inevitably a prolonged process, is a very necessary part – perhaps the most necessary part – of the repertoire of those involved in the work of peace-building.

Postscript

For some years to come, it is likely that Northern Ireland will struggle to ensure that its peace is sustainable and can survive the tensions that are the inevitable lot of a post-violence situation. These include satisfactory decommissioning, comprehensive victim strategies, removing the remnants of inequality, ensuring representative policing, and developing a more trusting political landscape. Society in Northern Ireland, has, however substantially changed, and the strategies outlined in this book have laid the foundations for a future society that is less segregated, less discriminatory, more tolerant, and more pluralist than ever in the history of the state. Such a foundation thus offers more positive prospects for peace than have been available for many decades, and will hopefully provide a secure infrastructure for the many political shifts that are now taking place through an agreed power-sharing process.

Like others, I look backwards to the nightmare that has been, and look forward with tentative hope to a future that will be brighter for our children. I live with my family in a rural area that is deeply Republican[70] and where tacit, and in some cases, active support for the campaign of the IRA has been widespread since the early 1970s. Because of this, it is an area that has been continually patrolled and searched by the army and the police. My two sons, born in the late 1970s, have been brought up to the constant sound of surveillance helicopters, landing frequently beside our house, and the recurrent sounds of bombs and gunfire. Their great aunt was the postmistress of the post office at the end of our lane, which was robbed so often by the IRA in pursuit of funding for their military campaign that it was eventually closed. Their uncle owns the nearby public house, which has been blown up both by Loyalist and by Republican paramilitaries in turn, and which for all of their lives has had most of its windows and doors blocked up against further attacks.

Our small village and the village area next to it, which is mostly Protestant, have between us suffered the death of 25 people at the hands of paramilitaries and security forces during the course of the conflict, as well as a few people who have killed themselves while preparing explosives intended for use on others. Attending the wakes and funerals of such victims – from both sides – has been a deeply traumatic experience, testifying as it has done to the tragic results of the failure of our political process to deal adequately with our conflicts.

The ceasefires of 1994 and 1996, and the subsequent Belfast Agreement of 1998, brought significant hope to Northern Ireland. In our area we no longer have to worry about our children being caught in crossfire between the IRA and the army and our youth are able to socialize in the local club without fear of the paramilitaries coming in to seize money or cars for a murder operation. For the first time in our children's lives they are able to see policemen on the streets without flak jackets, and their guns at the ready. The army has moved off the streets. The thuds that we hear are only demolition work, and not explosions. The shots that we hear are only the bird-scarers that the farmers used, and not the sound of the murder weapons that have so often disturbed the quiet of our green fields.

Much work still remains to be done to ensure that the dust of violence will permanently settle, but we look to the future with some hope, as we see how much has been achieved in creating a more positive infrastructure for peace in Ireland. This book has been a reflection of just how much work has been needed by so many to try to contain and resolve the conflict. The amount of effort and courage which such work has taken stands as a salutary recommendation for the development of preventive work both here and elsewhere in areas of incipient violence. The price that Northern Ireland has paid for the lack of such preventive work suggests that the best of our intellectual energies and financial resources, throughout the world, are needed to endorse the needs of peacemaking much more energetically, not just in Northern Ireland, but throughout our continuingly troubled world.

Appendix 1

This is the entire text of the "Belfast Agreement"

Note the section on decommissioning, it can be clearly seen that there is <u>NO</u> requirement for any paramilitary group to hand over weapons.

The Belfast Agreement

Agreement reached in the multi-party negotiations

TABLE OF CONTENTS

DECLARATION OF SUPPORT

- 1. We, the participants in the multi-party negotiations, believe that the agreement we have negotiated offers a truly historic opportunity for a new beginning.

2. The tragedies of the past have left a deep and profoundly regrettable legacy of suffering. We must never forget those who have died or been injured, and their families. But we can best honour them through a fresh start, in which we firmly dedicate ourselves to the achievement of reconciliation, tolerance, and mutual trust, and to the protection and vindication of the human rights of all.

3. We are committed to partnership, equality and mutual respect as the basis of relationships within Northern Ireland, between North and South, and between these islands.

4. We reaffirm our total and absolute commitment to exclusively democratic and peaceful means of resolving differences on political issues, and our opposition to any use or threat of force by others for any political purpose, whether in regard to this agreement or otherwise.

5. We acknowledge the substantial differences between our continuing, and equally legitimate, political aspirations. However, we will endeavour to strive in every practical way toconstituencys reconciliation and rapprochement within the framework of democratic and agreed arrangements. We pledge that we will, in

good faith, work to ensure the success of each and every one of the arrangements to be established under this agreement. It is accepted that all of the institutional and constitutional arrangements - an Assembly in Northern Ireland, a North/South Ministerial Council, implementation bodies, a British-Irish Council and a British-Irish Intergovernmental Conference and any amendments to British Acts of Parliament and the Constitution of Ireland - are interlocking and interdependent and that in particular the functioning of the Assembly and the North/South Council are so closely inter-related that the success of each depends on that of the other.

6. Accordingly, in a spirit of concord, we strongly commend this agreement to the people, North and South, for their approval.

CONSTITUTIONAL ISSUES

• 1. The participants endorse the commitment made by the British and Irish Governments that, in a new British-Irish Agreement replacing the Anglo-Irish Agreement, they will:

(i) recognise the legitimacy of whatever choice is freely exercised by a majority of the people of Northern Ireland with regard to its status, whether they prefer to continue to support the Union with Great Britain or a sovereign united Ireland;

(ii) recognise that it is for the people of the island of Ireland alone, by agreement between the two parts respectively and without external impediment, to exercise their right of self-determination on the basis of consent, freely and concurrently given, North and South, to bring about a united Ireland, if that is their wish, accepting that this right must be achieved and exercised with and subject to the agreement and consent of a majority of the people of Northern Ireland;

(iii) acknowledge that while a substantial section of the people in Northern Ireland share the legitimate wish of a majority of the people of the island of Ireland for a united Ireland, the present wish of a majority of the people of Northern Ireland, freely exercised and legitimate, is to maintain the Union and, accordingly, that Northern Ireland's status as part of the United Kingdom reflects and relies upon that wish; and that it would be wrong to make any change in the status of Northern Ireland save with the consent of a majority of its people;

(iv) affirm that if, in the future, the people of the island of Ireland exercise their right of self-determination on the basis set out in sections (i) and (ii) above to bring about a united Ireland, it will be a binding obligation on both Governments to introduce and support in their respective Parliaments legislation to give effect to that wish;

(v) affirm that whatever choice is freely exercised by a majority of the people of Northern Ireland, the power of the sovereign government with jurisdiction there shall be exercised with rigorous impartiality on behalf of all the people in the diversity of their identities and traditions and shall be founded on the principles of full respect for, and equality of, civil, political, social and cultural rights, of freedom from discrimination for all citizens, and of parity of esteem and of just and equal treatment for the identity, ethos, and aspirations of both communities;

(vi) recognise the birthright of all the people of Northern Ireland to identify themselves and be accepted as Irish or British, or both, as they may so choose, and accordingly confirm that their right to hold both British and Irish citizenship is accepted by both Governments and would not be affected by any future change in the status of Northern Ireland.

2. The participants also note that the two Governments have accordingly undertaken in the context of this comprehensive political agreement, to propose and support changes in, respectively, the Constitution of Ireland and in British legislation relating to the constitutional status of Northern Ireland.

ANNEX A

• DRAFT CLAUSES/SCHEDULES FOR INCORPORATION IN BRITISH LEGISLATION

1. (1) It is hereby declared that Northern Ireland in its entirety remains part of the United Kingdom and shall not cease to be so without the consent of a majority of the people of Northern Ireland voting in a poll held for the purposes of this section in accordance with Schedule 1.

(2) But if the wish expressed by a majority in such a poll is that Northern Ireland should cease to be part of the United Kingdom and form part of a united Ireland, the Secretary of State shall lay before Parliament such proposals to give effect to that wish as may be agreed between Her Majesty's Government in the United Kingdom and the Government of Ireland.

2. The Government of Ireland Act 1920 is repealed; and this Act shall have effect notwithstanding any other previous enactment.

SCHEDULE 1

POLLS FOR THE PURPOSE OF SECTION 1

1. The Secretary of State may by order direct the holding of a poll for the purposes of section 1 on a date specified in the order.

2. Subject to paragraph 3, the Secretary of State shall exercise the power under paragraph 1 if at any time it appears likely to him that a majority of those voting would express a wish that Northern Ireland should cease to be part of the United Kingdom and form part of a united Ireland.

3. The Secretary of State shall not make an order under paragraph 1 earlier than seven years after the holding of a previous poll under this Schedule.

4. (Remaining paragraphs along the lines of paragraphs 2 and 3 of existing Schedule 1 to 1973 Act.)

• ANNEX B

IRISH GOVERNMENT DRAFT LEGISLATION TO AMEND THE
CONSTITUTION

Add to Article 29 the following sections:

- 7.

1.
   1. The State may consent to be bound by the British-Irish Agreement done at
      Belfast on the day of 1998, hereinafter called the Agreement.

1.
   1. Any institution established by or under the Agreement may exercise the powers
      and functions thereby conferred on it in respect of all or any part of the island of
      Ireland notwithstanding any other provision of this Constitution conferring a like
      power or function on any person or any organ of State appointed under or
      created or established by or under this Constitution. Any power or function
      conferred on such an institution in relation to the settlement or resolution of
      disputes or controversies may be in addition to or in substitution for any like
      power or function conferred by this Constitution on any such person or organ of
      State as aforesaid.

1.
   1. If the Government declare that the State has become obliged, pursuant to the
      Agreement, to give effect to the amendment of this Constitution referred to
      therein, then, notwithstanding Article 46 hereof, this Constitution shall be
      amended as follows:

- i. the following Articles shall be substituted for Articles 2 and 3 of the Irish text:

  - "2. [Irish text to be inserted
    here]
    3. [Irish text to be inserted
    here]"

II. the following Articles shall be substituted for Articles 2 and 3 of the English text:

- "Article 2
  It is the entitlement and birthright of every person born in the island of Ireland,
  which includes its islands and seas, to be part of the Irish nation. That is also the
  entitlement of all persons otherwise qualified in accordance with law to be
  citizens of Ireland. Furthermore, the Irish nation cherishes its special affinity with
  people of Irish ancestry living abroad who share its cultural identity and heritage.

- Article 3
  - 1. It is the firm will of the Irish nation, in harmony and friendship, to unite all the people who share the territory of the island of Ireland, in all the diversity of their identities and traditions, recognising that a united Ireland shall be brought about only by peaceful means with the consent of a majority of the people, democratically expressed, in both jurisdictions in the island. Until then, the laws enacted by the Parliament established by this Constitution shall have the like area and extent of application as the laws enacted by the Parliament that existed immediately before the coming into operation of this Constitution.
    2. Institutions with executive powers and functions that are shared between those jurisdictions may be established by their respective responsible authorities for stated purposes and may exercise powers and functions in respect of all or any part of the island."
    - iii. the following section shall be added to the Irish text of this Article:
      "8. [Irish text to be inserted here]"
      and
      iv. the following section shall be added to the English text of this Article:
      "8. The State may exercise extra-territorial jurisdiction in accordance with the generally recognised principles of international law."

4. If a declaration under this section is made, this subsection and subsection 3, other than the amendment of this Constitution effected thereby, and subsection 5 of this section shall be omitted from every official text of this Constitution published thereafter, but notwithstanding such omission this section shall continue to have the force of law.

5. If such a declaration is not made within twelve months of this section being added to this Constitution or such longer period as may be provided for by law, this section shall cease to have effect and shall be omitted from every official text of this Constitution published thereafter.

STRAND ONE
DEMOCRATIC INSTITUTIONS IN NORTHERN IRELAND

1. This agreement provides for a democratically elected Assembly in Northern Ireland which is inclusive in its membership, capable of exercising executive and legislative authority, and subject to safeguards to protect the rights and interests of all sides of the community.

The Assembly

2. A 108-member Assembly will be elected by PR(STV) from existing Westminster constituencies.
3. The Assembly will exercise full legislative and executive authority in respect of those matters currently within the responsibility of the six Northern Ireland Government Departments, with the possibility of taking on responsibility for other matters as detailed elsewhere in this agreement.
4. The Assembly - operating where appropriate on a cross-community basis - will be the prime source of authority in respect of all devolved responsibilities.

Safeguards

5. There will be safeguards to ensure that all sections of the community can participate and work together successfully in the operation of these institutions and that all sections of the community are protected, including:

- (a) allocations of Committee Chairs, Ministers and Committee membership in proportion to party strengths;
  (b) the European Convention on Human Rights (ECHR) and any Bill of Rights for Northern Ireland supplementing it, which neither the Assembly nor public bodies can infringe, together with a Human Rights Commission;
  (c) arrangements to provide that key decisions and legislation are proofed to ensure that they do not infringe the ECHR and any Bill of Rights for Northern Ireland;

- (d) arrangements to ensure key decisions are taken on a cross-community basis;

- (i) <u>either</u> parallel consent, i.e. a majority of those members present and voting, including a majority of the unionist and nationalist designations present and voting;
  (ii) <u>or</u> a weighted majority (60%) of members present and voting, including at least 40% of each of the nationalist and unionist designations present and voting.

Key decisions requiring cross-community support will be designated in advance, including election of the Chair of the Assembly, the First Minister and Deputy First Minister, standing orders and budget allocations. In other cases such decisions could be triggered by a petition of concern brought by a significant minority of Assembly members (30/108).

(e) an Equality Commission to monitor a statutory obligation to promote equality of opportunity in specified areas and parity of esteem between the two main communities, and to investigate individual complaints against public bodies.

Operation of the Assembly

6. At their first meeting, members of the Assembly will register a designation of identity - nationalist, unionist or other - for the purposes of measuring cross-community support in Assembly votes under the relevant provisions above.

7. The Chair and Deputy Chair of the Assembly will be elected on a cross-community basis, as set out in paragraph 5(d) above.

8. There will be a Committee for each of the main executive functions of the Northern Ireland Administration. The Chairs and Deputy Chairs of the Assembly Committees will be allocated proportionally, using the d'Hondt system. Membership of the Committees will be in broad proportion to party strengths in the Assembly to ensure that the opportunity of Committee places is available to all members.

9. The Committees will have a scrutiny, policy development and consultation role with respect to the Department with which each is associated, and will have a role in initiation of legislation. They will have the power to:

- o consider and advise on Departmental budgets and Annual Plans in the context of the overall budget allocation;
- o approve relevant secondary legislation and take the Committee stage of relevant primary legislation;
- o call for persons and papers;
- o initiate enquiries and make reports;
- o consider and advise on matters brought to the Committee by its Minister.

10. Standing Committees other than Departmental Committees may be established as may be required from time to time.

11. The Assembly may appoint a special Committee to examine and report on whether a measure or proposal for legislation is in conformity with equality requirements, including the ECHR/Bill of Rights. The Committee shall have the power to call people and papers to assist in its consideration of the matter. The Assembly shall then consider the report of the Committee and can determine the matter in accordance with the cross-community consent procedure.

12. The above special procedure shall be followed when requested by the Executive Committee, or by the relevant Departmental Committee, voting on a cross-community basis.

13. When there is a petition of concern as in 5(d) above, the Assembly shall vote to determine whether the measure may proceed without reference to this special procedure. If this fails to achieve support on a cross-community basis, as in 5(d)(i) above, the special procedure shall be followed.

Executive Authority

14. Executive authority to be discharged on behalf of the Assembly by a First Minister

- and Deputy First Minister and up to ten Ministers with Departmental responsibilities.

15. The First Minister and Deputy First Minister shall be jointly elected into office by the Assembly voting on a cross-community basis, according to 5(d)(i) above.

16. Following the election of the First Minister and Deputy First Minister, the posts of Ministers will be allocated to parties on the basis of the d'Hondt system by reference to the number of seats each party has in the Assembly.

17. The Ministers will constitute an Executive Committee, which will be convened, and presided over, by the First Minister and Deputy First Minister.

18. The duties of the First Minister and Deputy First Minister will include, inter alia, dealing with and co-ordinating the work of the Executive Committee and the response of the Northern Ireland administration to external relationships.

19. The Executive Committee will provide a forum for the discussion of, and agreement on, issues which cut across the responsibilities of two or more Ministers, for prioritising executive and legislative proposals and for recommending a common position where necessary (e.g. in dealing with external relationships).

20. The Executive Committee will seek to agree each year, and review as necessary, a programme incorporating an agreed budget linked to policies and programmes, subject to approval by the Assembly, after scrutiny in Assembly Committees, on a cross-community basis.

21. A party may decline the opportunity to nominate a person to serve as a Minister or may subsequently change its nominee.

22. All the Northern Ireland Departments will be headed by a Minister. All Ministers will liaise regularly with their respective Committee.

23. As a condition of appointment, Ministers, including the First Minister and Deputy First Minister, will affirm the terms of a Pledge of Office (Annex A) undertaking to discharge effectively and in good faith all the responsibilities attaching to their office.

24. Ministers will have full executive authority in their respective areas of responsibility, within any broad programme agreed by the Executive Committee and endorsed by the Assembly as a whole.

25. An individual may be removed from office following a decision of the Assembly taken on a cross-community basis, if (s)he loses the confidence of the Assembly, voting on a cross-community basis, for failure to meet his or her responsibilities including, inter alia, those set out in the Pledge of Office. Those who hold office should use only democratic, non-violent means, and those who do not should be excluded or removed from office under these provisions.

Legislation

26. The Assembly will have authority to pass primary legislation for Northern Ireland in devolved areas, subject to:

- (a) the ECHR and any Bill of Rights for Northern Ireland supplementing it which, if the courts found to be breached, would render the relevant legislation null and void;
(b) decisions by simple majority of members voting, except when decision on a cross-community basis is required;

    - (c) detailed scrutiny and approval in the relevant Departmental Committee;
(d) mechanisms, based on arrangements proposed for the Scottish Parliament, to ensure suitable co-ordination, and avoid disputes, between the Assembly and the Westminster Parliament;
(e) option of the Assembly seeking to include Northern Ireland provisions in United Kingdom-wide legislation in the Westminster Parliament, especially on devolved issues where parity is normally maintained (e.g. social security, company law).

27. The Assembly will have authority to legislate in reserved areas with the approval of the Secretary of State and subject to Parliamentary control.
28. Disputes over legislative competence will be decided by the Courts.
29. Legislation could be initiated by an individual, a Committee or a Minister.

Relations with other institutions

30. Arrangements to represent the Assembly as a whole, at Summit level and in dealings with other institutions, will be in accordance with paragraph 18, and will be such as to ensure cross-community involvement.
31. Terms will be agreed between appropriate Assembly representatives and the Government of the United Kingdom to ensure effective co-ordination and input by Ministers to national policy-making, including on EU issues.
32. Role of Secretary of State:

    - (a) to remain responsible for NIO matters not devolved to the Assembly, subject to regular consultation with the Assembly and Ministers;
(b) to approve and lay before the Westminster Parliament any Assembly legislation on reserved matters;

    - (c) to represent Northern Ireland interests in the United Kingdom Cabinet;
(d) to have the right to attend the Assembly at their invitation.

33. The Westminster Parliament (whose power to make legislation for Northern Ireland would remain unaffected) will:

    - (a) legislate for non-devolved issues, other than where the Assembly legislates with the approval of the Secretary of State and subject to the control of Parliament;
(b) to legislate as necessary to ensure the United Kingdom's international obligations are met in respect of Northern Ireland;
(c) scrutinise, including through the Northern Ireland Grand and Select Committees, the responsibilities of the Secretary of State.

34. A consultative Civic Forum will be established. It will comprise representatives of the business, trade union and voluntary sectors, and such other sectors as agreed by the First Minister and the Deputy First Minister. It will act as a consultative mechanism on social, economic and cultural issues. The First Minister and the Deputy First Minister will by agreement provide administrative support for the Civic Forum and establish guidelines for the selection of representatives to the Civic Forum.

Transitional Arrangements

35. The Assembly will meet first for the purpose of organisation, without legislative or executive powers, to resolve its standing orders and working practices and make preparations for the effective functioning of the Assembly, the British-Irish Council and the North/South Ministerial Council and associated implementation bodies. In this transitional period, those members of the Assembly serving as shadow Ministers shall affirm their commitment to non-violence and exclusively peaceful and democratic means and their opposition to any use or threat of force by others for any political purpose; to work in good faith to bring the new arrangements into being; and to observe the spirit of the Pledge of Office applying to appointed Ministers.

Review

36. After a specified period there will be a review of these arrangements, including the details of electoral arrangements and of the Assembly's procedures, with a view to agreeing any adjustments necessary in the interests of efficiency and fairness.
Annex A

Pledge of Office
To pledge:

-
  -
    - (a) to discharge in good faith all the duties of office;
    - (b) commitment to non-violence and exclusively peaceful and democratic means;

(c) to serve all the people of Northern Ireland equally, and to act in accordance with the general obligations on government to promote equality and prevent discrimination;

-
  -
    - (d) to participate with colleagues in the preparation of a programme for government;

(e) to operate within the framework of that programme when agreed within the Executive Committee and endorsed by the Assembly;
(f) to support, and to act in accordance with, all decisions of the Executive Committee and Assembly;
(g) to comply with the Ministerial Code of Conduct.

CODE OF CONDUCT

Ministers must at all times:

- observe the highest standards of propriety and regularity involving impartiality, integrity and objectivity in relationship to the steconstituencyship of public funds;
- be accountable to users of services, the community and, through the Assembly, for the activities within their responsibilities, their steconstituencyship of public funds and the extent to which key performance targets and objectives have been met;
- ensure all reasonable requests for information from the Assembly, users of services and individual citizens are complied with; and that Departments and their staff conduct their dealings with the public in an open and responsible way;
- follow the seven principles of public life set out by the Committee on Standards in Public Life;
- comply with this code and with rules relating to the use of public funds;
- operate in a way conducive to promoting good community relations and equality of treatment;
- not use information gained in the course of their service for personal gain; nor seek to use the opportunity of public service to promote their private interests;
- ensure they comply with any rules on the acceptance of gifts and hospitality that might be offered;
- declare any personal or business interests which may conflict with their responsibilities. The Assembly will retain a Register of Interests. Individuals must ensure that any direct

or indirect pecuniary interests which members of the public might reasonably think could influence their judgement are listed in the Register of Interests;

•

STRAND TWO
NORTH/SOUTH MINISTERIAL COUNCIL
1. Under a new British/Irish Agreement dealing with the totality of relationships, and related legislation at Westminster and in the Oireachtas, a North/South Ministerial Council to be established to bring together those with executive responsibilities in Northern Ireland and the Irish Government, to develop consultation, co-operation and action within the island of Ireland - including through implementation on an all-island and cross-border basis - on matters of mutual interest within the competence of the Administrations, North and South.
2. All Council decisions to be by agreement between the two sides. Northern Ireland to be represented by the First Minister, Deputy First Minister and any relevant Ministers, the Irish Government by the Taoiseach and relevant Ministers, all operating in accordance with the rules for democratic authority and accountability in force in the Northern Ireland Assembly and the Oireachtas respectively. Participation in the Council to be one of the essential responsibilities attaching to relevant posts in the two Administrations. If a holder of a relevant post will not participate normally in the Council, the Taoiseach in the case of the Irish Government and the First and Deputy First Minister in the case of the Northern Ireland Administration to be able to make alternative arrangements.
3. The Council to meet in different formats:

•
        •
                •

• (i) in plenary format twice a year, with Northern Ireland representation led by the First Minister and Deputy First Minister and the Irish Government led by the Taoiseach;
(ii) in specific sectoral formats on a regular and frequent basis with each side represented by the appropriate Minister;
(iii) in an appropriate format to consider institutional or cross-sectoral matters (including in relation to the EU) and to resolve disagreement.
4. Agendas for all meetings to be settled by prior agreement between the two sides, but it will be open to either to propose any matter for consideration or action.
5. The Council:

•
        •
                •

• (i) to exchange information, discuss and consult with a view to co-operating on matters of mutual interest within the competence of both Administrations, North and South;
(ii) to use best endeavours to reach agreement on the adoption of common policies, in areas where there is a mutual cross-border and all-island benefit, and which are within the competence of both Administrations, North and South, making determined efforts to overcome any disagreements;
(iii) to take decisions by agreement on policies for implementation separately in each jurisdiction, in

relevant meaningful areas within the competence of both Administrations, North and South;

(iv) to take decisions by agreement on policies and action at an all-island and cross-border level to be implemented by the bodies to be established as set out in paragraphs 8 and 9 below.

6. Each side to be in a position to take decisions in the Council within the defined authority of those attending, through the arrangements in place for co-ordination of executive functions within each jurisdiction. Each side to remain accountable to the Assembly and Oireachtas respectively, whose approval, through the arrangements in place on either side, would be required for decisions beyond the defined authority of those attending.

7. As soon as practically possible after elections to the Northern Ireland Assembly, inaugural meetings will take place of the Assembly, the British/Irish Council and the North/South Ministerial Council in their transitional forms. All three institutions will meet regularly and frequently on this basis during the period between the elections to the Assembly, and the transfer of powers to the Assembly, in order to establish their modus operandi.

8. During the transitional period between the elections to the Northern Ireland Assembly and the transfer of power to it, representatives of the Northern Ireland transitional Administration and the Irish Government operating in the North/South Ministerial Council will undertake a work programme, in consultation with the British Government, covering at least 12 subject areas, with a view to identifying and agreeing by 31 October 1998 areas where co-operation and implementation for mutual benefit will take place. Such areas may include matters in the list set out in the Annex.

9. As part of the work programme, the Council will identify and agree at least 6 matters for co-operation and implementation in each of the following categories:

• (I) Matters where existing bodies will be the appropriate mechanisms for co-operation in each separate jurisdiction;

(ii) Matters where the co-operation will take place through agreed implementation bodies on a cross-border or all-island level.

10. The two Governments will make necessary legislative and other enabling preparations to ensure, as an absolute commitment, that these bodies, which have been agreed as a result of the work programme, function at the time of the inception of the British-Irish Agreement and the transfer of powers, with legislative authority for these bodies transferred to the Assembly as soon as possible thereafter. Other arrangements for the agreed co-operation will also commence contemporaneously with the transfer of powers to the Assembly.

11. The implementation bodies will have a clear operational remit. They will implement on an all-island and cross-border basis policies agreed in the Council.

12. Any further development of these arrangements to be by agreement in the Council and with the specific endorsement of the Northern Ireland Assembly and Oireachtas, subject to the extent of the competences and responsibility of the two Administrations.

13. It is understood that the North/South Ministerial Council and the Northern Ireland Assembly are mutually inter-dependent, and that one cannot successfully function without the other.

14. Disagreements within the Council to be addressed in the format described at paragraph 3(iii) above or in the plenary format. By agreement between the two sides, experts could be appointed to consider a particular matter and report.

15. Funding to be provided by the two Administrations on the basis that the Council and the implementation bodies constitute a necessary public function.

16. The Council to be supported by a standing joint Secretariat, staffed by members of the Northern Ireland Civil Service and the Irish Civil Service.
17. The Council to consider the European Union dimension of relevant matters, including the implementation of EU policies and programmes and proposals under consideration in the EU framework. Arrangements to be made to ensure that the views of the Council are taken into account and represented appropriately at relevant EU meetings.
18. The Northern Ireland Assembly and the Oireachtas to consider developing a joint parliamentary forum, bringing together equal numbers from both institutions for discussion of matters of mutual interest and concern.
19. Consideration to be given to the establishment of an independent consultative forum appointed by the two Administrations, representative of civil society, comprising the social partners and other members with expertise in social, cultural, economic and other issues.
ANNEX
Areas for North-South co-operation and implementation may include the following:

- 1. Agriculture - animal and plant health.
  2. Education - teacher qualifications and exchanges.
  3. Transport - strategic transport planning.
  4. Environment - environmental protection, pollution, water quality, and waste management.
  5. Waterways - inland waterways.
  6. Social Security/Social Welfare - entitlements of cross-border workers and fraud control.
  7. Tourism - promotion, marketing, research, and product development.
  8. Relevant EU Programmes such as SPPR, INTERREG, Leader II and their successors.
  9. Inland Fisheries.
  10. Aquaculture and marine matters
  11. Health: accident and emergency services and other related cross-border issues.
  12. Urban and rural development.

Others to be considered by the shadow North/ South Council.

STRAND THREE
BRITISH-IRISH COUNCIL

1. A British-Irish Council (BIC) will be established under a new British-Irish Agreement to promote the harmonious and mutually beneficial development of the totality of relationships among the peoples of these islands.
2. Membership of the BIC will comprise representatives of the British and Irish Governments, devolved institutions in Northern Ireland, Scotland and Wales, when established, and, if appropriate, elsewhere in the United Kingdom, together with representatives of the Isle of Man and the Channel Islands.
3. The BIC will meet in different formats: at summit level, twice per year; in specific sectoral formats on a regular basis, with each side represented by the appropriate Minister; in an appropriate format to consider cross-sectoral matters.
4. Representatives of members will operate in accordance with whatever procedures for democratic authority and accountability are in force in their respective elected institutions.
5. The BIC will exchange information, discuss, consult and use best endeavours to reach agreement on co-operation on matters of mutual interest within the competence of the

relevant Administrations. Suitable issues for early discussion in the BIC could include transport links, agricultural issues, environmental issues, cultural issues, health issues, education issues and approaches to EU issues. Suitable arrangements to be made for practical co-operation on agreed policies.

6. It will be open to the BIC to agree common policies or common actions. Individual members may opt not to participate in such common policies and common action.

7. The BIC normally will operate by consensus. In relation to decisions on common policies or common actions, including their means of implementation, it will operate by agreement of all members participating in such policies or actions.

8. The members of the BIC, on a basis to be agreed between them, will provide such financial support as it may require.

9. A secretariat for the BIC will be provided by the British and Irish Governments in co-ordination with officials of each of the other members.

10. In addition to the structures provided for under this agreement, it will be open to two or more members to develop bilateral or multilateral arrangements between them. Such arrangements could include, subject to the agreement of the members concerned, mechanisms to enable consultation, co-operation and joint decision-making on matters of mutual interest; and mechanisms to implement any joint decisions they may reach. These arrangements will not require the prior approval of the BIC as a whole and will operate independently of it.

11. The elected institutions of the members will be encouraged to develop interparliamentary links, perhaps building on the British-Irish Interparliamentary Body.

12. The full membership of the BIC will keep under review the workings of the Council, including a formal published review at an appropriate time after the Agreement comes into effect, and will contribute as appropriate to any review of the overall political agreement arising from the multi-party negotiations.

BRITISH-IRISH INTERGOVERNMENTAL CONFERENCE

1. There will be a new British-Irish Agreement dealing with the totality of relationships. It will establish a standing British-Irish Intergovernmental Conference, which will subsume both the Anglo-Irish Intergovernmental Council and the Intergovernmental Conference established under the 1985 Agreement.

2. The Conference will bring together the British and Irish Governments to promote bilateral co-operation at all levels on all matters of mutual interest within the competence of both Governments.

3. The Conference will meet as required at Summit level (Prime Minister and Taoiseach). Otherwise, Governments will be represented by appropriate Ministers. Advisers, including police and security advisers, will attend as appropriate.

4. All decisions will be by agreement between both Governments. The Governments will make determined efforts to resolve disagreements between them. There will be no derogation from the sovereignty of either Government.

5. In recognition of the Irish Government's special interest in Northern Ireland and of the extent to which issues of mutual concern arise in relation to Northern Ireland, there will be regular and frequent meetings of the Conference concerned with non-devolved Northern Ireland matters, on which the Irish Government may put forward views and proposals. These meetings, to be co-chaired by the Minister for Foreign Affairs and the Secretary of State for Northern Ireland, would also deal with all-island and cross-border co-operation on non-devolved issues.

6. Co-operation within the framework of the Conference will include facilitation of co-operation in security matters. The Conference also will address, in particular, the areas of rights, justice, prisons and policing in Northern Ireland (unless and until responsibility is devolved to a Northern Ireland administration) and will intensify co-operation between the two Governments on the all-island or cross-border aspects of these matters.

7. Relevant executive members of the Northern Ireland Administration will be involved in meetings of the Conference, and in the reviews referred to in paragraph 9 below to discuss non-devolved Northern Ireland matters.

8. The Conference will be supported by officials of the British and Irish Governments, including by a standing joint Secretariat of officials dealing with non-devolved Northern Ireland matters.

9. The Conference will keep under review the workings of the new British-Irish Agreement and the machinery and institutions established under it, including a formal published review three years after the Agreement comes into effect. Representatives of the Northern Ireland Administration will be invited to express views to the Conference in this context. The Conference will contribute as appropriate to any review of the overall political agreement arising from the multi-party negotiations but will have no power to override the democratic arrangements set up by this Agreement.

RIGHTS, SAFEGUARDS AND EQUALITY OF OPPORTUNITY
Human Rights

1. The parties affirm their commitment to the mutual respect, the civil rights and the religious liberties of everyone in the community. Against the background of the recent history of communal conflict, the parties affirm in particular:

- the right of free political thought;
- the right to freedom and expression of religion;
- the right to pursue democratically national and political aspirations;
- the right to seek constitutional change by peaceful and legitimate means;
- the right to freely choose one's place of residence;
- the right to equal opportunity in all social and economic activity, regardless of class, creed, disability, gender or ethnicity;
- the right to freedom from sectarian harassment; and
- the right of women to full and equal political participation.

United Kingdom Legislation

2. The British Government will complete incorporation into Northern Ireland law of the European Convention on Human Rights (ECHR), with direct access to the courts, and remedies for breach of the Convention, including power for the courts to overrule Assembly legislation on grounds of inconsistency.

3. Subject to the outcome of public consultation underway, the British Government intends, as a particular priority, to create a statutory obligation on public authorities in Northern Ireland to carry out all their functions with due regard to the need to promote equality of opportunity in relation to religion and political opinion; gender; race; disability; age; marital status; dependants; and sexual orientation. Public bodies would be required to draw up statutory schemes showing how they would implement this obligation. Such schemes would cover arrangements for policy appraisal, including an assessment of impact on relevant categories, public consultation, public access to information and services, monitoring and timetables.

4. The new Northern Ireland Human Rights Commission (see paragraph 5 below) will be invited to consult and to advise on the scope for defining, in Westminster legislation, rights supplementary to those in the European Convention on Human Rights, to reflect the particular circumstances of Northern Ireland, drawing as appropriate on international instruments and experience. These additional rights to reflect the principles of mutual respect for the identity and ethos of both communities and parity of esteem, and - taken together with the ECHR - to constitute a Bill of Rights for Northern Ireland. Among the issues for consideration by the Commission will be:

- • the formulation of a general obligation on government and public bodies fully to respect, on the basis of equality of treatment, the identity and ethos of both communities in Northern Ireland; and
  - a clear formulation of the rights not to be discriminated against and to equality of opportunity in both the public and private sectors.

New Institutions in Northern Ireland

5. A new Northern Ireland Human Rights Commission, with membership from Northern Ireland reflecting the community balance, will be established by Westminster legislation, independent of Government, with an extended and enhanced role beyond that currently exercised by the Standing Advisory Commission on Human Rights, to include keeping under review the adequacy and effectiveness of laws and practices, making recommendations to Government as necessary; providing information and promoting awareness of human rights; considering draft legislation referred to them by the new Assembly; and, in appropriate cases, bringing court proceedings or providing assistance to individuals doing so.

6. Subject to the outcome of public consultation currently underway, the British Government intends a new statutory Equality Commission to replace the Fair Employment Commission, the Equal Opportunities Commission (NI), the Commission for Racial Equality (NI) and the Disability Council. Such a unified Commission will advise on, validate and monitor the statutory obligation and will investigate complaints of default.

7. It would be open to a new Northern Ireland Assembly to consider bringing together its responsibilities for these matters into a dedicated Department of Equality.

8. These improvements will build on existing protections in Westminster legislation in respect of the judiciary, the system of justice and policing.

Comparable Steps by the Irish Government

9. The Irish Government will also take steps to further strengthen the protection of human rights in its jurisdiction. The Government will, taking account of the work of the All-Party Oireachtas Committee on the Constitution and the Report of the Constitution Review Group, bring forconstituency measures to strengthen and underpin the constitutional protection of human rights. These proposals will draw on the European Convention on Human Rights and other international legal instruments in the field of human rights and the question of the incorporation of the ECHR will be further examined in this context. The measures brought forconstituency would ensure at least an equivalent level of protection of human rights as will pertain in Northern Ireland. In addition, the Irish Government will:

  - • establish a Human Rights Commission with a mandate and remit equivalent to that within Northern Ireland;
  - proceed with arrangements as quickly as possible to ratify the Council of Europe Framework Convention on National Minorities (already ratified by the UK);
  - implement enhanced employment equality legislation;
  - introduce equal status legislation; and
  - continue to take further active steps to demonstrate its respect for the different traditions in the island of Ireland.

A Joint Committee

10. It is envisaged that there would be a joint committee of representatives of the two Human Rights Commissions, North and South, as a forum for consideration of human rights issues in the island of Ireland. The joint committee will consider, among other matters, the possibility of establishing a charter, open to signature by all democratic political parties, reflecting and endorsing agreed measures for the protection of the fundamental rights of everyone living in the island of Ireland.

Reconciliation and Victims of Violence

11. The participants believe that it is essential to acknowledge and address the suffering of the victims of violence as a necessary element of reconciliation. They look forconstituency to the results of the work of the Northern Ireland Victims Commission.

12. It is recognised that victims have a right to remember as well as to contribute to a changed society. The achievement of a peaceful and just society would be the true memorial to the victims of violence. The participants particularly recognise that young people from areas affected by the troubles face particular difficulties and will support the development of special community-based initiatives based on international best practice. The provision of services that are supportive and sensitive to the needs of victims will also be a critical element and that support will need to be channelled through both statutory and community-based voluntary organisations facilitating locally-based self-help and support networks. This will require the allocation of sufficient resources, including statutory funding as necessary, to meet the needs of victims and to provide for community-based support programmes.

13. The participants recognise and value the work being done by many organisations to develop reconciliation and mutual understanding and respect between and within communities and traditions, in Northern Ireland and between North and South, and they see such work as having a vital role in consolidating peace and political agreement. Accordingly, they pledge their continuing support to such organisations and will positively examine the case for enhanced financial assistance for the work of reconciliation. An essential aspect of the reconciliation process is the promotion of a culture of tolerance at every level of society, including initiatives to facilitate and encourage integrated education and mixed housing.

RIGHTS, SAFEGUARDS AND EQUALITY OF OPPORTUNITY
Economic, Social and Cultural Issues

1. Pending the devolution of powers to a new Northern Ireland Assembly, the British Government will pursue broad policies for sustained economic growth and stability in Northern Ireland and for promoting social inclusion, including in particular community development and the advancement of women in public life.

2. Subject to the public consultation currently under way, the British Government will make rapid progress with:

> • (i) a new regional development strategy for Northern Ireland, for consideration in due course by a the Assembly, tackling the problems of a divided society and social cohesion in urban, rural and border areas, protecting and enhancing the environment, producing new approaches to transport issues, strengthening the physical infrastructure of the region, developing the advantages and resources of rural areas and rejuvenating major urban centres;
> (ii) a new economic development strategy for Northern Ireland, for consideration in due course by a the Assembly, which would provide for short and medium term economic planning linked as appropriate to the regional development strategy; and
> (iii) measures on employment equality included in the recent White Paper ("Partnership for Equality") and covering the extension and strengthening of anti-discrimination legislation, a review of the national security aspects of the present fair employment legislation at the earliest possible time, a new more focused Targeting Social Need initiative and a range of measures aimed at combating unemployment and progressively eliminating the differential in unemployment rates between the two communities by targeting objective need.

3. All participants recognise the importance of respect, understanding and tolerance in relation to linguistic diversity, including in Northern Ireland, the Irish language, Ulster-Scots and the languages of the various ethnic communities, all of which are part of the cultural wealth of the island of Ireland.

4. In the context of active consideration currently being given to the UK signing the Council of Europe Charter for Regional or Minority Languages, the British Government will in particular in relation to the Irish language, where appropriate and where people so desire it:
   • • take resolute action to promote the language;
   • facilitate and encourage the use of the language in speech and writing in public and private life where there is appropriate demand;
   • seek to remove, where possible, restrictions which would discourage or work against the maintenance or development of the language;
   • make provision for liaising with the Irish language community, representing their views to public authorities and investigating complaints;
   • place a statutory duty on the Department of Education to encourage and facilitate Irish medium education in line with current provision for integrated education;
   • explore urgently with the relevant British authorities, and in co-operation with the Irish broadcasting authorities, the scope for achieving more widespread availability of Teilifis na Gaeilige in Northern Ireland;
   • seek more effective ways to encourage and provide financial support for Irish language film and television production in Northern Ireland; and
   • encourage the parties to secure agreement that this commitment will be sustained by a new Assembly in a way which takes account of the desires and sensitivities of the community.
5. All participants acknowledge the sensitivity of the use of symbols and emblems for public purposes, and the need in particular in creating the new institutions to ensure that such symbols and emblems are used in a manner which promotes mutual respect rather than division. Arrangements will be made to monitor this issue and consider what action might be required.

DECOMMISSIONING

1. Participants recall their agreement in the Procedural Motion adopted on 24 September 1997 "that the resolution of the decommissioning issue is an indispensable part of the process of negotiation", and also recall the provisions of paragraph 25 of Strand 1 above.
2. They note the progress made by the Independent International Commission on Decommissioning and the Governments in developing schemes which can represent a workable basis for achieving the decommissioning of illegally-held arms in the possession of paramilitary groups.
3. All participants accordingly reaffirm their commitment to the total disarmament of all paramilitary organisations. They also confirm their intention to continue to work constructively and in good faith with the Independent Commission, and to use any influence they may have, to achieve the decommissioning of all paramilitary arms within two years following endorsement in referendums North and South of the agreement and in the context of the implementation of the overall settlement.
4. The Independent Commission will monitor, review and verify progress on decommissioning of illegal arms, and will report to both Governments at regular intervals.
6. Both Governments will take all necessary steps to facilitate the decommissioning process to include bringing the relevant schemes into force by the end of June.

SECURITY

1. The participants note that the development of a peaceful environment on the basis of this agreement can and should mean a normalisation of security arrangements and practices.
2. The British Government will make progress toconstituencys the objective of as early a return as possible to normal security arrangements in Northern Ireland, consistent with the level of threat and with a published overall strategy, dealing with:
   • (i) the reduction of the numbers and role of the Armed Forces deployed in Northern Ireland to levels compatible with a normal peaceful society;

(ii) the removal of security installations;
(iii) the removal of emergency powers in Northern Ireland; and
(iv) other measures appropriate to and compatible with a normal peaceful
society.
3. The Secretary of State will consult regularly on progress, and the response to any
continuing paramilitary activity, with the Irish Government and the political parties, as
appropriate.
4. The British Government will continue its consultation on firearms regulation and control
on the basis of the document published on 2 April 1998.
5. The Irish Government will initiate a wide-ranging review of the Offences Against the
State Acts 1939-85 with a view to both reform and dispensing with those elements no
longer required as circumstances permit.

POLICING AND JUSTICE
1. The participants recognise that policing is a central issue in any society. They equally
recognise that Northern Ireland's history of deep divisions has made it highly emotive,
with great hurt suffered and sacrifices made by many individuals and their families,
including those in the RUC and other public servants. They believe that the agreement
provides the opportunity for a new beginning to policing in Northern Ireland with a police
service capable of attracting and sustaining support from the community as a whole.
They also believe that this agreement offers a unique opportunity to bring about a new
political dispensation which will recognise the full and equal legitimacy and worth of the
identities, senses of allegiance and ethos of all sections of the community in Northern
Ireland. They consider that this opportunity should inform and underpin the development
of a police service representative in terms of the make-up of the community as a whole
and which, in a peaceful environment, should be routinely unarmed.
2. The participants believe it essential that policing structures and arrangements are such
that the police service is professional, effective and efficient, fair and impartial, free from
partisan political control; accountable, both under the law for its actions and to the
community it serves; representative of the society it polices, and operates within a
coherent and co-operative criminal justice system, which conforms with human rights
norms. The participants also believe that those structures and arrangements must be
capable of maintaining law and order including responding effectively to crime and to any
terrorist threat and to public order problems. A police service which cannot do so will fail
to win public confidence and acceptance. They believe that any such structures and
arrangements should be capable of delivering a policing service, in constructive and
inclusive partnerships with the community at all levels, and with the maximum delegation
of authority and responsibility, consistent with the foregoing principles. These
arrangements should be based on principles of protection of human rights and
professional integrity and should be unambiguously accepted and actively supported by
the entire community.
3. An independent Commission will be established to make recommendations for future
policing arrangements in Northern Ireland including means of encouraging widespread
community support for these arrangements within the agreed framework of principles
reflected in the paragraphs above and in accordance with the terms of reference at
Annex A. The Commission will be broadly representative with expert and international
representation among its membership and will be asked to consult widely and to report
no later than Summer 1999.
4. The participants believe that the aims of the criminal justice system are to:
• deliver a fair and impartial system of justice to the community;
be responsive to the community's concerns, and encouraging community involvement where
appropriate;
• • have the confidence of all parts of the community; and
• deliver justice efficiently and effectively.
5. There will be a parallel wide-ranging review of criminal justice (other than policing and
those aspects of the system relating to the emergency legislation) to be carried out by the

British Government through a mechanism with an independent element, in consultation with the political parties and others. The review will commence as soon as possible, will include wide consultation, and a report will be made to the Secretary of State no later than Autumn 1999. Terms of Reference are attached at Annex B.

6. Implementation of the recommendations arising from both reviews will be discussed with the political parties and with the Irish Government.

7. The participants also note that the British Government remains ready in principle, with the broad support of the political parties, and after consultation, as appropriate, with the Irish Government, in the context of ongoing implementation of the relevant recommendations, to devolve responsibility for policing and justice issues.

ANNEX A

- **COMMISSION ON POLICING FOR NORTHERN IRELAND**
  Terms of Reference

  - Taking account of the principles on policing as set out in the agreement, the Commission will inquire into policing in Northern Ireland and, on the basis of its findings, bring forconstituency proposals for future policing structures and arrangements, including means of encouraging widespread community support for those arrangements.

    Its proposals on policing should be designed to ensure that policing arrangements, including composition, recruitment, training, culture, ethos and symbols, are such that in a new approach Northern Ireland has a police service that can enjoy widespread support from, and is seen as an integral part of, the community as a whole.

    Its proposals should include recommendations covering any issues such as re-training, job placement and educational and professional development required in the transition to policing in a peaceful society.

    Its proposals should also be designed to ensure that:

- the police service is structured, managed and resourced so that it can be effective in discharging its full range of functions (including proposals on any necessary arrangements for the transition to policing in a normal peaceful society);
- the police service is delivered in constructive and inclusive partnerships with the community at all levels with the maximum delegation of authority and responsibility;
- the legislative and constitutional framework requires the impartial discharge of policing functions and conforms with internationally accepted norms in relation to policing standards;
- the police operate within a clear framework of accountability to the law and the community they serve, so:

  - • they are constrained by, accountable to and act only within the law;
  - their powers and procedures, like the law they enforce, are clearly established and publicly available;
  - there are open, accessible and independent means of investigating and adjudicating upon complaints against the police;
  - there are clearly established arrangements enabling local people, and their political representatives, to articulate their views and concerns about policing and to establish publicly policing priorities and influence policing policies, subject to safeguards to ensure police impartiality and freedom from partisan political control;
  - there are arrangements for accountability and for the effective, efficient and economic use of resources in achieving policing objectives;
  - there are means to ensure independent professional scrutiny and inspection of the police service to ensure that proper professional standards are maintained;

- the scope for structured co-operation with the Garda Siochana and other police forces is addressed; and
- the management of public order events which can impose exceptional demands on policing resources is also addressed.

The Commission should focus on policing issues, but if it identifies other aspects of the criminal justice system relevant to its work on policing, including the role of the police in prosecution, then it should draw the attention of the Government to those matters.

The Commission should consult widely, including with non-governmental expert organisations, and through such focus groups as they consider it appropriate to establish.

The Government proposes to establish the Commission as soon as possible, with the aim of it starting work as soon as possible and publishing its final report by Summer 1999.

- ANNEX B

REVIEW OF THE CRIMINAL JUSTICE SYSTEM
Terms of Reference

Taking account of the aims of the criminal justice system as set out in the Agreement, the review will address the structure, management and resourcing of publicly funded elements of the criminal justice system and will bring forconstituency proposals for future criminal justice arrangements (other than policing and those aspects of the system relating to emergency legislation, which the Government is considering separately) covering such issues as:

- the arrangements for making appointments to the judiciary and magistracy, and safeguards for protecting their independence;
- the arrangements for the organisation and supervision of the prosecution process, and for safeguarding its independence;
- measures to improve the responsiveness and accountability of, and any lay participation in the criminal justice system;
- mechanisms for addressing law reform;
- the scope for structured co-operation between the criminal justice agencies on both parts of the island; and
- the structure and organisation of criminal justice functions that might be devolved to an Assembly, including the possibility of establishing a Department of Justice, while safeguarding the essential independence of many of the key functions in this area.

The Government proposes to commence the review as soon as possible, consulting with the political parties and others, including non-governmental expert organisations. The review will be completed by Autumn 1999.

-

PRISONERS

1. Both Governments will put in place mechanisms to provide for an accelerated programme for the release of prisoners, including transferred prisoners, convicted of scheduled offences in Northern Ireland or, in the case of those sentenced outside Northern Ireland, similar offences (referred to hereafter as qualifying prisoners). Any such arrangements will protect the rights of individual prisoners under national and international law.

2. Prisoners affiliated to organisations which have not established or are not maintaining a complete and unequivocal ceasefire will not benefit from the arrangements. The situation in this regard will be kept under review.

3. Both Governments will complete a review process within a fixed time frame and set prospective release dates for all qualifying prisoners. The review process would provide for the advance of the release dates of qualifying prisoners while allowing account to be taken of the seriousness of the offences for which the person was convicted and the need to protect the community. In addition, the intention would be that should the

circumstances allow it, any qualifying prisoners who remained in custody two years after the commencement of the scheme would be released at that point.

4. The Governments will seek to enact the appropriate legislation to give effect to these arrangements by the end of June 1998.

5. The Governments continue to recognise the importance of measures to facilitate the reintegration of prisoners into the community by providing support both prior to and after release, including assistance directed toconstituencys availing of employment opportunities, re-training and/or re-skilling, and further education.

VALIDATION, IMPLEMENTATION AND REVIEW
Validation and Implementation

1. The two Governments will as soon as possible sign a new British-Irish Agreement replacing the 1985 Anglo-Irish Agreement, embodying understandings on constitutional issues and affirming their solemn commitment to support and, where appropriate, implement the agreement reached by the participants in the negotiations which shall be annexed to the British-Irish Agreement.

2. Each Government will organise a referendum on 22 May 1998. Subject to Parliamentary approval, a consultative referendum in Northern Ireland, organised under the terms of the Northern Ireland (Entry to Negotiations, etc.) Act 1996, will address the question: "Do you support the agreement reached in the multi-party talks on Northern Ireland and set out in Command Paper 3883?". The Irish Government will introduce and support in the Oireachtas a Bill to amend the Constitution as described in paragraph 2 of the section "Constitutional Issues" and in Annex B, as follows: (a) to amend Articles 2 and 3 as described in paragraph 8.1 in Annex B above and (b) to amend Article 29 to permit the Government to ratify the new British-Irish Agreement. On passage by the Oireachtas, the Bill will be put to referendum.

3. If majorities of those voting in each of the referendums support this agreement, the Governments will then introduce and support, in their respective Parliaments, such legislation as may be necessary to give effect to all aspects of this agreement, and will take whatever ancillary steps as may be required including the holding of elections on 25 June, subject to parliamentary approval, to the Assembly, which would meet initially in a "shadow" mode. The establishment of the North-South Ministerial Council, implementation bodies, the British-Irish Council and the British-Irish Intergovernmental Conference and the assumption by the Assembly of its legislative and executive powers will take place at the same time on the entry into force of the British-Irish Agreement.

4. In the interim, aspects of the implementation of the multi-party agreement will be reviewed at meetings of those parties relevant in the particular case (taking into account, once Assembly elections have been held, the results of those elections), under the chairmanship of the British Government or the two Governments, as may be appropriate; and representatives of the two Governments and all relevant parties may meet under independent chairmanship to review implementation of the agreement as a whole.

Review procedures following implementation

5. Each institution may, at any time, review any problems that may arise in its operation and, where no other institution is affected, take remedial action in consultation as necessary with the relevant Government or Governments. It will be for each institution to determine its own procedures for review.

6. If there are difficulties in the operation of a particular institution, which have implications for another institution, they may review their operations separately and jointly and agree on remedial action to be taken under their respective authorities.

7. If difficulties arise which require remedial action across the range of institutions, or otherwise require amendment of the British-Irish Agreement or relevant legislation, the process of review will fall to the two Governments in consultation with the parties in the Assembly. Each Government will be responsible for action in its own jurisdiction.

8. Notwithstanding the above, each institution will publish an annual report on its operations. In addition, the two Governments and the parties in the Assembly will

convene a conference 4 years after the agreement comes into effect, to review and report on its operation.

AGREEMENT
BETWEEN THE GOVERNMENT OF
THE UNITED KINGDOM OF
GREAT BRITAIN AND NORTHERN IRELAND
AND
THE GOVERNMENT
OF IRELAND

The British and Irish Governments:

Welcoming the strong commitment to the Agreement reached on 10th April 1998 by themselves and other participants in the multi-party talks and set out in Annex 1 to this Agreement (hereinafter "the Multi-Party Agreement");

Considering that the Multi-Party Agreement offers an opportunity for a new beginning in relationships within Northern Ireland, within the island of Ireland and between the peoples of these islands;

Wishing to develop still further the unique relationship between their peoples and the close co-operation between their countries as friendly neighbours and as partners in the European Union;

Reaffirming their total commitment to the principles of democracy and non-violence which have been fundamental to the multi-party talks;

Reaffirming their commitment to the principles of partnership, equality and mutual respect and to the protection of civil, political, social, economic and cultural rights in their respective jurisdictions;

Have agreed as follows:

ARTICLE 1

The two Governments:

(i) recognise the legitimacy of whatever choice is freely exercised by a majority of the people of Northern Ireland with regard to its status, whether they prefer to continue to support the Union with Great Britain or a sovereign united Ireland;

(ii) recognise that it is for the people of the island of Ireland alone, by agreement between the two parts respectively and without external impediment, to exercise their right of self-determination on the basis of consent, freely and concurrently given, North and South, to bring about a united Ireland, if that is their wish, accepting that this right must be achieved and exercised with and subject to the agreement and consent of a majority of the people of Northern Ireland;

(iii) acknowledge that while a substantial section of the people in Northern Ireland share the legitimate wish of a majority of the people of the island of Ireland for a united Ireland, the present wish of a majority of the people of Northern Ireland, freely exercised and legitimate, is to maintain the Union and accordingly, that Northern Ireland's status as part of the United Kingdom reflects and relies upon that wish; and that it would be wrong to make any change in the status of Northern Ireland save with the consent of a majority of its people;

(iv) affirm that, if in the future, the people of the island of Ireland exercise their right of self-determination on the basis set out in sections (i) and (ii) above to bring about a united Ireland, it will be a binding obligation on both Governments to introduce and support in their respective Parliaments legislation to give effect to that wish;

(v) affirm that whatever choice is freely exercised by a majority of the people of Northern Ireland, the power of the sovereign government with jurisdiction there shall be exercised with rigorous impartiality on behalf of all the people in the diversity of their identities and traditions and shall be founded on the principles of full respect for, and equality of, civil, political, social and cultural rights, of freedom from discrimination for all citizens, and of parity of esteem and of just and equal treatment for the identity, ethos and aspirations of both communities;

(vi) recognise the birthright of all the people of Northern Ireland to identify themselves and be accepted as Irish or British, or both, as they may so choose, and accordingly confirm that their right to hold both British and Irish citizenship is accepted by both Governments and would not be affected by any future change in the status of Northern Ireland.

ARTICLE 2

The two Governments affirm their solemn commitment to support, and where appropriate implement, the provisions of the Multi-Party Agreement. In particular there shall be established in accordance with the provisions of the Multi-Party Agreement immediately on the entry into force of this Agreement, the following institutions:

- (i) a North/South Ministerial Council;
- (ii) the implementation bodies referred to in paragraph 9 (ii) of the section entitled "Strand Two" of the Multi-Party Agreement;
- (iii) a British-Irish Council;
- (iv) a British-Irish Intergovernmental Conference.

ARTICLE 3

- (1) This Agreement shall replace the Agreement between the British and Irish Governments done at Hillsborough on 15th November 1985 which shall cease to have effect on entry into force of this Agreement.
- (2) The Intergovernmental Conference established by Article 2 of the aforementioned Agreement done on 15th November 1985 shall cease to exist on entry into force of this Agreement.

ARTICLE 4

(1) It shall be a requirement for entry into force of this Agreement that:

- (a) British legislation shall have been enacted for the purpose of implementing the provisions of Annex A to the section entitled "Constitutional Issues" of the Multi-Party Agreement;
- (b) the amendments to the Constitution of Ireland set out in Annex B to the section entitled "Constitutional Issues" of the Multi-Party Agreement shall have been approved by Referendum;
- (c) such legislation shall have been enacted as may be required to establish the institutions referred to in Article 2 of this Agreement.

(2) Each Government shall notify the other in writing of the completion, so far as it is concerned, of the requirements for entry into force of this Agreement. This Agreement shall enter into force on the date of the receipt of the later of the two notifications.

(3) Immediately on entry into force of this Agreement, the Irish Government shall ensure that the amendments to the Constitution of Ireland set out in Annex B to the section entitled "Constitutional Issues" of the Multi-Party Agreement take effect.

In witness thereof the undersigned, being duly authorised thereto by the respective Governments, have signed this Agreement.

Done in two originals at Belfast on the 10th day of April 1998.

For the Government of the United Kingdom of Great Britain and Northern Ireland	For the Government of Ireland

ANNEX 1

The Agreement Reached in

the Multi-Party Talks

ANNEX 2

Declaration on the Provisions of

Paragraph (vi) of Article 1

In Relationship to Citizenship

The British and Irish Governments declare that it is their joint understanding that the term "the people of Northern Ireland" in paragraph (vi) of Article 1 of this Agreement means, for the purposes of giving effect to this provision, all persons born in Northern Ireland and having, at the time of their birth, at least one parent who is a British citizen, an Irish citizen or is otherwise entitled to reside in Northern Ireland without any restriction on their period of residence.

Notes

1. "Republican" is the term used in Northern Ireland to denote those Catholics who are more inclined to support the use of violence to achieve their goal of a politically united island of Ireland. "Nationalist" is the term usually used to denote Catholics who want a united Ireland, but do not support violence. The term "paramilitary" denotes those people belonging to illegal militias who seek to leverage a political outcome through violence. This term is the one most frequently used in Northern Ireland, rather than guerrilla, terrorist, or illegal militia, and hence its usage throughout the book.

2. I have used the term "Catholic" as a shorthand for those, mainly of the Catholic faith, who seek to achieve a unification of the island of Ireland. The term "Roman Catholic" should technically be used to signify those who adhere to Rome rather than the reformed Protestant traditions for their faith, but the term "Catholic" is more generally used in Northern Ireland. I have used the term "Protestant" to refer to those, mainly of the Protestant faith, who seek to keep Northern Ireland as part of the United Kingdom of Great Britain and Ireland.

3. "Loyalist" is the term usually used to denote those Protestants more willing to use militia violence to achieve their aim of ensuring that Northern Ireland remains part of Britain. The "loyalty" is loyalty to the British monarch.

4. http://cain.ulst.ac.uk/events/peace/docs/clmc131094.htm

5. Good Friday is the Christian remembrance day of the death of Christ on the cross, preceding his "Resurrection" on the following Easter Sunday. The Agreement is more commonly known as the Belfast Agreement.

6. The Community Conflict Skills Project. The book resulting from this project is Fitzduff (1988).

7. The term "community relations" work, which literally means work promoting good relations within and between communities on conflict issues, is a term that is commonly used in Northern Ireland to denote what is often called conflict resolution work elsewhere. The fashions for terminology to describe this work have varied in Northern Ireland, e.g. anti-sectarian work and co-existence work have been used at various times.

8. For websites on many of these conflicts see the Conflict Data Service country guides at UNU/INCORE's web site at www.incore.ulst.ac.uk

9. INCORE (Institution for Conflict Resolution) is a joint United Nations University/University of Ulster initiative, set up in 1993, and based in Derry/Londonderry, Northern Ireland.

10. The northern part of the island in general consisted of the province of Ulster – the other three provinces in Ireland were Munster in the south, Leinster in the east, and Connaught in the west of the island.

11. The Reformation refers to the "reform" of the Christian church based in Rome, which resulted in the division of the Christian church into Protestants who rebelled against many of the traditions of Rome and Roman Catholics who remained faithful to the older traditions. Ironically, many of the settlers who came to Northern Ireland from Scotland were Presbyterian Protestants

who were fleeing from the discrimination which was exercised by the established Protestant Church of England following the reformation.

12. Green is the colour used to denote Irish Nationalism/Republicanism, and
orange to denote Unionism.

13. This is the result of a variety of factors, not the least of which is believed
to be the Catholic church's insistence on the children of mixed marriages being
brought up as Catholics. In addition, however, the number of Protestant men
who died fighting in World War II was far greater than the number of Catholics.

14. The number of Catholics has grown steadily since then. In 1993 the
Catholic population was approximately 42 per cent, but the proportion of
school children who were Catholic was 55 per cent. It has been estimated that
there could be a Catholic voting majority in Northern Ireland by 2020.

15. Quoted in De Paor (1970: 154).

16. Orange Halls belong to the Protestant Orange Order, and Hibernian to
the Catholic Hibernian Association. Both orders are exclusively male.

17. This event became known as Bloody Sunday. The government contracted
a much-contested report that suggested that the soldiers who killed the men
had been involved in self-defence against what they perceived as IRA violence
(Widgery, 1972). In 2000, a tribunal was set to investigate the facts of the
killings. It is estimated that the Tribunal will take three years to complete and
cost at least $150 million.

18. A review of the changing election results for all parties is available on
http://cain.ulst.ac.uk/issues/politics/politics.htm#election

19. These were a commitment by the parties to use democratic and exclusively peaceful means of resolving political issues, to the total disarmament of
all paramilitary organizations, verifiable to the satisfaction of an independent
commission, to renounce and to oppose the use of force to influence the course
or the outcome of all-party negotiations, to abide by the terms of any agreement reached in all-party negotiations, to only use democratic and exclusively
peaceful methods in trying to alter any aspect of that outcome with which they
may disagree; and to urge that "punishment" killings and beatings stop and to
take effective steps to prevent such actions.

20. There are over 3,000 parades in Northern Ireland every year, most of
them by the Protestant Orange Order. Because of changing demography, many
of their traditional parade routes now go through Catholic areas, which often
provoke tension and violence on the streets.

21. A copy of the Belfast Agreement can be found in Appendix 1.

22. The proportionate number of deaths in a country the size of the US would
be over 600,000. It has been estimated that over 50 per cent of the population
have relatives who been directly affected by these deaths and or injuries.

23. Great Britain refers to England, Scotland, and Wales, whereas the term
Britain refers to these areas plus Northern Ireland. United Kingdom refers to
all areas in total.

24. The original civil rights campaign also had a small percentage of Protestants as participants, although many of these left as the violence escalated.

25. Protestants call it Londonderry, Catholics call it Derry. For the sake of inclusiveness, I call it Derry/Londonderry throughout the book.

26. http://cain.ulst.ac.uk/othelem/research/nisas/rep2c8.htm#housing

27. Fair Employment Commission Annual Reports.

28. http://cain.ulst.ac.uk/csc/reports/one.htm

29. Registrar General Northern Ireland, Department of Health and Social Services (1993) *The Northern Ireland Census 1991 Religion Report*. Belfast: HMSO.

30. For a fuller review of such work, see the website of the Community Relations Council at http://www.community-relations.org.uk/community-relations

31. Previously known as Cooperation North.

32. Within this programme, the promotion of sustainable cooperative processes between all sections and institutions in the community is paramount.

33. Union Jack or Ulster flags in Loyalist areas, and Tricolours, the green, white, and orange Irish flag in many Nationalist areas.

34. There is considerable discussion about whether it is a language or a dialect of English. Although it has been accepted by the European Charter as "one of Europe's traditional minority languages" the debate continues.

35. This language/dialect is spoken in the lowlands of Scotland, from whence came many of the settlers.

36. See Chapter 1.

37. For more information see www.diversity21.co.uk

38. The figure for police included approximately 8,000 full time police officers, and 4,000 reserve.

39. See Chapter 7.

40. Supergrass trials were trials in which many people were convicted on the evidence of one informer, in return for promises of a new identity and a new home. Both Loyalist and Republicans were used as supergrasses.

41. The figures for conflict related deaths have been taken mainly from Fay et al. (1997).

42. Such consultative work began in the early nineties. Although the work was seen by such groups as necessary to improve the interface between the security forces and the community, it often has to happen with some degree of confidentiality, as undertaking it was seen as "collusion" by Republicans, and those undertaking it were threatened for doing such work.

43. There has been a tradition of Irish regiments in the British army providing careers for many men from the Republic of Ireland, who wish to join a large army rather than the small Irish army.

44. So called because it was chaired by Chris Patten, a former Conservative Minister for Northern Ireland.

45. Although outside of Northern Ireland the term paramilitary is often used to refer to semi-state forces, in Northern Ireland the term paramilitaries is used to refer to illegal militias that use violence to achieve political leverage.

46. Over 4,500 people were killed in this war. For an excellent account see Bardon (1992).

47. In 1969, the IRA split, mostly on the use of violence. The "Official" IRA

went into politics, and became a socialist party in both Northern Ireland and the Republic of Ireland. The "Provisional" IRA continued to use violence for political ends.

48. Catholic and Nationalist (those who support an independent and united island of Ireland) are usually interchangeable terms as the number of Protestants who support a United Ireland is about 2 per cent.

49. In 2000, a new inquiry opened in Derry/Londonderry to try and ascertain the truth of this incident which became known as "Bloody Sunday". It is estimated that this new inquiry will take two years to complete and will cost $150 million.

50. A further split resulted in the development of the the Irish Nationalist Liberation Army (INLA) in 1974, a group infamous for its particularly gruesome violence.

51. Until the end of the 1990s, Amnesty International confined itself to criticizing illegal state violence. As most of the violence (approximately 90 per cent) was carried out by paramilitaries, AI was seen by many in the community to be avoiding criticizing the paramilitaries, who were perpetrating most of the violence.

52. A wake is a period of a few days, following a death, when people visit the family to pay their respects and mourn with the family and friends of the deceased.

53. Ironically, by 2002, ETA had as yet failed to successfully use this tactic to end its own campaign of violence.

54. See particularly "The Management of Peace Processes," an INCORE project now detailed in Darby and MacGinty (2000).

55. The terms of this Assembly were not very different from those eventually agreed in the Belfast Agreement in 1998.

56. While it is accepted by most people in Northern Ireland that the membership of Sinn Fein and the IRA is not necessarily the same, it is generally believed that the links between them are substantial in so far as many Sinn Fein politicians have served jail sentences for membership/activity of the IRA.

57. The DUP refused to attend.

58. A copy of the Agreement is contained in Appendix 1.

59. Shuttle diplomacy is where a mediator tries to increase understanding of differing perspectives through sequential conversations with the participants, rather than through contact between them.

60. Such work included contact work, rumour clarification, institutional antisectarian work, rights work, church dialogue work, work on issues of identity, and political discussion work.

61. This centre deals with issues of European Community concern to Northern Ireland.

62. The Civic Forum was the idea of the Northern Ireland Women's Coalition, a party set up in 1996, and dedicated to cross-community dialogue between the political parties. They have two elected members in the Assembly.

63. At that time, I was Director of the Community Relations Council.

64. At INCORE, along with many other organizations involved in the Lessons

Learned project, particularly the European Platform for Conflict Prevention, we are seeking to develop more satisfactory approaches to the evaluation of interventions, and in particular macro-evaluation, i.e. understanding how or whether cumulative work, at many different levels, can contribute to the overall development of a peace process. We are aware that most of the frameworks that we have are less than satisfactory, particularly when addressing issues of macro-evaluation.

65. Which at least partially explains the community rioting in this area in late 2001, and early 2002.

66. In November 2001, John Hume, the long-term leader of the SDLP, resigned from the party, and was replaced by Mark Durcan, who received this invitation.

67. Northern Ireland Life and Times Surveys, http://www.qub.ac.uk/nilt

68. The original documents setting up the CRC noted the need for both approaches as being paramount to robust and successful conflict management e.g. Frazer and Fitzduff (1986).

69. For a description of such processes see Darby and MacGinty (2000).

70. The area is known as "The Killing Fields" because of the number of murders that have happened in the area.

References

Arthur, P. (2000), *Special Relationships: Britain, Ireland and the Northern Ireland Problem*. Belfast: Blackstaff Press.

Bardon, J. (1992), *A History of Ulster*. Belfast: Blackstaff Press.

Barritt, D. and Carter, C. (1962), *The Problem in Northern Ireland: A Study in Group Relations*. Oxford: Oxford University Press.

Barry, E. and Higgins, P. (1999), *Getting Off the Fence*. Belfast: CRC.

Bean, K. (1994), *The New Departure. Recent Developments in Republican Ideology and Structure*. Liverpool: University of Liverpool.

Bishop, P. and Mallie, E. (1987), *The Provisional IRA*. London: Heinemann.

Bloomfield, D. (1997), *Peacemaking Strategies in Northern Ireland: Building Complementarity in Conflict Management*. London: Macmillan.

Boyle, K. and Hadden, T. (1994), *Northern Ireland: The Choice*. London: Penguin.

Brocklehurst, H., Stott, N., Hamber, B., and Robinson, G. (2000), *Lessons Drawn from Negotiated Transitions in Northern Ireland and South Africa*. Paper presented at American Political Science Association, http://www.incore.ulst.ac.uk/home/research/ongoing/confpapers.html

Bruce, S. (1992), *The Red Hand: Protestant Paramilitaries in Northern Ireland*. Oxford: Oxford University Press.

Cairns, E. (1987), *Caught in the Crossfire: Children in the Northern Ireland Conflict*. Centre for the Study of Conflict, Coleraine: University of Ulster.

—— (1994), *A Welling up of Deep Unconscious Forces*. Occasional Paper, Centre for the Study of Conflict, Coleraine: University of Ulster.

—— (2001), *An Evaluation of the Contact Hypothesis in Promoting Positive Intergroup Relations in Northern Ireland*. Paper presented at the

British Psychological Association Centenary Conference, Glasgow, March.

CAJ (1992), *Adding Insult to Injury*. Belfast: CAJ.

Cameron Report (1969), *Disturbances in Northern Ireland: Report of a Commission Appointed by the Governor of Northern Ireland*. Belfast: HMSO.

Census Report (1990), Belfast: HMSO.

CIRAC (1993), *Report on Anti-Intimidation*. Belfast: CRC.

Connolly, P. (1998), *Early Years Anti-Sectarian Television*. Belfast: CRC.

—— (1999), *Community Relations Work with Pre-School Children*. Belfast: CRC.

Connolly, P. and Maginn, P. (1999), *Sectarianism, Children and Community Relations in Northern Ireland*. Centre for the Study of Conflict, Coleraine: University of Ulster.

Cooperation North (1992), *Annual Report*. Belfast/Dublin: Cooperation North.

Counteract (1993), *Annual Report*. Belfast: Counteract.

CRC (1990, 1994), *Annual Reports*. Belfast: CRC.

—— (1992), *Transport Needs and Resources for Groups in Northern Ireland*. Belfast: CRC.

—— (1995), *"Of Mutual Benefit": The Capacity of Economic Development to Contribute to Community Relations*. Belfast: CRC.

—— (1997), *Doing Business in a Divided Society*. Belfast: CRC.

—— (1998), *Dealing with Difference: A Guide to Peace, Reconciliation and Community Relations Projects in Northern Ireland*. Belfast: CRC.

—— (1999), *Youth Worker's Handbook to Cultural Diversity*. Belfast: CRC.

—— (2000), *Bridging the Gap: A Report on Projects Funded under the European Funding Programme*. Belfast: CRC.

Darby, J. ed. (1983), *Northern Ireland: The Background to the Conflict.* Belfast: Appletree.

—— (1997), *Scorpions in a Bottle: The Case of Northern Ireland.* Minority Rights Group: London.

—— (1993), *What's Wrong with Conflict.* Centre for the Study of Conflict, Coleraine: University of Ulster.

Darby, J. and MacGinty, R., eds. (2000), *The Management of Peace Processes.* London: Macmillan.

Darby, J., Dodge, N., and Hepburn, A., eds. (1990), *Political Violence.* Belfast: Appletree.

De Paor, L. (1970), *Divided Ulster.* Penguin: Harmondsworth.

Doherty, M. and Dickson, A. (1993), *Life Lines: A Youth Workers Guide for Cross Community Work.* Belfast: Youth Action.

Doob, L. and Foltz, W. (1974), "The impact of a workshop upon grassroots leaders in Belfast", *Journal of Conflict Resolution*, Vol. 18, No. 2, pp. 237–56.

Dugan, M. (1994), Making the Connection: Peace Studies and Conflict Resolution. Unpublished manuscript.

Dunn, S. and Morgan, V., eds. (1999), *Service Delivery in a Divided Society.* Belfast: CRC.

Elliott, R. and Lockhart, W. (1980), "Characteristics of scheduled and juvenile offenders in a society under stress" in J. Harbison, ed., *Children and Young People in Northern Ireland.* Somerset: Penn Books.

Equality Commission (1999), *Monitoring Report No. 10.* Belfast: Equality Commission.

Eyben, K., Morrow, D. and Wilson, D. (1997), *A Worthwhile Venture? Practically Investing in Equity, Diversity and Interdependence in Northern Ireland.* Coleraine: University of Ulster.

Farrell, M. (1983), *Arming the Protestants: The Formation of the Ulster Special Constabulary and the Royal Ulster Constabulary 1920–1927.* Brandon Pass, Co. Kerry: Dingle.

Fay, M., Morrissey, M., Smyth, M., and Wong, T. (1997), *The Cost of the Troubles Study: Report on the Northern Ireland Survey*. Derry/Londonderry: UNU/INCORE.

FEC (1993), *Annual Report*. Belfast: FEC.

Fitzduff, M. (1988), *Community Conflict Skills*. Belfast: CRC.

—— (1989a), *A Typology of Community Relations Work and Contextual Necessities*. Belfast: Policy Planning and Research Unit. Reprinted as Fitzduff, M. (1993), *Approaches to Community Relations Work*. Belfast: CRC.

—— (1989b), From Ritual to Consciousness: a study of change in progress in Northern Ireland. Unpublished PhD Thesis, Londonderry: University of Ulster.

—— (2000), *From Shelf to Field: Functional Knowledge for Conflict Management*. Paper presented at the "Facing Ethnic Conflicts" Conference, December 2000 at the Centre for Development Research of the University of Bonn. Bonn, http://www.incore.ulst.ac.uk/home/policy/policy/

Frazer, H. and Fitzduff, M. (1986), *Improving Community Relations*. Belfast: Standing Advisory Commission on Human Rights.

Gallagher, A.M. (1991), *Majority Minority Review 2: Employment, Unemployment and Religion in Northern Ireland*. Centre for the Study of Conflict, Coleraine: University of Ulster.

Gallagher, T. (1998), *Religious Divisions in Schools in Northern Ireland*. British Educational Research Association Annual Conference.

Gormley, C. (2000), *From Protagonist to Pragmatist – Political Leadership in Societies in Transition*. INCORE research project 1999–2001, Derry/Londonderry: http://www.incore.ulst.ac.uk/home/research/ongoing/leadership.html

Grant, D. (1994), *Playing the Wild Card – Community Drama*. Institute of Irish Studies, Belfast: Queen's University.

Hamilton, A. (1995), *Policing a Divided Society*. Centre for the Study of Conflict, Coleraine: University of Ulster.

Harbison, J., ed. (1980), *Children and Young People in Northern Ireland*. Somerset: Penn Books.

Harris, R. (1972), *Prejudice and Tolerance in Ulster*. Manchester: Manchester University.

Hewstone, M. and Browne, R. (1986), *Contact and Conflict in Intergroup Behaviour*. London: Basil Blackwell.

Hillyard, P. (1983), "Law and order" in J. Darby, ed., *Northern Ireland: The Background to the Conflict*, Belfast: Appletree.

Hinds, J. (1994), *A Guide to Peace, Reconciliation and Community Relations Projects in Ireland*. Belfast: CRC.

Horgan, J. and Taylor, M. (1999), "Playing the Green Card – Financing the Provisional IRA: Part 1", *Terrorism and Political Violence*, Vol. 11, No. 2, pp. 1–38.

Hughes, J. and Donnelly, C. (1998), "Single Identity Community Relations in Northern Ireland: final report", *Ulster Papers in Public Policy and Management* No. 77. Jordanstown: University of Ulster.

Hughes, J. and Knox, C. (1997), "Ten Years Wasted Effort? An overview of community relations in Northern Ireland", *Ulster Papers in Public Policy and Management*, No. 64. Jordanstown: University of Ulster.

International Alert (2000), *The Business of Peace: The Private Sector as a Partner in Conflict Prevention and Resolution*. International Alert: London, http://www.international-alert.org/publications.htm#business

Jackson, H. (1971), *The Two Irelands*. London: Minority Rights Group.

Jarman, N. (1999), *Material Conflicts: Parades and Visual Displays in Northern Ireland*. Berg: Oxford.

Jarman, N. and O'Hallaron, C. (2000), *Peacelines and Battlefields? Responding to Conflict in Interface Areas. Research and Policy Reports*, No. 1. Belfast: North Belfast Community Development Centre.

Keegan, J. (1993), *A History of Warfare*. London: Hutchinson.

Kelly, G. (1997), *Mediation in Practice*. Derry/Londonderry: UNU/INCORE.

Kendall, S. and Macdonald, M. (1992), "After consensus, what? Performance criteria for the United Nations in the post-cold war era", *Journal of Peace Research*, Vol. 129, No. 3.

Knox, C. and Hughes, J. (1994), *Community Relations and Local Government*. Centre for the Study of Conflict, Coleraine: University of Ulster.

Kraybill, R. and Buzzard, L. (1982), *Mediation: A Reader*. Akron, PA: Mennonite Central Committee.

Kriesberg, L., Terrel A.N. and Thorson S., eds. (1989), *Intractable Conflicts and Their Transformation*. Syracuse Studies on Peace and Conflict Resolution, Syracuse: Syracuse University.

Lederach, J.P. (1991), "Mediating conflict in South America", *Journal of Peace Research*, Vol. 28, No. 1.

—— (1995), "Beyond violence", in A. Williamson, ed., *Beyond Violence*. Belfast: CRC and the University of Ulster.

Lessons Learned (2000), Information available on http://www.incore.ulst.ac.uk/home/policy/eval/lessonsinconflict.html

LeVine, R. and Campbell, D. (1972), *Ethnocentrism: Theories of Conflict, Ethnic Attitudes and Group Behaviour*. New York: Wiley.

Logue, K. (1993), *Anti-Sectarian Work*. Belfast: CRC.

Lund, M. (1996), *Preventing Deadly Conflict*. Washington, DC: US Institute of Peace Press.

McCartney, C. (1994a), "Contact diagram" in *Community Relations Information Pack*. Belfast: CRC.

—— (1994b), *Clashing Symbols?* Institute of Irish Studies, Belfast: Queen's University.

McGowan and Patterson (2001), *Hear and Now ... And Then ... Developments in Victims and Survivors Work*. Belfast: Northern Ireland Voluntary Trust.

McMaster, J. and Higgins, C. (2001), *Churches Working Together: A Practical Resource*. Belfast: CRC.

Mitchell, C. (1966), *Cutting Losses*, Occasional Paper No 9. Virginia: ICAR.

Montville, J. (1990/1991), *The Psychodynamics of International Relationships*, Vols. 1, 2. PA: Lexington Books.

Morrow, D. (1994), *Churches and Inter-Community Relationships*. Centre for the Study of Conflict, Coleraine: University of Ulster.

—— (2000), *What Have We Learned: Community Relations and Peace Building*. Belfast: CRC.

Murphy, D. (1978), *A Place Apart*. Dublin: John Murray.

Murphy, J. and Murray, F. (1998), *A Cultural Diversity Directory*. Belfast: CRC.

Murtagh, B. (1999), *Community and Conflict in Rural Ulster*. Centre for the Study of Conflict, Coleraine: University of Ulster.

Nolan, P. (1993), *Screening the Message*. Belfast: CCRU.

Registrar General Northern Ireland, Department of Health and Social Services (1993), *The Northern Ireland Census 1991 Religion Report*. Belfast: HMSO.

O'Leary, B. and McGarry, J. (1993), *The Politics of Antagonism: Understanding Northern Ireland*. Athlone: Athlone Press.

O'Halloran, C. and McIntyre, G. (1999), *Inner East Outer West: Addressing Conflict in Two Interface Areas*. Belfast: Belfast Interface Project.

Playboard (1997), *Play and Community Relations: Games Not Names*. Belfast: CRC.

Pollak, A. (1993), *A Citizen's Inquiry: The Opsahl Report on Northern Ireland*. Belfast: Lilliput.

Poole, M. (1990), "The geographical location of violence in Northern Ireland" in J. Darby, N. Dodge, and A. Hepburn, eds., *Political Violence*. Belfast: Appletree.

RISCT (1991), *Reappraising Republican Violence*. London: RISCT.

—— (1992), *Reappraising Loyalist Violence*. London: RISCT.

Rose, R. (1971), *Governing without Consensus: An Irish Perspective*. London: Faber.

Ross, M. (1993), *The Culture of Conflict-Interpretations and Interest in Comparative Perspective*. Yale and London: Yale University Press.

—— (2000), " 'Good-Enough' Isn't So Bad: Thinking About Success And Failure", *Ethnic Conflict Management Peace and Conflict: Journal of Peace Psychology*, Vol. 6, No. 1.

Rothman, J. (1992), *From Conflict to Cooperation: Resolving Ethnic and Regional Conflicts in the Middle East and Beyond*. Beverly Hills: Sage Publications.

RUC (1993), *Chief Constable's Report*. Belfast: RUC.

Ryan, S. (1995), *"Peace-Building and Conflict Transformation,"* in *Ethnic Conflict and International Relations*, 129–52. Dartmouth: Dartmouth Publishing.

Ryder, C. (1991), *The Ulster Defence Regiment*. London: Methuen.

—— (1994), *Cultural Traditions 1989–94*. Belfast: CRC.

Scarman, Lord (1972), *Government of Northern Ireland: Violence and Civil Disturbances in Northern Ireland in 1969*, Report of Tribunal of Inquiry. London: HMSO.

Shara, L. (1994), "Thugs and Hooligans?", *Fortnight*, Belfast.

Shirlow, P. (2001), The State They Are Still In. Republican Ex-Prisoners and Their Families: An Independent Evaluation, http://cain.ulst.ac.uk/issues/prison/shirlow01.htm

Smith, A. (1999), *Education and the Peace Process in Northern Ireland*. Paper presented to the Annual Conference of the American Education Research Association, Montreal, http://cain.ulst.ac.uk/issues/education/docs/smith99.htm

Smyth, A. (2000), *Implications of Segregation for Transport within Northern Ireland by 2000*. Belfast: CRC.

Stevens, J. (1990), *Report to Chief Constable.* Belfast: Royal Ulster Constabulary.

Sugden, J. and Bairnen, A. (1993), *Sport, Sectarianism and Society in Northern Ireland.* Leicester: Leicester University Press.

Sugden, J. and Harvie, S. (1995), *Sport and Community Relations in Northern Ireland.* Centre for the Study of Conflict, Coleraine: University of Ulster.

The Belfast Agreement, http://www.nio.gov.uk/issues/agreement.htm

Urban, M. (1992), *Big Boys' Rules: The Secret Struggle against the IRA.* London: Faber and Faber.

Ury, B. (2000), *The Third Side.* New York: Penguin.

Volkan, V.D. (1988), *The Need to Have Enemies and Allies: From Clinical Practice International Relationships.* New York: Random House.

Widgery, Lord (1972), *Report of the Widgery Tribunal.* London: HMSO.

Williamson, A. (1995), *Beyond Violence.* Belfast: CRC and the University of Ulster.

Zartman, W. (1989), *Ripe for Resolution: Conflict and Intervention in Africa.* Oxford: Oxford University Press.

Index

Catalogue Request

Name: _____

Address: _____

_____

Tel: _____

Fax: _____

E-mail: _____

To receive a catalogue of UNU Press publications kindly photocopy this form and send or fax it back to us with your details. You can also e-mail us this information. Please put "Mailing List" in the subject line.

 **United Nations University Press**

53-70, Jingumae 5-chome
Shibuya-ku, Tokyo 150-8925, Japan
Tel: +81-3-3499-2811 Fax: +81-3-3406-7345
E-mail: sales@hq.unu.edu http://www.unu.edu